Making Managers in Canada, 1945–1995

Management education and training was a key influence on Canadian capital and labour in the post-World War II decades; however, it has been the subject of comparatively little academic inquiry. In many ways, historians have frequently learned about management behavior in unionized workplaces by examining labor-management relations. The management experience has thus often been seen through the eyes of rank-and-file workers rather than from the perspective of managers themselves. This book discusses how managers were trained and educated in Canada in the years following the Second World War.

Making Managers in Canada, 1945–1995 seeks to shed light on the experience of workers who have not received much attention in business history: managers. This book approaches management training from both institutional and social history perspectives. Drawing from community colleges, universities, and companies in British Columbia, Ontario, and Québec, this book reveals the nature of management education and training in English and French Canada, It integrates institutional analysis, and examines how factors such as gender and social class shaped the development of Canadian management in the post-war years, and illustrates the various international influences on Canadian management education.

Jason Russell is an Associate Professor at Empire State College – SUNY, USA.

Routledge International Studies in Business History
Series editors: Jeffrey Fear and Christina Lubinski

The Rise and Fall of the Italian Film Industry
Marina Nicoli

Foundations of Scenario Planning
The Story of Pierre Wack
Thomas J. Chermack

World Market Transformation
Inside the German Fur Capital Leipzig 1870–1939
Robrecht Declercq

Industries and Global Competition
A History of Business Beyond Borders
Bram Bouwens, Pierre-Yves Donzé, and Takafumi Kurosawa

Commodity Trading, Globaliation and the Colonial Word
Spinning the Web of the Global Market
Christof Dejung

Family Dynasties
The Evolution of Global Business in Scandinavia
Hans Sjögren

Multinational Business and Transnational Regions
A transnational business history of energy transition in the Rhine region, 1945–1973
Marten Boon

Making Managers in Canada, 1945–1995
Companies, Community Colleges, and Universities
Jason Russell

For a full list of titles in this series, please visit www.routledge.com

Making Managers in Canada, 1945–1995

Companies, Community Colleges, and Universities

Jason Russell

Routledge
Taylor & Francis Group

LONDON AND NEW YORK

First published 2018 by Routledge

2 Park Square, Milton Park, Abingdon, Oxfordshire OX14 4RN

52 Vanderbilt Avenue, New York, NY 10017

Routledge is an imprint of the Taylor & Francis Group, an informa business

First issued in paperback 2020

Library of Congress Cataloging-in-Publication Data
Names: Russell, Jason, 1968– author.
Title: Making managers in Canada, 1945–1995 / Jason Russell.
Description: New York, NY : Routledge, 2018. | Series:
   Routledge international studies in business history |
   Includes bibliographical references.
Identifiers: LCCN 2018014064 | ISBN 9781138691315
   (hardback) | ISBN 9781315535494 (ebook)
Subjects: LCSH: Executives—Canada—History—20th century. |
   Executives—Training of—Canada—History—20th century. |
   Management—Study and teaching—Canada—History—20th
   century.
Classification: LCC HD38.25.C2 R87 2018 | DDC
   658.0071/171—dc23
LC record available at https://lccn.loc.gov/2018014064

ISBN: 978-1-138-69131-5 (hbk)
ISBN: 978-0-367-85950-3 (pbk)

Typeset in Sabon
by Apex CoVantage, LLC

Contents

Acknowledgements   vi

Introduction   1

1   Management in Canada to 1945   11

2   Companies   35

3   Community Colleges   67

4   Universities and Undergraduate Management
    Education   97

5   Universities and Graduate Management Education   145

6   The Meaning of Management Education and
    Training in Canada   203

    Bibliography   231
    Index   241

Acknowledgements

This book is the product of interest in the historical development of the workplace that I have had since I first became a wage worker. I have known many people in my life who have been managers and, especially when I was young, I wondered about what it meant to be in management. I am grateful to be able publish this book about Canadian management, and there are many people whom I want to thank for making it possible. Historians rely heavily on archivists and librarians in order to conduct their research and writing, and I am no exception. I want to thank Erwin Wodarczak and Candice Bjur at the University of British Columbia Archive for their assistance with the Sauder School of Business Fonds, and Joanne Rajotte for arranging access to the Vancouver Community College Records at the Langara College Library. I also thank Paule Desjardins for her enormous help at the archive of École des hautes études commerciales de Montréal, and France Hamel at Bibliothèque et Archives nationales du Québec for providing access to materials pertaining to Collége Ahuntsic. Lise Noel kindly granted me access to the Bell Canada archive. Theresa Regnier at the Archive and Research College Centre at Western University Canada was unfailing helpful in providing access to the Clarence Fraser Papers, the Walter Thompson Fonds, and the Labatt Brewing Company Collection. Clay Thibodeau made me very welcome at the George Brown College Archives, and several staff members at the Archives of Ontario facilitated access to the T. Eaton Company Fonds and documents pertaining to the Ontario Management Development Program. I am particularly indebted to Gordana Vitez and Bianca Parisi for granting me access to a rich trove of unorganized archival documents at Niagara College. I also thank the staff at the Thomas Fisher Rare Book Library at the University of Toronto for making the Guelph Business College guide and Ronalds Company document accessible. I additionally thank Philip Mohtadi at Sears Canada, Shelley Panetta at Niagara College, Candace Bjur, and Paule Desjardins for granting permission to use the images included in this book.

I have benefited from comments provided by colleagues over the years on the research that has gone into this book, including useful feedback following conference paper presentations. I thank the members of the Toronto Labour Studies Group and participants in the former Canadian Business History Group for their comments on aspects of my research. I also want to recognize the assistance that the Canadian Business History Association provided in the form of a travel grant, and the faculty development funding assistance that I have received from Empire State College over several years. I thank Routledge International Studies in Business History series editors Geoffrey Fear and Christina Lubinski and the peer reviewers who commented on the proposal for this book. I should note that some content in chapters 1 and 2 is based on an article that I previously published in *Management and Organizational History* vol. 10, 3–4 (2015), copyright Taylor & Francis, available at www.tand fonline.com, 30 October 2015 date of issue. I also want to recognize the support of David Varley, Brianna Ascher, and Mary Del Plato at Routledge. I often thought of my son Thomas Russell while I worked on this book, as he is now at an age where he can work for wages and will soon deal with management in its many forms. This book is for Thomas, and I hope that it helps him make sense of what comes next.

Introduction

This is a book about management in Canada, but its origins are in a study of a local union in London, Ontario, from 1950 to 1990. That study of UAW/CAW Local 27 primarily focused on the local's internal development, relations with the national and international parent union, and its place in the community. The way in which relations with management changed over a four-decade period was also discussed. I had already been in a full-time job for many years when I began that study of Local 27 as a doctoral dissertation, and I had long thought about why managers acted and how the management field in Canada had evolved over time. Management became important in Canada in the post–World War II years, and this trend was represented in the development and expansion of management training and education programs of different types. Companies, colleges, and universities created new management training programs that were intended for managers and supervisors working in private corporations. Management education and training programs varied in terms of the scope of their content and duration. Some programs only involved listening to audio cassette tapes or watching films and videos, while others were held in classrooms on evenings and weekends. More comprehensive programs required completion of one- or two-year diplomas through part-time or evening study, while graduate degrees called for full-time study over two years.[1]

The Canadian experience relates to ideas developed about management over time. Sociologist C. Wright Mills discussed the rise of professional workers and other groups in the 1950s and described corporate executives as the organizers of a system of private property that had corporations located at its centre.[2] Senior corporate leaders were generalists, while middle-level managers below them had to be specialists, although it was the person who was the generalist who appeared to rise to the top of hierarchies.[3] In Mills' view, the foreman or front-line supervisor was the person in management structures who had "been so grievously affected by the rationalization of equipment and organization."[4] He also argued that middle managers were increasingly concerned with the management of people, and even went so far to say that "middle managers do not count for very much beyond their individual bureaucracies."[5] The 1950s were also the era of the organization men described by William H. Whyte.[6] The people analyzed by Mills and Whyte would become more numerous in the decades after the 1950s, and they were also found in Canada.

This book describes how Canada's organization men and women were educated and trained, and it addresses one main question: what were people taught about being a manager in business organizations from 1945 to 1995, and did they learn to manage corporations? It does not address the experience of working as a manager in the public sector. This analysis is intended to more empirical than theoretical. It uses historical materialism methodology in order to reveal something about the lived experience of managers. It principally relates to management history but also links to labour history, the history of capitalism, and the history of post-secondary education in Canada. There are several related sub-issues related to this overall question, including what was taught in different management education and training environments, the people who led training programs or taught at post-secondary institutions, the students who participated in training programs, and how this form of education and training reflected changes in Canadian society. Management is fundamentally about dealing with people, as Mills suggested, and this analysis is going to pay particular attention to what Canadian managers were taught about handling human issues in organizations.

Management in Canada altered considerably from 1945 to 1995, and a substantial education and training network shaped the changes that came during that period. An analysis of the development of management education and training in Canada also requires referring to social class, which is what Mills also did through his work. Canadian managers assumed different roles in organizational hierarchies, but they shared a common purpose and interests. Edward Thompson forcefully argued that a social class forms when people "as a result of common experiences (inherited or shared) feel and articulate the identity of their interests as between themselves, and as against other men whose interests are different from (and usually opposed to) theirs" while further arguing that "the class experience is largely determined by the productive relations into which men (people) are born."[7] A managerial class was created in Canada that shared common educational experiences, although people in this group were stratified according to the positions that they assumed in management hierarchies. They were also differentiated according to the type of education program in which they participated and where it was offered. The manner in which people in that group were educated and trained had a significant impact on what they would have thought about the role of management, particularly in relation to people with whom they would interact during their careers. Management became an important social institution and academic discipline, the role of the manager developed into an important occupational classification that was not necessarily a profession, and managing became a practice that could be studied. Canadian management developed unique characteristics through education and training programs and practices, and they had a significant impact on the education choices and career aspirations of many students. Management education and training programs covered many functions of business organizations, but there were crucial aspects that were not sufficiently taught.

The Rise of Modern Management

There is a well-established English language literature on the emergence of modern management, primarily in the United States, and the Canadian experience is reflected in different aspects of it. The existing work has been written by historians, sociologists, and people from a range of other academic disciplines. Management from 1945 onward had origins in the Industrial Revolution. Sydney Pollard's influential study traced the origins of management in the United Kingdom in the late eighteenth century.[8] John F. Wilson and Andrew Thomson have examined the development in management in the United Kingdom from the same early period as Pollard and continued to the 1980s and 1990s.[9] From the American perspective, Alfred Chandler's study of the rise of management had a lasting impact on how historians view the development of modern corporations.[10] The important influence of the engineering profession on management has been frequently noted. Pollard described the role of people with the title engineer as early as the late seventeenth century.[11] Wilson and Thomson also described the role engineers as managers beginning in the 1880s.[12] Chandler identified the military origins of the American engineering profession and subsequent influence on major projects like the building of turnpikes and railroads.[13] David Noble has placed even greater emphasis on the rise of engineering, technology, and corporate capitalism. In his view, engineering was making management into a technical occupation by the 1880s.[14] In contrast to authors like Pollard and Chandler, who wrote largely empirical analyses of the rise of management, Noble's narrative is a Marxist critique of management and corporations.

The practice of management has been described by a range of commentators, and Chester Barnard and Peter Drucker were among the more influential of them. Barnard had risen through managerial ranks, and his ideas about the functions of executives were informed by his long career working at American Telephone and Telegraph (AT&T).[15] Drucker had much less practical business experience and was instead an academic theorist. He described what management did at different levels of an organization and used specific case studies to illustrate his arguments.[16] Barnard and Drucker came from markedly different backgrounds and theoretical eras. As subsequent analysis will show, Barnard was part of a group of essentially self-taught management theorists, while Drucker was the first of the major post–World War II academic management thinkers.

What it meant to be a manager has been discussed by a further range of authors, and they often described working in an occupation that was far more complex than was suggested by Chandler. Melville Dalton's study of how American managers actually managed revealed that the people in those roles had to deal with conflicting pressures within their organizations and often shifting career expectations.[17] A more expansive British study with arguments similar to Dalton's was written by Roy Lewis and Rosemary Stewart.[18] Vance Packard's analysis of executive behaviour described a working environment of tremendous complexity that involved as many unwritten rules and norms as those that were written down.[19] The overarching need to conform to corporate culture appeared in Packard's analysis and also in Rosabeth Moss Kanter's study of management in one large American firm.[20] Robert Jackall discussed the occupational ethics of corporate management in a study conducted years after Packard and Moss Kanter.[21] The psychology of management is prominent in the work of those authors.

Management is not necessarily portrayed by Lewis, Stewart, Packard, Moss Kanter, and Jackall as a desirable occupation. The overall collective thrust of the work that has been described here on the development of management is that it became an important practice, and that managers were central to the running of corporations. The experience of being a manager was ultimately difficult because of the various aspects of the role, both formal and informal, that had to be navigated. With the exception of Moss Kanter, management was generally presented as an exclusively male vocation. Packard noted that, at the time that he wrote in the 1950s, women suffered the most discrimination of any occupational group.[22] Practicing management and being a manager meant adapting to organizations and their practices while also shaping them. The functions of managers were described by authors like Barnard and Drucker, and others like Chandler placed management development in a historical context. The ethics and legal obligations of management were not central to most analyses, with issues like the nature of organizational structures being more paramount. For instance, the creation of the modern holding company was the main legal innovation noted by Chandler.[23] Most recently, Stephen Cummings, Todd Bridgman, John Hassard, and Michael Rowlinson have reconsidered established ideas about such issues as the origins of modern management, scientific management, the Human Relations School, and the impact of Harvard Business School.[24]

Management Education History

There is considerable literature on the development of management education in English-speaking countries, but comparatively little has been written about Canada's experience with it. The work that has been written has tended of focus on graduate management education rather than undergraduate or college programs. For example, Rakesh Khurana's book described the transformation of American business schools from the late nineteenth century to the latter part of the twentieth century.[25] Carter Daniel wrote an earlier volume that recounted the history of the Master of Business Administration (MBA) degree that covered the period from the early 1900s to the late 1980s.[26] A collection of essays on the history of university business education in Canada was edited by Barbara Austin.[27] There have been comparative analyses of the development of business and management programs, including Robert Locke's study of American and Japanese influence practices in West Germany, Britain, and France.[28] A more recent comparative book that included essays on management education in several European countries, the United States, and Japan was edited by Lars Engwall and Vera Zamagni.[29] Comparisons between Europe, Japan, and the United States regarding management education and its link to competitiveness were also made in a book by Rolv Amdam.[30] Richard Whitley, Alan Thomas, and Jane Marceau produced a study that compared and contrasted British and French business schools and their graduates from 1973 to 1978.[31] Nancy Harding produced a detailed study of specific textbooks used in management education courses to illustrate the social construction of management.[32] Henry Mintzberg is Canada's leading critic of how graduate business school developed over time, and he wrote an analysis of what he thought was wrong with MBA programs and how to improve management education.[33]

The works mentioned above were written by academics and intended to be read by people in universities, with perhaps the exception of Mintzberg who appears to have been trying to speak to both academic and popular audiences. He did not reject the idea of graduate management education, just the MBA in the form that it existed at the time that he was writing. There have been more popular commentaries written about business schools that are highly critical about what is taught in them and their social influence. For example, Stuart Crainer and Des Dearlove wrote a highly critical book that emphasized the role of money on business schools.[34] Robert Locke collaborated with J.C. Spencer on a volume that was highly critical of business schools for enabling the rise of managerialist ideology.[35] Duff McDonald recently published a book that identified a litany of faults with Harvard Business School (HBS) and its MBA program, including HBS's focus on case teaching methodology.[36]

Graduate business education has received a lot of attention from different writers, but schools that are less elevated in the post-secondary education hierarchy have not received equal scrutiny. Community colleges became key providers of management education in the post–World War II decades. They are found in Canada and the United States and are approximately equal to further education colleges in the United

Kingdom. The community college in its present form was created to educate members of the baby boom generation. Canadian community colleges developed differently depending on the province where they were founded. There is much less academic literature on their programs than is available on undergraduate and graduate programs at universities.[37] Analyses of corporate management and supervisory training programs have been included in works written by authors such as Sanford Jacoby who have considered management training programs within the context of what corporate executives and owners hoped to achieve in terms of overall company policy, especially as it related to personnel administration.[38] Management is mentioned in Canadian business historiography, including research by Graham Taylor and Peter Baskerville.[39] Management attitudes about matters such as the role of the state have been described in research by Christopher Armstrong and H. Vivian Nelles.[40] Learning about the history of management in Canada often means having to look at how companies were operated from the perspective of workers and their unions.

Trying to learn about the history of management education and training in existing literature becomes more challenging as proximity to work on graduate business education lessens. There is literature on the role of class and education that relates to this book. Peter W. Cookson and Caroline Hodges Persell examined the role of education and elite socialization in a study of boarding schools in the United States.[41] Paul Willis revealed the role of education in the lives of working-class youth in the United Kingdom.[42] Those authors researched opposite ends of the social hierarchy and in different countries, but socialization was the key aspect of their analyses. Socialization was also part of management education and training.

Making Managers in Canada

This book will reference all the works mentioned above in subsequent analysis while addressing gaps in what historians know about management education in training in Canada in environments that have not yet been examined in comparison. The book will be divided into six chapters, with considerable primary source material found throughout. The first chapter will discuss the history of management in Canada from the time of European colonization to the immediate post–World War II period. It will emphasize the impact of British labour and employment law on the rights of management in Canada, the emergence of industrialization, the important role of geography in shaping business in Canada, the rise of organized labour, and management theory prior to the late 1940s. The career of one of Canada's first management theorists will also be revealed. This chapter will also serve as a review of existing research on the history of management in Canada.[43]

The second chapter will discuss management education and training programs at three Canadian companies: Bell Canada, T. Eaton Company, and Labatt Brewing. These companies were chosen because they were prominent in Canadian public life, and they were also owned by Canadian shareholders. This chapter will be mainly composed of research materials found at the Bell Canada Archive, the Archive of Ontario, and the Archives and Research Collections Centre at Western University Canada (formerly the University of Western Ontario). The third chapter will describe the creation of three community colleges in Canada and the management and supervisory programs that they offered over a five-decade period. The colleges are Vancouver Community College (VCC) in British Columbia, Collège Ahuntsic in Québec, and Niagara College in Ontario. Canadian universities operate their own archives and are usually diligent about retaining historical records. In contrast, community colleges often do not possess organized archives. The VCC records that are referenced here are held by Langara College, which was previously a VCC campus. The Collège Ahuntsic documents that are described in this narrative are housed at the Bibliothèque et Archives nationales du Québec (BAnQ). Niagara College has considerable archival holdings, and they thankfully permitted access even though the materials are not formally organized.

The fourth chapter discusses undergraduate business and management education programs offered by the University of British Columbia (UBC) in Vancouver, École des hautes études commerciales (HEC) in Montréal, and the University of Western Ontario (UWO) in London, Ontario. There are a range of archival materials available at all three universities, including program guides and records, with more documents available at UBC and HEC than at UWO. The fifth chapter will draw upon many of the same primary sources to discuss graduate management and short-duration programs offered by the same three universities. The final chapter will summarize the arguments made in the preceding five chapters, refer to key developments in Canadian history from 1945 to 1995 that pertain to the history of management, and conclude by discussing the meaning of management education and training in Canada in the different forms in which it was conducted.

It is important to note that virtually all the archival materials about Collège Ahuntsic and HEC are written in French, and any errors in translation that may be found are the author's alone. The archival materials that will be referenced came in different forms. Earlier sources from corporate records are in print form, while those from later decades came in audio and video formats. Materials pertaining to university and college programs are in print format. The three oral interviews were with former UWO Business School professor Donald Thain, former Niagara College faculty member Sherri Rosen, and a man who will be referred to as John who worked in corporate film and video production and preferred to remain anonymous. The interviews were conducted in order to add to what is found in the other forms of archival sources. Each type of research source has its own strength and limitations, but they collectively provide enormous insights into the meaning of management in Canada in the post–World War II decades.

Management, managing, and managers are important in Canadian society even if their impact is not always readily identifiable. There have been people performing management roles in Canada since Europeans first sailed across the Atlantic Ocean and began exploiting the North American continent's natural resources. The idea of designating one or more people with the authority to organize and direct work in an organization existed well before Canada became a new country in 1867. Functions in an organization may be managed by someone who does not have people reporting directly to him or her, but being a manager usually means organizing and directing the work of other people. Managers have wide discretion over how organizations function, and decisions that they make can make a company thrive and make it a provider of profit and employment, or they can quickly cause widespread failure. Major institutions in Canada—companies, community colleges, and universities—decided that teaching managerial skills was important, and the people whom they educated and trained were part of the country's development in the post–World War II decades. They often pursued education and training objectives with extensive help from the state. This is why it is important to think about how management developed in its many forms across Canada. Everyone who works for wages has at some time been managed, engaged in management, or interacted with a manager. This book helps explain how managers were made during important decades in Canada's history.

Notes

1 Jason Russell, *Our Union: UAW/CAW Local 27 from 1950 to 1990* (Edmonton: Athabasca University Press, 2011).
2 C. Wright Mills, *The Power Elite* (Oxford: Oxford University Press, 1956), 119.
3 Mills, *The Power Elite*, 135–136.
4 C. Wright Mills, *White Collar: The American Middle Classes* (New York: Oxford University Press, 1953), 87.
5 Mills, *White Collar*, 86.
6 William H. Whyte, *The Organization Man* (New York: Simon and Schuster, 1959).
7 E.P. Thompson, *The Making of the English Working Class* (London: Penguin, 1991), 8–9.
8 Sidney Pollard, *The Genesis of Modern Management: A Study of the Industrial Revolution in Great Britain* (Cambridge, MA: Harvard University Press, 1965).
9 John F. Wilson and Andrew Thompson, *The Making of Modern Management: British Management in Historical Perspective* (Oxford: Oxford University Press, 2006).

10 Alfred Chandler, *The Visible Hand: The Managerial Revolution in American Business* (Cambridge, MA: Belknap, 1977).

11 Pollard, *The Genesis of Modern Management*, 86.

12 Wilson and Thomson, *The Making of Modern Management*, 81.

13 Chandler, *The Visible Hand*, 95.

14 David Noble, *America By Design: Science, Technology, and the Rise of Corporate Capitalism* (Oxford: Oxford University Press, 1977), 41.

15 Chester Barnard, *The Functions of the Executive* (Cambridge, MA: Harvard University Press, 1938).

16 Peter Drucker, *The Practice of Management* (New York: Harper and Brothers, 1954).

17 Melville Dalton, *Men Who Manage: Fusions of Feeling and Theory in Administration* (New York: John Wiley and Sons, 1959).

18 Roy Lewis and Rosemary Stewart, *The Boss: The Life and Times of the British Business Man* (London: Phoenix House, 1961).

19 Vance Packard, *The Pyramid Climbers* (New York: McGraw-Hill, 1962).

20 Rosabeth Moss Kanter, *Men and Women of the Corporation* (New York: Basic Books, 1977).

21 Robert Jackall, *Moral Mazes: The World of Corporate Managers* (Oxford: Oxford University Press, 1988).

22 Packard, *The Pyramid Climbers*, 30.

23 Chandler, *The Visible Hand*, 155.

24 Stephen Cummings, Todd Bridgman, John Hassard, and Michael Rowlinson, *A New History of Management* (Cambridge: Cambridge University Press, 2017).

25 Rakesh Khurana, *From Higher Aims to Hired Hands: The Social Transformation of American Business Schools and the Unfulfilled Promise of Management as a Profession* (Princeton: Princeton University Press, 2007).

26 Carter Daniel, *MBA: The First Century* (Lewisburg: Bucknell University Press, 1998).

27 Barbara Austin, ed., *Capitalizing Knowledge: Essays on the History of Business Education in Canada* (Toronto: University of Toronto Press, 2000).

28 Robert R. Locke, *Management and Higher Education Since 1940: The Influence of America and Japan on West Germany, Great Britain, and France* (Cambridge: Cambridge University Press, 1989).

29 Lars Engwall and Vera Zamagni, ed., *Management Education in Historical Perspective* (Manchester: Manchester University Press, 1998).

30 Rolv Amdam, *Management Education and Competitiveness: Europe, Japan and the United States* (Abingdon: Routledge, 1996).

31 Richard Whitley, Alan Thomas, and Jane Marceau, *Masters of Business: Business Schools and Business Graduates in Britain and France* (London: Tavistock Publications, 1991).

32 Nancy Harding, *The Social Construction of Management: Texts and Identities* (London: Routledge, 2003).

33 Henry Mintzberg, *Managers Not MBAs: A Hard Look at the Soft Practice of Managing and Management Development* (San Francisco: Berrett-Koehler Publishers, 2004).

34 Stuart Crainer and Des Dearlove, *Gravy Training: Inside the Business of Business Schools* (San Francisco: Jossey-Bass Publishers, 1999).

35 Robert Locke and J.C. Spender, *Confronting Managerialism: How the Business Elite and Their Schools Threw Our Lives Out of Balance* (London: Zed Books, 2011).

36 Duff McDonald, *The Golden Passport: Harvard Business School, the Limits of Capitalism, and the Moral Failure of the MBA Elite* (New York: Harper Collins, 2017).

37 For an overview of the history of higher education policy in Canada see David M. Cameron, *More Than an Academic Question: Universities, Government, and Public Policy in Canada* (Halifax: The Institute for Research on Public Policy, 1991).

38 Sanford Jacoby, *Modern Manors: Welfare Capitalism Since the New Deal* (Princeton: Princeton University Press, 1997).

39 Graham D. Taylor and Peter Baskerville, *A Concise History of Business in Canada* (Oxford: Oxford University Press, 1994).

40 Christopher Armstrong and H. Vivian Nelles, *Monopoly's Moment: The Organization and Regulation of Canadian Utilities, 1830–1930* (Philadelphia: Temple University Press, 1986).

41 Peter W. Cookson Jr. and Caroline Hodges Persell, *Preparing for Power: America's Elite Boarding Schools* (New York: Basic Books, 1985).

42 Paul Willis, *Learning to Labour: How Working Class Kids Get Working Class Jobs* (Westmead, Farnborough, Hampshire, England: Gower, 1980).

43 Chapters 1 and 2 will include some content that has previously been presented by the author in Jason Russell, "Organization Men and Women: Making Managers at Bell Canada from the 1940s to the 1960s", *Management and Organizational History* 10, 3–4 (2015), pp. 213–229.

1 Management in Canada to 1945

The practice of management had common aspects regardless of the organization in which it occurred and where it happened. Variation in management practice occurs over time and place and is also shaped by a range of social, economic, cultural, and political influences. The practice of management in Canada has also historically been shaped by these different factors, and this chapter will describe how Canadian management developed over time. It will consider one key question: how did management develop in Canada prior to 1945, and what was unique about it? There are several related sub-issues that pertain to this overall question, including what roles geography, education, gender, race, ethnicity, technology, and relations with other nations played in shaping Canadian management. The manner in which an early managerial class was formed in Canada is also a key issue. Management in Canada developed features that related to each other to create a unique form of management that would nonetheless have been recognizable to anyone looking at the country from abroad. It also reflected the wider socio-economic development of the country.

There is literature on the history of business development in Canada, but much less research on the development of Canadian management. Since this chapter is focused on the making of managers, considering how managers of different forms learned to do their jobs is a central part of this chapter. This analysis will begin by discussing existing historical literature, with particular emphasis on labour and working-class history because Canadian labour historians have said much more about management than their colleagues in business history even though they have primarily described management through the eyes of workers. Canadian management practice was also shaped by ideas about hierarchy and class that later manifested themselves in theories that were framed around workplace organization. This chapter will describe how these theories and beliefs guided the shaping of managers.

Geography has often been fundamental to analyses of economic development in Canada, and it is also helps explain how organizations in the country were formed and managed. Canadian political economist

Harold Adams Innis postulated in his Staples Thesis that Canada's economy was essentially shaped by natural resources. He was principally concerned with how European settlers used natural resources while being influenced by them. Canada did not exist as a political entity at the time of European settlement, at least not in terms recognizable to Europeans. Indigenous peoples had been relying on natural resources in North America for thousands of years prior to European settlement, and the first settlers to come from Britain and France were immediately struck by the enormous size of the country. The idea of the North American continent being vast became part of standard national narratives. Canada was also linked to wider global economic networks from the moment that Europeans arrived.[1]

A second major theory of economic development in Canada was developed by Donald Creighton, who had also been influenced by Innis. Creighton postulated the idea that Canada's economy had grown around the St. Lawrence River, and his theory was called the Laurentian Thesis.[2] The idea of the nature of land and geography influencing the progress of commercial development was at the forefront of Creighton's thinking, as it was with Innis. That idea of the land shaping human activity rather than the other way around became a central part of historical analysis in Canada until the 1970s. In contrast, the idea of the land shaping human agency arguably did not become a popular stream in American historiography until authors like William Cronon began writing about it in the 1980s and 1990s.[3]

The Staples and Laurentian theses described Canada's economy through sequential periods of development, but they did not focus on resources that would become crucial to Canada's modern economic developments: hydro-electric power and hydrocarbons. The state began making lasting economic policy decisions within a few years of Confederation in 1867. The widely known National Policy of Sir John A. MacDonald's Conservative Party was introduced in 1879. It featured three key policies that would foster the development of a country that had achieved independence from Great Britain: a high tariff to protect emerging domestic manufacturing, an ambitious plan to populate western Canada with European immigrants, and a railway that would cross the country from east to west. Canada is in many ways a hydrocarbon country because the European immigrants who organized it into its current form could not have done so unless its great physical expanse could be traversed.

The concept of management as developed in Canada has European roots. Indigenous populations that lived in North America prior to European colonization had nothing equivalent to the legal structures that underpinned what would later be called managerial authority. The legal origins of management in Canada are primarily found in English common law, since the country became part of the British Empire. As Douglas Hay and Paul Craven have noted, master and servant laws set the boundaries for relations between employers and workers throughout the empire for more than 500 years.[4] These laws established employment as a private contract that gave employers the power to command and obliged workers to obey.[5] Such laws appeared in different forms across the empire, but the key point is that the employer and those wielding authority were supported by a legal system that gave them enormous influence over how employment would function. Indeed, as Craven additionally noted, the 1349 Statute of Labourers introduced in England following the Black Death was a forerunner to subsequent laws, and it gave justices of the peace the power to force able-bodied men and women to work for any master that required his or her services.[6]

Early forms of business organization in Canada were supported by an established legal system, but the forms that they took varied in complexity. Master craftsmen and farmers represented basic forms of free market production. The corporation was another much more complex form of business organization that emerged in Canada in the seventeenth century. The Hudson's Bay Company (HBC) was founded in 1670 to facilitate the expansion of the fur trade.[7] There is a significant literature on the role of corporations in founding and expanding the British Empire, most notably on the British East India Company.[8] HBC was part of that system. The people who ran it and other companies in the British Empire had no training as managers, even though they executed managerial functions.

The administrators of HBC were concerned with ensuring that a supply of furs was shipped to Britain at a profit and that there was a sufficient supply of labour to ensure that the company operated. The firm's operations were spread across a wide swath of territory. The people who operated HBC were thus Canada's earliest managers although they lacked formal training. As Pollard noted, "formal management training was so rare as to be negligible" in the late eighteenth century, and managers thus learned on the job.[9] Early European settlement in North America involved an almost constant shortage of labour. Efforts to try and compel indigenous people to adapt to European work practices were usually unsuccessful. As Burley has described, HBC brought indentured labourers from Britain and preferred people who came from areas such as the Orkney Islands because it was thought that they would be obedient.[10] The company faced ongoing labour recruitment problems for much of the eighteenth and early nineteenth centuries. Burley argues that it was a conservative, paternalistic, and authoritarian organization that operated using pre-industrial processes.[11] HBC had a hierarchical structure, with its directors based in London, England. It would be the forerunner of future business structures in Canada.

H. Clare Pentland discussed the importance of indentured servitude to the Canadian economy during the pre-1800 colonial period. Indeed, a person coming to the Caribbean during that period was likely to be an

African slave, while someone coming to more northern colonies was an indentured servant.[12] The need to identify and import labour was a key challenge for Canadian employers from the pre-Confederation period prior to 1867, and in the following decades. The terms "personnel" and "human resource management" were obviously not used in the nineteenth century, but dealing with labour matters was a central function for anyone running a business. As Peter Way illustrated, a class system emerged in North America between 1786 and 1860 that was predicated on industrial capitalism.[13] Divisions between skilled and unskilled labour increased, and employers in Canada and the United States continued to identify specific immigrant groups for jobs depending on their ethnicity. In the case of canal construction, Irish immigrants who lived in poor conditions were often used.[14] However, as Way also argues, the emergence of the engineering profession in North America was grounded in canal construction. Way also notes differing roles played by governments in Canada and the United States when it came to major capital projects like canals, as there was more state intervention in Canada.[15]

The role of the state in shaping early economic development in Canada and, in turn, the management of enterprises, has been examined in depth by Michael Bliss. He described a Canadian economy in the late eighteenth and early nineteenth centuries that was heavily dependent on British military spending, which exceeded the value of the fur trade.[16] Pentland argued that nineteenth-century Canadians had become accustomed to state economic intervention and held qualified opinions regarding free market competition.[17] This was also true of people who ran commercial enterprises. The state was a major consumer of commercial goods, and it also created a statutory framework that was intended to protect domestic business.

There was some rudimentary formal training for managers and business owners in Canada by the late nineteenth century, but it focused on basic aspects of business operation rather than presenting corporations as large integrated entities. For example, an 1889 compendium for a school in Guelph, Ontario, presented business as important and advised students:

> Do not anticipate an easy marc to the goal of your present ambition. Be prepared rather for meeting difficulties, but be thoroughly determined by faithful self-application to overcome them. Don't lean for support upon the skill or strength of others, but draw upon your own power of will, and exercise your own mental faculties, study system and save time. Life is short: waste no part of it in trifling; be in earnest. . . . Thus you will justly earn the Diploma of the College, and go out with confidence from this miniature world of business to contend on that broader arena where fortune and fame await the competent.[18]

Guelph Business College focused on bookkeeping and other financial aspects of running a business, and a basic form of case teaching methodology. For example, the Third Set problem presented to students stated:

> You will open this set at No. 144 Main St., St John, N.B., and there conduct a Wholesale Dry Goods and Commission Business. The books to be used are the Day Book, Journal, Cash Book, Invoice Book, Sales Book, and Ledger, with some auxiliary books in the former sets.[19]

Students were advised that they were embarking on a daunting program of study but that they could succeed by applying themselves. They were not industrial managers but instead small business people who wanted to learn basic aspects of commercial enterprise. They learned to manage business functions and were not managers like those found in new large corporations. Relations between workers and employers, the role of government, marketing, and other aspects of later business practice were not part of their studies.

The size and scope of businesses in Canada increased from the mid-nineteenth century to the turn of the twentieth century. Paul Craven described relations between labour and management in one railway firm in Ontario from the 1850s to the 1880s. The Great Western Railway (GWR), like predecessor firms such as HBC, had directors and shareholders based in England. Employer paternalism, already long-established in Canada, was a core feature of GWR management methodology.[20] The railway industry was one in which people could develop actual careers, and Craven described several people in management positions at GWR who had begun theirs with companies in England before being recruited to work in Canada.[21] This was a departure from earlier forms of business organization in Canada where perhaps the only person who would have had a career would have been the actual owner of a company. The fact that the owners and shareholders of the railway were in Britain meant that the profits that they would receive were entirely dependent on what non-owning managers did on the other side of the Atlantic Ocean.

Workers who reported to the emerging management class in Canada also experienced important changes. Organizing in labour organizations had long been considered a conspiracy in restraint of trade under common law, and a group of workers from Dorsetshire were famously convicted and transported to New South Wales (Australia) in 1834 before they were subsequently released.[22] Some of them, including George Loveless, eventually settled outside of London, Ontario. Organizing a union was consequently not lightly contemplated, and unions were legalized in Canada in 1872 with the passage of the Trade Unions Act.[23] Labour unions were organized, with many of them in Ontario. The Knights of Labor (KoL) had been founded in Philadelphia in 1869.[24] It was the first labour organization of its type that operated in both Canada and the United

States. Different historians, especially Greg Kealey and Bryan Palmer, have argued that the KoL was also the most important union in Canada prior to 1900.[25] It was formed at a time when Canada was experiencing enormous industrial growth. For instance, the number of business establishments capitalized at $50,000 increased by 50 percent between 1870 and 1890.[26] The phenomenon of Canadian workers joining American unions while also increasingly working for employers based in the United States would be a defining aspect of Canada's economy as the country entered the twentieth century. This was especially true of membership in unions that were linked to the American Federation of Labor (AFL) that was founded in 1886.[27] Canadian business significantly expanded in the late nineteenth century, grew in complexity, and saw the emergence of a countervailing force in the form of organized labour.

Relations between management and labour were fractious into the twentieth century even though unions had become legal. As Eric Tucker has discussed, industrial workplaces were dangerous, and working conditions were adversely impacted by new hazards and forms of work organization.[28] The legal view of employment continued to be that it was a form of contract, and that working conditions were not germane to that contract.[29] It was extraordinarily difficult to prove employer liability in court, often because of a biased judiciary.[30] The influx of women and children into the unskilled industrial workforce, and the dangers that they faced on the job, was the main impetus for the introduction of Ontario's first Factory Act in 1884.[31] Tucker argued that this law did not alter the balance of power between management and workers in industrial workplaces.[32] It did represent an improvement in the position of labour in Ontario, which was Canada's leading industrialized province. Race also played a key role in how Canada's economy developed. The racialization of work was evident in different areas of the country. For example, as Donald Avery has shown, Chinese immigrant workers played a key role in building the Canadian Pacific Railway that was part of the Macdonald government's national policy, but they were also subjected to a head tax.[33] David Goutor described opposition to immigration within the Canadian labour movement, with race having been a motivating factor over concerns about Asian workers as a menace to white society.[34] As Avery further showed, race and ethnicity would play a role in labour and employment in Canada into the latter part of the twentieth century.

The companies that emerged in the early twentieth century, and the managers who ran them, faced some organized opposition in the form of early unions. They were regulated by the state but, as the case of workplace safety shows, this did not happen in punitive manner. The Canadian state was instead often central to the development of commercial activity. The policies and practices used by companies began to significantly alter at the turn of the century, and this is also when early management theory appeared. The labour process was rationalized into its constituent parts partly in order to improve efficiency and profitability but also to enhance managerial control over organizations. Harry Braverman argued that management appeared when workers were concentrated in one production location. New industries appeared, such as sugar refining and distilling, that were not artisanal in nature, while others like iron smelting were transformed. Braverman argued, "All of these required conceptual and coordination functions which in capitalist industry took the form of management."[35]

A similar narrative on the emergence of modern management practices and work processes with in a Canadian context has been developed by James Rinehart. Like Braverman, Rinehart identifies the rise of scientific management as a major reason for changes in work organization in the early twentieth century.[36] American Frederick Winslow Taylor was the person behind scientific management, with his ideas having been articulated in his 1911 book *The Principles of Scientific Management*. Taylor stressed that "the management must take over and perform much of the work which is now left to the men."[37] Managers would plan work in advance, and workers would perform it.[38] Those workers actually doing tasks lost control and discretion over what they did, while management would exercise sole control over the work process. The Taylorist work system became an integral part of Canadian industry and management practice into the twentieth century. This was particularly evident in the steel industry, which Craig Heron has described as being "a small, fragile edifice" in the 1890s in comparison to its American and European counterparts.[39] This situation changed in the 1900s, especially when the Steel Company of Canada (Stelco) was formed by the amalgamation of a group of smaller companies then opened new blast furnaces and mills in Hamilton, Ontario.[40] Stelco was owned and run by Canadian business interests, not by British or American investors. The company's managers oversaw a workforce that was largely composed of European immigrants.[41] Heron notes that, prior to the turn of the twentieth century, factory management was handled by the people who owned them along with the assistance of a small number of clerks and foremen.[42] This situation changed markedly in the 1900s as managerial systems that had previously been created by railway companies were implemented in manufacturing.[43] The managers who ran new manufacturing firms viewed themselves as professionals and sought recognition of their new status.[44] Taylorism became known in Canada in 1911 and gained currency among some employers while also raising the ire of skilled workers.[45]

The managerial systems that were used in railways, then in other business organizations in Canada, have been most notably explained by American historian Alfred Chandler. He showed that the model of corporation organization was hierarchical and divided into functions with successive layers of management.[46] Chandler described the introduction of scientific management and Frederick Winslow Taylor's central role in implementing it.[47] He also described a wave of mergers that happened in the 1880s that led to the emergence of large corporations run by managers.[48] The end result was that "managers assumed command in the central sectors of the American economy."[49] The same was true of their place in Canada's economy as companies like Stelco and Dofasco were formed and expanded. Canadian businesses merged years after their American counterparts, and they eventually used the same methods as their peers south of the border to run new business structures.

Canadian managers, such as those at Stelco or other domestically owned firms, were influenced by ideas from outside the country such as those developed by Frederick Winslow Taylor. They also shared views with their counterparts in the United States. Managers could be punitive and felt that they had an inherent right to run business in an unfettered manner. Employer paternalism was still widely practiced and was often manifested through corporate welfare programs. In the case of some firms such as steel company Dofasco, it enabled managers to avoid unionization into the 1930s and 1940s and maintain complete control over the production process.[50] The emergence of modern management also appeared in non-manufacturing environments. Graham Lowe has described how office automation facilitated managerial control.[51] New processes like cost accounting changed the nature of administrative work.[52] The introduction of the upright Underwood typewriter was a leading mechanical innovation that altered clerical work.[53] Lowe overall identified three key changes in office work: mechanization, feminization, and managerial control.[54] Office work became women's work as it became more rationalized, while men who had previously been clerks in less automated environments assumed managerial roles.[55]

Mechanization, job rationalization, managerial control, and paternalism were popular methods used for running companies into the 1920s in manufacturing and beyond in Canada. As Donica Belisle has shown, paternalism was also a preferred management technique in the retailing industry from 1880 to 1940.[56] Laurel Sefton-McDowell described how Canadian firms formed industrial councils in order to dissuade workers from joining unions.[57] William Lyon Mackenzie King, who would become Canada's longest-serving prime minister, wrote a book about the need to ensure industrial peace between workers and employers.[58] His ideas were based on work he had done for the Rockefeller family in the United States. Paternalism and welfare capitalism were influenced by the work of George Elton Mayo, who became synonymous with a series of studies conducted at Western Electric's Hawthorne Works.[59] Mayo's work propelled the creation of the Human Relations School of management, which also appeared in Canada.

Corporate welfarism in Canada has been described by Margaret McCallum. She argues that it served specific goals for employers: the productive and efficient use of labour, control over production and personnel, and securing worker acceptance of a class-based social order.[60] The problem was that it faltered in the face of economic catastrophe in the 1930s. There is a broader literature in the United States on work and labour in the years of the Great Depression, but much of what American historians have found applies to Canada. Lizabeth Cohen described the use of welfare capitalism plans at Chicago meatpacking companies like Armour, Swift, Wilson, and Morris in the 1920s and how those plans fell into decline while worker militancy rose.[61] Rising labour militancy blunted the effectiveness of many welfare capitalism programs. However, there were companies that maintained such programs during the rise of industrial unions in the New Deal era. Kodak was one firm that spent considerable sums on employee amenities like cafeterias and bowling alleys.[62]

The Canadian economy leading into the late 1930s and early 1940s was increasingly dominated by large firms in different industries. Retailers like T. Eaton Company, which is discussed in a subsequent chapter, was one example. Manufacturing firms like Stelco were another type of large firm. The role of the state continued to be very evident in the years preceding World War II. For example, the crown corporation became an important corporate form in twentieth-century Canada. It would eventually take many forms, including transportation firms in airlines and railways. Hydroelectric power was another industry in which the crown corporation became important. Such entities functioned as corporations, but the state was the shareholder and the firms often operated in monopoly conditions. For instance, Graham Taylor and Peter Baskerville have described the landmark founding of the 1910 Ontario Hydroelectric Commission.[63] The enormous kinetic energy of Niagara Falls was harnessed to electrify the province, and smaller privately owned electricity producers were forced to become part of the publicly owned monopoly.

Analyses of publicly owned corporations in Canadian historiography differ from what is found in American historical literature. Chandler talked about the role of government in stopping the 1930s economic crisis, and gradual changes in relations between business and government into the 1940s.[64] In contrast, as shown with Bliss, Taylor and Baskerville, and Christopher Armstrong and H.V. Nelles, the role of government in economic development is often central to historical analysis Canada.[65] The role of government was central to business production during both world wars. Canadian industry produced $1.25 billion worth of munitions and armaments for the Imperial Munitions Board between 1914 and 1918, and the wartime economy increased efficiency and profitability.[66] Similar patterns were found in World War II, with close to $10 billion worth of war materials produced.[67] Such was the extent of the government's involvement in the war effort that a new crown entity, the Polymer Corporation, was established to produce synthetic rubber to meet war production demands.[68] However, while the Canadian state pursued interventionist economic policies, the country also became more economically linked to the United States as the war further frayed links to Britain. Taylor and Baskerville cite the 1941 Hyde Park declaration between Canada and the United States as a significant economic turning point as much as it represented a strategic wartime decision.[69]

The interwar years were, as Don Nerbas has argued, a period of crisis for Canadian business leaders. People like Royal Bank of Canada president Sir Herbert Holt thought in 1929 that the years ahead would be much like the preceding fifty-year period of prosperity that began with the National Policy.[70] They instead found themselves dealing with momentous change as long-standing conditions such as the economic influence of Britain waned while American influence increased.[71] Owners and executives of large enterprises chafed against the more state-oriented form of capitalism brought in by senior federal government minister C.D. Howe during World War II.[72] Nonetheless, the business-owning class in Canada that sat at the top of the Canadian elite continued to wield influence in both commercial and political spheres.[73] Peter C. Newman would eventually describe that group as the Canadian establishment.[74]

Canadian management in the 1940s did not have a business philosophy that emphasized relentless pursuit of profit, but instead emphasized prudence. An internal document produced by the Ronalds Company of Montréal in 1940 summarized the views of many people running Canadian business:

> The primary job of the management of business is to make a fair distribution of income among customers, employees, and investors. Some people have another idea of the job of management. They believe that the primary job of management is to increase income so that there will be more money to distribute. That belief is not entirely sound. There is no ordinance or law requiring a business to have any particular income, but there is an economic law that requires a business to live within its income (whatever it is) or fail. The principles of management in business are the same as the principles that apply to the management of one's personal affairs. Every man who has a job wants to earn more money. That's a natural desire, and it is supported by a willingness to study and work for advancement, it can be properly called an ambition. But it is not, necessarily, a form of management. Management is the practical task of keeping one's expenses within one's income.[75]

Canadian businesses, and the managers who ran them, entered a post–World War II world that was much different than what they had experienced in the decades up to the start of war. The country's economy had expanded enormously, the need for managerial skills had increased along with the expansion of business activity, and the state was more active than it had ever been in economic affairs. On the other hand, as Bliss noted, corporations in the immediate post-war years publicly seemed to be run by faceless managers who knew each other through personal and professional networks.[76] This reinforced a significant issue that was the focus of an important analysis by Adolph Berle and Gardiner Means, who argued that a corporate system had emerged by the early 1930s that should be regarded as a social institution.[77] Berle and Means suggested that "In its new aspect the corporation is a means whereby the wealth of innumerable individuals has been concentrated into huge aggregate and where by control over this wealth has been surrendered to a unified direction."[78] The unified direction was provided by managers who controlled wealth but did not actually own it. This situation still fundamentally prevailed in the post–World War II years.

Workers had also acquired new legal rights, and a vast expansion of unions occurred as the result of the introduction of industrial legislation modeled after the National Labor Relations Act in the United States, but management attitudes toward labour had not significant altered from the 1920s. As Howell Harris has described, American management in the 1940s wanted workers and the general public to agree with the same view of social order held by business executives.[79] In his analysis, management had a unitary ideology regarding how workplaces would function, and businessmen were quite determined that there was no room for democracy in industry.[80] The border between Canada and the United States was no physical barrier to this view of how the workplace should function. American firms like General Motors and Ford Motor Company had been operating in Canada since immediately after the turn of the twentieth century, with the latter firm establishing a Canadian subsidiary in 1904.[81] This was the beginning of the branch-plant aspect of Canada's economy, and it brought American management ideology.

Corporations continued to adopt new technologies, and manufacturing industries like steel and automotive were not the only places where such changes were found. As Ian Radforth explained, logging was transformed as management introduced new technology. The early twentieth century logging industry relied on a lot of immigrant labour, much like the Hudson's Bay Company in prior centuries.[82] There was a shortage of workers by the 1950s, which led to changes in production processes.[83] Mechanization was a solution to labour shortages and also increased production. As Radforth notes, it was welcomed by both workers and their managers.[84] As subsequent analysis will show, technological change had an ongoing effect on Canadian businesses and how they trained the people whom they employed.

Canadian workers formed unions in major numbers in the late 1930s and into the war years, and many of those unions were part of the AFL or the Congress of Industrial Organizations (CIO). The unions, including the United Steel Workers of America (USWA) and the United Auto Workers (UAW), would organize hundreds of thousands of Canadian workers even though they were based in the United States. The National Labor Relations Act (NLRA) passed in the United States in 1935 ensured that workers could form unions and obliged employers to engage in collective bargaining.[85] This law, commonly referred to by the name of the senator who sponsored it—Robert Wagner—was not immediately copied in Canada. A Wagner-based labour relations system began in Canada with the wartime introduction of Privy Council 1003 (PC1003) in 1944.[86] The meaning and consequences of the post-war Wagner system have been the focus of many academic analyses in both Canada and the United States. The key point is that industrial unionism was thriving as the 1940s ended, while managers still wanted unfettered control of workplaces.

Management was a hierarchical function, as shown by Chandler, and lower-level supervisors, commonly called foremen from the early 1900s well into to the post–World War II decades, were at the lowest rung of the management structure. They were not the people described by Berle and Means who wielded control over the profits of corporations. They were instead largely anonymous and from the same social class backgrounds as the workers whom they supervised. However, as Charles Larrowe illustrated, senior management was determined that foremen view themselves as being firmly on the side of business and not confused by conflicted loyalties. A union called the Foreman's Association of America (FAA) was formed at the Ford Rouge plant in 1941 and had grown to 50,000 members across twenty American states and Canada.[87] It was expanding into other industries such as steel and rubber by that point. In 1946, the US National Labor Relations Board ordered the Packard Motor Company to begin bargaining with a foreman's union formed in its organization.[88] American business was extremely concerned that the lowest level of the management hierarchy could become unionized and successfully lobbied to have management unionization banned under the 1947 Taft-Hartley Act.[89] Management would also face barriers to organizing in Canada. Nonetheless, there was increasing disenchantment among foremen. In 1950, 73 percent of American foremen who were surveyed by Opinion Research Corporation expressed satisfaction with the way that they were treated by senior management.[90] A white collar occupation was not something to which a lot of blue collar workers aspired and Ely Chinoy found in a 1955 study of an American manufacturing company that manual workers had little interest in white collar jobs.[91] They were aware of management hierarchy—some had seen company executives—but rising to the rank of foreman was the most that any of them wanted to attain if they harboured ambitions of promotion.[92] Being a foreman was surely viewed as a difficult job that did not come with sufficient rewards. This sentiment was also surely prevalent in Canada among blue collar workers who grew up from the 1920s to the 1940s.

Canadian businesses continued to be segregated in different ways, with gender as a key consideration. Women streamed into industrial employment during World War II and sought to join unions. For employers, the need to maintain war production at a time of labour shortages was a paramount consideration, so hiring women for men's jobs was a necessary choice. However, as Pamela Sugiman revealed, women encountered challenges when entering those wartime workplaces and continued to do so into the post-war era.[93] By the war's end, the standard employment relationship (SER) was the aspiration for workers regardless of gender across Canada and the United States. Leah Vosko described the SER as "lifelong, continuous, continuous employment relationship where the worker has one employer and normally works on the employer's premises or under his or her direct supervision."[94] The forty-hour work week with middle-class wages and benefits were features of the type of job that Canadians wanted. Large corporations were suppliers of those kinds of jobs, and the manager's role fit nicely into the SER description.

The people who ran Canadian business were not theoretical thinkers. They were instead practically minded people who were interested in expanding their enterprises and profits and who would have paid attention to the words of management theorists if they felt that it would beneficial to do so. As already seen from the work of Frederick Winslow Taylor and George Elton Mayo, theory had a profound impact on the way in which businesses operated from the early nineteenth century onward. Management theories do not stand in isolation from each other, and there were a range of people writing about workplace organization up until the late 1940s other than Taylor and Mayo. Patricia Genoe McLaren and Albert Mills have argued that there is an absence of management theory in Canada that is distinct from what is found in the United States.[95] There were people in Canada in the 1930s and 1940s who began thinking about management, and one of them was even a self-taught theorist named Clarence Fraser.

Thinking About Management Theory

Clarence H. Fraser was a figure in Canadian history who enjoyed influence during his career but has been otherwise forgotten. Although he only now exists in archival documents, his writing and consulting work surely had an impact on thousands of managers at various levels in organizations across North America. Fraser was, after William Lyon Mackenzie-King, one of Canada's first management consultants. Like many management theorists of the pre–World War II decades, he was not a formally trained academic. As subsequent discussion will show, the seemingly scholarly theories of people like Peter Drucker were preceded by a number of highly influential works produced by essentially self-taught theorists.

Fraser joined Bell Telephone in Montréal in 1923 as a traffic student. At this time, Bell job titles that included references to traffic usually meant working in routing or monitoring phone calls. The Bell system had little automation and was staffed by large numbers of telephone operators, and other administrative staff—often female—handled the routine and often demanding work of operating Canada's largest telephone system. Fraser had been promoted to traffic supervisor by 1929 and advanced to the position of general personnel supervisor for Bell by 1940. As Fraser noted in a brief autobiography, Bell did not possess a major personnel function prior to 1940. His promotion to personnel supervisor brought him into close working contact with vice presidents responsible for various different functions within the corporation.[96]

By his own admission, Clarence Fraser knew little about the personnel function when he began working in it in 1934. He nonetheless developed a keen interest in all aspects of it—especially career planning for management—and he developed an enduring fascination with it for the rest of his career. In a 1933 memorandum to senior Bell management, Fraser noted the rapid expansion of the Bell network in Ontario and Québec and the central role of foremen in company operations. His interest in personnel matters grew out of his field experience "to the point where it far outweighs any other phase of Traffic activity." He furthermore planned to take a leave of absence from Bell to travel to Britain and Europe to studying industrial relations practice.[97]

Fraser did not make it to continental Europe, but he did travel to the United States and initiated correspondence with leading 1930s American management thinkers and with theorists in Britain. He was profoundly shaped by what he saw developing with the New Deal in the United States and came away from a 1933 trip to New York City swept up on a wave of progressive fervour:

> There is a movie house on Broadway where the news of the world is shown for one hour. The place was jammed with people, the motley which is the population of New York. A figured appeared on the screen, President Roosevelt ending his address to the American Legion in Chicago. His voice rang out "comrades, you who wore the colours." One could feel the response about one, stirring to the call from the leader . . . another crusade is underway, with a great leader a crusading knight. That is the main impression. The others are supplementary to it.[98]

Fraser was inspired by Roosevelt to mount his own crusade.

Fraser began to compile his own thoughts on the importance of good employment relations in 1934. He was aware of Elton Mayo and the human relations approach to employment relations, and his ideas were congruent with what Mayo and others advocated.[99] He felt it was important to "shake oneself loose from the limitations of viewing employee and employer relations as two organizations charts greeting each other across a table." Fraser further postulated that "employee-employer negotiation is definitely a social undertaking . . . designed to further certain deep-rooted interests on both sides."[100] He was not a contemporary of Abraham Maslow—the creator of a well-known hierarchy of needs—but his ideas were very similar. Fraser argued that there were basic human desires, including the need for earning, security, leisure, and sharing. These themes would appear in subsequent writing. Fraser commenced a copious correspondence with people in both the United States and Britain at the same time that he began working in personnel at Bell. This eventually involved exchanging letters with groups like the American Management Association, with executives from General Motors and American Telephone and Telegraph, and with British management theorist Lyndall Urwick. Fraser both sought and offered advice on personnel management issues. He also began publishing papers in early personnel management journals. Fraser had developed a sufficient reputation as a personnel management thinker that, by the early 1940s, his opinion was sought by federal ministers dealing with wartime employment issues.[101]

Fraser's principal piece of management thought was called "A Career Plan for Every Man." It was written in 1949 and, while likely not extensively circulated outside of industry groups, it had an impact on managerial thought in Canada. This is because, while Fraser appears to have devoted tremendous effort to writing, reading, and corresponding about personnel management issues, he also continued his employment with Bell. At the very least, the large Bell conglomerate, which also included equipment manufacturing, would have been a testing ground for Fraser's theories. Employer groups in other regions of North America requested copies of his career plan.[102]

Fraser's plan comprised aspects of both the Human Relations School and Taylorism. He indicated that the plan "aims to identify individual's needs for development, protection, direction and encouragement" while also seeing a need to "cultivate human resources for useful purposes."[103] The plan was "no new religion" and "was based on age-old truths on what people want."[104] Career planning was the key theme underlying the entire plan. Fraser generally wrote about male employees, as did the vast majority of management theorists, and stressed that they were to be guided through a rewarding career plan that would enable them to accept, if not rationalize, their own career progress. Fraser claimed that the plan "pays as much attention to men who will not be promoted as those who will."[105] It applied to all levels of an organization and ensured that "every member of the organization develops to the limits of his capacities."[106]

At one point in his narrative, Fraser referred to a "God-Father Relationship" to describe interaction between management and subordinates.[107]

He did not use the terms welfare capitalism or paternalism in reference to his plan—or even corporate social responsibility—but the idea of management being benevolent and paternal was central to his theories. Fraser felt that every person should be regarded as "a career man or career woman" and should see their careers as a series of satisfying jobs and challenges.[108] Much of this would be accomplished by comprehensive feedback on job performance. Employees would go through a thorough review every year, and the process was to be as objective as possible. That particular part of Fraser's plan drew the attention of General Motors, and it was implemented throughout the Bell system in Canada as, in all probability, was his larger guide to career success.

What Fraser proposed was not significantly different from the ideas promulgated by other theorists. There was a human relations aspect to his writing, as he believed that work should be fulfilling and that employers needed to be cognizant of the need to engage employees in a positive manner. Undergoing seemingly objective scrutiny, being agreeable, taking a positive outlook on work, and navigating the intricacies of documents like flow charts would lead to career success. One of the more notable aspects of Fraser's plan is that, while it mentions compensation, there is no discussion of wages. This suggests that he was either disinterested in the details of wage administration or felt that salary amounts were secondary to management's intrinsic rewards. This is a marked contrast with how non-managerial staff wage issues, particularly union wage matters, have traditionally been handled in North American workplaces. The emphasis that Fraser placed on the need to be contented at work is also noteworthy. He may not have specifically known anything about the mental hygiene movement, but his efforts to encourage managers to feel contented rather than resigned with their roles indicates that his theories were as much about conditioning as they were about education.

Fraser must have looked back on his career progress in the late 1940s and felt himself to have made contributions equal to the work done by his intellectual idols including Mary Parker Follett, Henri Fayol, Chester Barnard, and Lyndall Urwick. His theories and background were remarkably similar to theirs in key ways. Follett has been rediscovered in recent years, but Fayol, Barnard, and Urwick have largely disappeared from much contemporary management writing. Like Fraser, it was them, not Peter Drucker and those who came after World War II, who formed the foundations of modern management theory, and it is important to note who they were and why they inspired Clarence Fraser. Henri Fayol was a founder of modern management practice who could be considered equal in importance to Frederick Winslow Taylor, the originator of scientific management. Whereas Taylor focused on breaking the work process into its constituent parts, Fayol emphasized the importance of organizational structure and differing functions within a firm. Fayol essentially rationalized a firm down to six key administrative areas: technical, commercial, financial, security, accounting, and administrative. Those and other ideas were presented in a relatively short book, and Fayol based his views on his long experience working at one mining company. Frederick Winslow Taylor had similarly based much of his ideas on what he observed during his employment at the Midvale Steel Company.[109]

Parker-Follett was unique among early twentieth-century management thinkers because she was a woman and could not assume a major leadership role in a corporation. On the other hand, she had perhaps the best formal education of any of the early theorists, as she attended the Harvard Annex (later Radcliffe College) and demonstrated far greater strength of intellect than someone like Taylor. Much of Parker-Follett's early writing focused on public governance, and her first book was on the United States House of Representatives. She was intensely interested in fostering worker creativity, but also once remarked that the "main purpose of life is testing, verifying, comparing."[110] Such was the force of Parker-Follett's arguments that Lyndall Urwick said that when he met her "in two minutes flat I was at her feet, and I stayed there as long as she lived."[111] Urwick surely did stay there, and Clarence Fraser was sitting at all of their feet in his own way.

In the 1930s and 1940s, Lyndall Urwick enjoyed stature that was somewhat equal to Peter Drucker's in the 1950s and 1960s. His academic training was, however, entirely different from that obtained by the latter two men. Urwick was born in England in 1891 and was the only child in his prosperous middle-class family. His father had been a partner in a glove manufacturing business—Fownes Brothers—and was expected to eventually take over the family business. This life plan was interrupted by service in World War I. Urwick distinguished himself as a junior officer, and later read history at Oxford.

Urwick's family sold their interest in Fownes and, in any event, the firm was not successful. The years that Urwick spent working at Rowntree in the 1920s were the most formative of his career. Firm owner Seebohm Rowntree was also a self-taught management theorist, and Urwick began to form theories of his own under Rowntree's tutelage. His transformation into a management thinker was well underway when he left Rowntree in 1929 to become director of the International Management Institute in Geneva.[112] Clarence Fraser's personal papers suggest that Lyndall Urwick had a marked influence on his own thinking about workplace organization. Urwick felt that there was a need for more formal management education and believed that American universities were doing a better job of providing business education than British universities like Oxford and Cambridge.[113] He prized good personal qualities over anything else when it came to training managers: courage, determination, flexibility of mind, knowledge, and integrity.[114] Urwick was also determined to make management into a profession to such an extent that, in 1956, he felt compelled to argue that it was an intelligent and vital occupation.[115] This suggests that perhaps he continued to be troubled about criticism of business management.

In addition to his great affection for Parker-Follett's work, Urwick was the first person to begin referencing Fayol in English. Fayol's work had not received widespread attention in Britain, the United States, and Canada because it was written in French. He was more commonly known in continental Europe. Urwick considered Fayol the equal of Frederick Winslow Taylor and became a great advocate of rationalization.[116] By 1933, Urwick joined with John Leslie Orr to form Urwick-Orr and Partners. The firm would soon be Britain's principal management consultancy. Its founding also coincided with the start of Clarence Fraser's journey down the intellectual road to solve the problems of personnel management.

Fraser shared numerous similarities with his intellectual idols. Like Taylor, Fayol, and Urwick, he was interested in organizational planning and wanted to help raise intellectual inquiry regarding management to a more professional level. He also based his ideas on his long career at one firm: Bell Telephone. The idea that the personnel solutions employed by a telephone company may not have been useful at a manufacturing firm, a retailer, or a government office seems to have never entered Fraser's mind. Work at Bell was also frequently rationalized and difficult, but Fraser appears not to have noticed this issue. Then again, such doubts do not have seemed to have plagued Urwick, Fayol, or Taylor. Fraser, like his idols, came from an upper middle-class socio-economic background and viewed work largely as an intellectual concept rather than a source of physical and mental distress. He was also an admirer of the work of American engineer Henry Gantt—inventor of an eponymous chart that became favoured in organizational planning—and Gantt was also self-taught and sought professional respect. Parker-Follett was in many ways an outsider who earned respect from business and government leaders. Such people would have seemed incredibly inspiring to an intellectually curious if entirely anonymous traffic supervisor in the late 1920s like Fraser.[117]

Fraser shared a major common trait with other pre–World War II management thinkers, as they all believed that workplace issues, especially the management of firms, were socially important. They did not view work as necessarily being a means of simply gaining economic rewards. Fraser was like Urwick as he also did not sufficiently discuss the importance of compensation in the employment contract. They instead viewed workers as a key part of the organization, but, in beginning to use the term human resources, they reinforced the view that labour was a production input like any other. Fraser was self-taught at a time when people with similar backgrounds dominated management theory. He did not consider himself an amateur. On the contrary, he read widely across the management writing of his time and thought himself worthy enough to produce a theory of his own. The fact that those theories were based on relatively anecdotal observations did not seem to trouble Fraser. It is noteworthy that, even though early management thought was dominated by such thinkers, they knew each other's work. Clarence Fraser, in his own way, brought a Canadian viewpoint to the discussion. The work that he and other self-taught management theorists were doing was having the effect that they desired as it began to have an impact on corporate management practices.

Management in the Late 1940s

The foregoing discussion of how Canadian management evolved up to the late 1940s and the immediate post–World War II years, and the theory that was eventually integrated into management practice, shows both evolution and continuity. Chandler postulated that modern management was a stratified structure, but this was the case since Europeans first arrived on the North American continent. Masters and servants gradually became managers and workers, but the legal regime on which modern management was established had its basic roots in the fourteenth century. Management as an institution, and managers as individuals, had vast prerogatives when it came to running businesses. Managers devoted considerable time and resources to dealing with issues pertaining to work and labour. Colonization required a steady supply of workers from Europe. The transition to industrialization brought further workplace problems for management as labour stratified into unskilled, semi-skilled, and skilled work. Workers demonstrated agency by forming unions, and those organizations were often founded in the United States. Work was shaped by gender, race, class, and ethnicity.

The United States was a constant influence on Canadian management from the start of industrialization. Americans business began consolidating and growing at an earlier period than was experienced in Canada, but the Canadian experience was heavily informed by what occurred south of the border. Britain also continued to have economic influence in Canada into the post–World War I years. Being part of the British Empire meant that government spending was a major part of Canada's domestic product when it was a colony, and it continued to be after Confederation in 1867. The role of the state was evident in the accelerated wave of industrialization that occurred when large Canadian businesses like Stelco were formed and when crown corporations like the Ontario Hydroelectric Commission were created. The Canadian economy experienced enormous expansion during both world wars, and businesses produced more finished goods. The state played an active role in organizing the activities of capital during World War II, but established Canadian business interests were not always receptive to the state's new role. Primary resources like lumber continued to have a prominent role in the country's economy. Many of the new, large manufacturing companies were branches of larger American parent firms like General Motors and Ford, while primary resource companies were often domestically owned.

Theories of business and work organization that originated in the United States, Britain, and France were referenced and implemented in Canada. Taylor and Mayo are the most commonly known early management thinkers, with Taylor having the most profound influence prior to the late 1940s. Managers in cities like Hamilton, Ontario, sought to integrate Taylor's methods into manufacturing. Mayo's influence was felt through the welfare capitalism programs that were implemented at different companies. The work of people like Mary Parker Follet and Lyndall Urwick was also influential in the pre–World War II decades, as was the work of Henri Fayol. These theorists did not stand at odds with each other. They instead successively built on each other's work. The 1930s in particular were a period when a range of authors—from Adolph Berle and Gardiner Means to Chester Barnard—devoted considerable effort to thinking about how modern corporations were formed and who ran them.

People who had job titles relating to the managing and overseeing of business functions had grown in number from the early twentieth century to the late 1940s. Owners of large business enterprises and the executives who ran them sat at the apex of the management hierarchy. They may have attended one of the early university business programs that will be discussed in subsequent chapters. Middle and front-line managers were below them in organizational hierarchies. People in those positions, usually men, often rose from the ranks of the workers whom they would supervise. Their training in managerial methods was an apprenticeship rather than a type of academic study. They learned on the job and, in terms of their place in organizational hierarchies, were closer to the workers they managed rather than bosses to whom they reported. Nonetheless, legal structures put in place in North America in the post–World War years compelled front-line foremen to view themselves as part of management even if they felt more affinity with workers. Management was a key corporate function in late 1940s Canada, as it involved coordinating everything going on within a corporation. People had differing titles depending on their place in the organizational hierarchy but were all involved in doing some kind of managing. Some of them directly managed people, while others may have managed functions but not had anyone reporting to them. Management as a field of academic study was still in comparative infancy, despite the proliferation of management theory in the 1930s, as it was just beginning to be introduced into colleges and universities in the form of degrees and other programs. That situation would begin to quickly change by 1950.

Notes

1 See Harold Adams Innis, *The Fur-Trade of Canada* (Toronto: Oxford University Press, 1927).
2 See Donald Creighton, *Empire of the St. Lawrence* (Toronto: Macmillan, 1956).

3 See William Cronon, *Nature's Metropolis: Chicago and the Great West* (New York: W.W. Norton, 1991).
4 Douglas Hay and Paul Craven, ed., *Masters, Servants, and Magistrates in Britain and the Empire, 1562–1955* (Chapel Hill: University of North Carolina Press, 2004), 1.
5 Hay and Craven, *Masters, Servants, and Magistrates in Britain and the Empire, 1562–1955*, 2.
6 Paul Craven, "The Law of Master and Servant in Mid-Nineteenth Century Ontario", in D.H. Flaherty, ed., *Essays in the History of Canadian Law I* (Toronto: University of Toronto Press, 1981), 182.
7 Edith Burley, *Servants of the Right Honourable Company: Work, Discipline and Conflict in the Hudson's Bay Company, 1779–1870* (Toronto: Oxford University Press, 1997), 2.
8 For example see Philip J. Stern, *The Company-State: Corporate Sovereignty and the Early Modern Foundations of the British Empire in India* (Oxford: Oxford University Press, 2011).
9 Pollard, *The Genesis of Modern Management*, 122.
10 Burley, *Servants of the Right Honourable Company*, 4.
11 Burley, *Servants of the Right Honourable Company*, 2.
12 H. Clare Pentland, *Labour and Capital in Canada, 1650–1860* (Toronto: James Lorimer and Company, 1981), 8.
13 Peter Way, *Common Labour: Workers and the Digging of North American Canals, 1780–1860* (Cambridge: Cambridge University Press, 1993), 3.
14 Way, *Common Labour*, 97.
15 Way, *Common Labour*, 53.
16 Michael Bliss, *Northern Enterprise: Five Centuries of Canadian Business* (Toronto: McClelland Stewart, 1987), 110.
17 Pentland, *Labour and Capital*, 159.
18 Thomas Fisher Rare Book Library, University of Toronto, *Business Compendium: Guelph Business College, 1889*, 3.
19 *Guelph Business College*, 10.
20 Paul Craven, "Labour and Management on the Great Western Railway", Paul Craven, ed., *Labouring Lives: Work and Workers in Nineteenth-Century Ontario* (Toronto: OHSS, 1995), pp. 335–336.
21 Craven, "Labour and Management", 341–345.
22 See Andrew Norman, *The Story of George Loveless and the Tolpuddle Martyrs* (Tiverton: Halsgrove, 2008) for an account of the Tolpuddle Martyrs.
23 Craig Heron, *The Canadian Labour Movement: A Short History, second edition* (Toronto: Lorimer, 1996), 14.
24 Greg Kealey and Bryan Palmer, *Dreaming of What Might Be: The Knights of Labor in Ontario, 1880–1900* (Cambridge: Cambridge University Press, 1982), 57.
25 Kealey and Palmer, *Dreaming of What Might Be*, 57.
26 Kealey and Palmer, *Dreaming of What Might Be*, 29.
27 Heron, *The Canadian Labour Movement*, 30.
28 Eric Tucker, *Administering Danger in the Workplace: The Law and Politics of Occupational Health and Safety Regulation in Ontario, 1850–1914* (Toronto: University of Toronto Press, 1990), 15.
29 Tucker, *Administering Danger in the Workplace*, 45.
30 Tucker, *Administering Danger in the Workplace*, 59.
31 Tucker, *Administering Danger in the Workplace*, 101.
32 Tucker, *Administering Danger in the Workplace*, 210.
33 Donald Avery, *Reluctant Host: Canada's Response to Immigrant Workers, 1896–1994* (Toronto: McClelland and Stewart, 1995), 46–47.

34 David Goutor, *Guarding the Gates: The Canadian Labour Movement and Immigration, 1872–1934* (Vancouver: University of British Columbia Press, 2007), 4–5.
35 Harry Braverman, *Labor and Monopoly Capital: The Degradation of Work in the Twentieth Century* (New York: Monthly Review Press 1974), 41.
36 James Rinehart, *The Tyranny of Work: Alienation and the Labour Process, fourth edition* (Toronto: Harcourt Canada, 2001), 38–41.
37 Frederick Winslow Taylor, *The Principles of Scientific Management* (New York: Harper and Brothers Publishers, 1911), 26.
38 Taylor, *The Principles*, 39.
39 Craig Heron, *Working in Steel: The Early Years in Canada, 1883–1935* (Toronto: McClelland and Stewart, 1988), 16.
40 Heron, *Working in Steel*, 19.
41 Heron, *Working in Steel*, 77.
42 Craig Heron, *Lunch-Bucket Lives: Remaking the Workers' City* (Toronto: Between the Lines, 2015), 239.
43 Heron, *Lunch-Bucket Lives*, 239.
44 Heron, *Lunch-Bucket Lives*, 240.
45 Heron, *Lunch-Bucket Lives*, 241.
46 Chandler, *The Visible Hand*, 2.
47 Chandler, *The Visible Hand*, 275.
48 Chandler, *The Visible Hand*, 320.
49 Chandler, *The Visible Hand*, 484.
50 See Robert Storey, "Unionization Versus Corporate Welfare: The 'Dofasco Way' ", *Labour/Le Travail* 12 (Autumn, 1983), pp. 7–42.
51 Graham Lowe, "Mechanization, Feminization, and Managerial Control in the Early Twentieth Century Canadian Office", Craig Heron and Robert Storey, ed., *On the Job: Confronting the Labour Process in Canada* (Montréal: McGill-Queen's, 1986), 183.
52 Lowe, "Mechanization, Feminization, and Managerial Control in the Early Twentieth Century Canadian Office", 178–179.
53 Lowe, "Mechanization, Feminization, and Managerial Control in the Early Twentieth Century Canadian Office", 184.
54 Lowe, "Mechanization, Feminization, and Managerial Control in the Early Twentieth Century Canadian Office", 199.
55 Lowe, "Mechanization, Feminization, and Managerial Control in the Early Twentieth Century Canadian Office", 199.
56 Donica Belisle, *Retail Nation: Department Stores and the Making of Modern Canada* (Vancouver: University of British Columbia Press, 2011), 84–85.
57 Laurel Sefton-McDowell, "Company Unionism in Canada", Bruce E. Kaufman and Daphne Gottlieb Taras, ed., *Nonunion Employee Representation: History, Contemporary Practice, and Policy* (Armonk: M.E. Sharpe, 2000), 102–109.
58 William Lyon Mackenzie King, *Industry and Humanity: A Study in the Principles Underlying Industrial Reconstruction* (New York: Houghton-Mifflin, 1918).
59 See Elton Mayo, *The Human Problems of an Industrial Civilization* (New York: Macmillan, 1933) for a description of experiments that Mayo helped oversee at the Western Electric's Hawthorne Works in Hawthorne, Illinois; and for a discussion of the basis of the Human Relations School. See Richard Gillespie, *Manufacturing Knowledge: A History of the Hawthorne Experiments* (Cambridge: Cambridge University Press, 1991) for a very insightful analysis of what actually occurred at Hawthorne.
60 Margaret McCallum, "Corporate Welfarism in Canada: 1919–1939", *Canadian Historical Review* March 71, 1 (1990), 46.

61 Lizabeth Cohen, *Making a New Deal: Industrial Workers in Chicago, 1919–1939* (Cambridge: Cambridge University Press, 1990).

62 Jacoby, *Modern Manors*, 80.

63 Taylor and Baskerville, *A Concise History of Business*, 270–271.

64 Chandler, *The Visible Hand*, 496–497.

65 See Armstrong and Nelles, *Monopoly's Moment*.

66 Bliss, *Northern Enterprise*, 374.

67 Bliss, *Northern Enterprise*, 448.

68 On the creation of Polymer Corporation see Matthew Bellamy, *Profiting the Crown: Canada's Polymer Corporation, 1942–1990* (Montréal: McGill-Queen's, 2005).

69 Taylor and Baskerville, *A Concise History of Business*, 399.

70 Don Nerbas, *Dominion of Capital: The Politics of Big Business and the Crisis of the Canadian Bourgeoisie, 1914–1947* (Toronto: University of Toronto Press, 2013), 4.

71 Nerbas, *Dominion of Capital*, 6.

72 Nerbas, *Dominion of Capital*, 203.

73 Nerbas, *Dominion of Capital*, 11.

74 Peter C. Newman, *The Canadian Establishment, volume one* (Toronto: McClelland and Stewart, 1975) and *The Canadian Establishment, volume two: The Acquisitors* (Toronto: McClelland and Stewart, 1981).

75 Thomas Fisher Rare Book Library, University of Toronto, The Ronalds Company Ltd., "The Story of Business: An informal study of the basic principles of our Canadian was of doing business, showing why Capital and Labour need each other, what responsibilities each has to the other, and why we must work together" (Montréal, 1940), 71.

76 Bliss, *Northern Enterprise*, 469.

77 Adolph Berle and Gardiner Means, *The Modern Corporation and Private Property* (New York: Macmillan, 1932), 1.

78 Berle and Means, *The Modern Corporation*, 2.

79 Howell John Harris, *The Right to Manage: Industrial Relations Policies of American Business in the 1940s* (Madison: University of Wisconsin Press, 1982), 10.

80 Harris, *The Right to Manage*, 99.

81 Taylor and Baskerville, *A Concise History of Business*, 328.

82 Ian Radforth, *Bushworkers and Bosses: Logging in Northern Ontario, 1900–1980* (Toronto: University of Toronto Press, 1987), 29.

83 Radforth, *Bushworkers and Bosses*, 160.

84 Radforth, *Bushworkers and Bosses*, 221.

85 Eric Tucker and Judy Fudge, *Labour Before the Law: The Regulation of Workers' Collective Action in Canada, 1900–1948* (Oxford: Oxford University Press, 2001), 194.

86 Tucker and Fudge, *Labour Before the Law*, 264.

87 Charles P. Larrowe, "A Meteor on the Industrial Relations Horizon: The Foremen's Association of America", *Labor History* vol. 2, no. 3 (1961), 260.

88 Larrowe, "A Meteor on the Industrial Relations Horizon", 259.

89 Larrowe, "A Meteor on the Industrial Relations Horizon", 261.

90 Larrowe, "A Meteor on the Industrial Relations Horizon", 261.

91 Ely Chinoy, *Automobile Workers and the American Dream* (Garden City, New York: Doubleday, 1955), 48.

92 Chinoy, *Automobile Workers*, 47.

93 See Pamela Sugiman, *Labour's Dilemma: The Gender Politics of Auto Workers in Canada, 1937–1979* (Toronto: University of Toronto Press, 1994).

94 Leah Vosko, *Temporary Work: The Gendered Rise of a Precarious Employment Relationship* (Toronto: University of Toronto Press, 2000), 24.

95   Patricia Genoe McLaren and Albert J. Mills, "History and the Absence of Canadian Management Theory", in Patricia Genoe McLaren, Albert J. Mills, and Terrance G. Weatherbee, ed., *The Routledge Companion to Management and Organizational History* (Abingdon: Routledge, 2015), 304–331.

96   Archives and Research Collection Centre (hereafter ARCC) Western University Canada, Clarence Fraser Papers, B5084, loose leaf, "Statement on Work of Clarence H. Fraser".

97   ARCC, Clarence Fraser Papers, B5084, loose leaf, "Statement on Work of Clarence H. Fraser".

98   ARCC, Clarence Fraser Papers, B5081–2, Impressions of the NRA in Action—A Week in New York—October 1935.

99   See Mayo, *The Human Problems of an Industrial Civilization*, and Gillespie, *Manufacturing Knowledge* for a very insightful analysis of what actually occurred at Hawthorne.

100 ARCC, Clarence Fraser Papers, B5081–2, loose leaf, "Statement on Work of Clarence H. Fraser".

101 ARCC, Clarence Fraser Papers, B5085, Binder "Publications and Talk", "Management Control of Industrial Relations in Canada To-Day and To-Morrow", *Journal of Institute of Labour Management*, March, 1938. B5083, file B.M. Stewart. In April, 1942 Fraser corresponded with Bryce Stewart, Deputy Minister of Labour, regarding the possibility of him working with the federal government on wartime labour and employment issues. He indicated to Stewart that he had previously been approached about performing similar duties in the United States.

102 ARCC, Clarence Fraser Papers, B5084, "A Career Plan for Every Man". B5084, an example is a letter from the Hawaii Employers Council to Fraser, 13 March 1947 requesting a copy of "A Plan for Every Man".

103 ARCC, Clarence Fraser Papers, B5084 "A Career Plan for Every Man", 1.

104 ARCC, Clarence Fraser Papers, B5084 "A Career Plan for Every Man", 2.

105 ARCC, Clarence Fraser Papers, B5084 "A Career Plan for Every Man", 3.

106 ARCC, Clarence Fraser Papers, B5084 "A Career Plan for Every Man", 3.

107 ARCC, Clarence Fraser Papers, B5084 "A Career Plan for Every Man", 34.

108 ARCC, Clarence Fraser Papers, B5084 "A Career Plan for Every Man", 19.

109 Henri Fayol, *Industrial and General Administration* (Paris: SRL Durand, 1916), 4.

110 Joan C. Tonn, *Mary Parker-Follett: Creating Democracy, Transforming Management* (New Haven: Yale University Press, 2003), 375.

111 Tonn, *Mary Parker-Follett*, 427.

112 Edward Brech, Andrew Thomson, and John F. Wilson, *Lyndall Urwick, Management Pioneer: A Biography* (Oxford: Oxford University Press, 2011), 44–49.

113 Lyndall Urwick, *Leadership in the Twentieth Century* (London: Sir Issac Pitman and Sons, 1957).

114 Urwick, *Leadership in the Twentieth Century*, 52.

115 Lyndall Urwick, "Management Can Be An Intelligent Occupation", *Advanced Management*, February 1956.

116 Brech, Thomson, and Wilson, *Lyndall Urwick, Management Pioneer*, 77.

117 On the nature of work in the Bell systems see Venus Green, *Race on the Line: Gender, Labor and Technology in the Bell System, 1880–1980* (Durham: Duke University Press, 2001) for an American perspective and Joan Newman Kuyek, *The Phone Book: Working at the Bell* (Toronto: Between the Lines, 1983) for the Canadian experience. Kuyek notes the highly rationale nature of the work process, while Green examines how gender and race shaped working at Bell.

2 Companies

As previously noted, analyses of management education and training tend to focus on degree-granting programs at universities. The training that occurs in private organizations is often not examined, mainly because of the challenge of accessing suitable sources. This chapter is going to discuss how managers were educated and trained at three major Canadian-owned firms: Bell Canada, John Labatt Limited, and T. Eaton Company. Bell was founded in Canada in 1880, and Labatt is a brewing firm that was initially founded in 1847 in London, Ontario, by John Labatt. T. Eaton Company was founded in Toronto, Ontario, by Timothy Eaton in 1869. Bell continues to operate in Canada, Labatt is now a subsidiary of Anheuser-Busch/InBev, and Eaton went bankrupt in 1999. All three firms historically occupied important socio-economic positions in post-war Canada because of the scope of their operations and because of the ubiquity of the products that they sold and services that they provided.

This analysis of Bell, Eaton, and Labatt will focus more on front-line and middle-level management. Bell's programs in the 1950s and 1960s, Eaton's programs from the 1940s to the early 1990s, and those at Labatt from the early 1970s to the 1990s will be discussed. The chapter will address key issues including what was taught and who participated in training programs. The companies provided training to managers; however, this training was principally about adapting to the culture and organizational needs of the firm rather than developing skills needed to guide the strategic direction of the organization. Furthermore, the cases of Eaton's and Labatt's both show that being in a more front-line managerial role was a vocational experience that was predicated on a practical learning in the work environment. Participating in training programs was a key aspect of the management role at these companies. The impact of changes in training methods, especially the use of technology, also significantly shaped the management experience.

Bell Canada

Bell Canada was a key part of Canada's economy in the post–World War II decades. It was initially founded in 1880 and had 3.1 million subscribers and a budget of $1 billion by 1958.[1] Bell Canada was linked to American company American Telephone and Telegraph (AT&T) from its initial founding, and the Canadian Bell system was patterned after its American counterpart.[2] The company became a proponent of the new management theories that appeared during the 1940s and 1950s. Clarence Fraser's work contributed to personnel management practice at Bell Canada, but the company implemented additional methods to shape its managers. Bell principally provided phone service to customers in Ontario and Québec, and it was an essential part of Canada's post–World War II economic expansion.

Bell began to implement plans in the late 1940s to train mid-level managers who were above the level of front-line supervisor and who had demonstrated the potential for further promotion in the firm. The company also developed a plan to indoctrinate new managers who had been recruited directly out of university, and those programs were based on practices found among the Bell companies in the United States. The American Bell companies hired 2,000 college and university graduates per year by the mid-1950s, and 10,000 Bell employees were promoted into managerial jobs from front-line ranks. Comparable numbers for Bell Canada are not available, but, based on national population comparisons, it is reasonable to conclude that perhaps a tenth of the number of people hired and promoted in the Bell companies in the United States were similarly selected and promoted in Canada.[3]

Management training emphasized key corporate objectives that were communicated to new employees early in their careers. New graduates hired by Bell Canada in 1955 were advised that the company's overall policy was "To furnish the best possible telephone service at the lowest cost consistent with a reasonable and regular return to investors and just treatment of employees."[4] The main managerial functions, such as traffic and engineering, were explained along with the responsibilities of each level of management. New managerial employees were advised on the span and control of each level of management and the degree of specialization involved with each one.[5] The need for careful measurement of traffic flow was ascribed to the fact that Bell managers "cannot see, feel, or handle our product."[6] Good public relations were strongly emphasized, with one company vice president stating that "public relations is everybody's business."[7] Basic concepts of managerial authority were explained. New management recruits were advised that Bell Canada wanted "to promote the maximum delegation of responsibility and authority" within the organization.[8]

Employment relations and handling personnel problems were managerial functions covered in far more detail than other functions within the organization. New Bell Canada managers were told that good wages and benefits were the main motivation for people who sought employment.[9] The value of Bell's overall compensation package was explained during the induction course but actual wage levels for front-line managers and supervisors were notably not described. Employment relations was a major function in Bell Canada after World War II. Bell had 29,000 employees in 1955 who were covered by five different collective agreements, although it is crucial to note that those workers were in associations and organized into unions several years later.[10] New managers were told that membership in the Bell Canada unions (they were not described as company unions or associations) was voluntary, and that the company would engage in good-faith bargaining.[11] How Bell Canada would respond to unions that were not aligned with the company was not explained, but new managers were advised that:

> In some Labour Relations activities it would appear that there are people who think that the economic laws have been repealed. The drive for higher pay for less work, coupled with restrictive regulations with regard to seniority and work assignments has created management problems in some industries which, in a competitive economy, are well-nigh insurmountable.[12]

Senior Bell Canada management may well have had the Congress of Industrial Organizations (CIO) and the Trades and Labour Congress (TLC) of Canada in mind when this passage was composed. Training on labour relations had one particular purpose, as delineated in the preamble to a labour relations course that was offered in 1940:

> Being in a position to do this (define labour relations policy) is also of direct importance to every supervisor, because he cannot otherwise maintain his natural and logical position of leadership upon which his own effectiveness as a supervisor depends.[13]

Labour relations were also closely linked to overall company policy:

> Any discussion of company policies must start with a consideration of the basic policy of the company, inasmuch as all other policies are subordinate thereto and, if sound, must be supportive thereof.[14]

Bell Canada had a clear ideology when it came to the employment relationship, with management prerogatives and overall company policy as the main considerations in the labour relations process. A manager had to be in a position of authority at all times. The possibility that such an approach may lead to "conflict and divergence" was erroneous and should be considered an "optical illusion."[15]

Bell Canada's senior management wanted there to be no doubt that working at the firm was important because it played a vital role in the communities it served, and that being a Bell manager was a serious occupation. As with Clarence Fraser's work on career planning, salary details did not form part of the formal discussions at Bell management training programs. Being a Bell manager was the main reward, and wages may well have been considered of secondary importance. This is noteworthy considering that, in contrast, discussions of the rewards of unionized jobs almost invariably revolve around wages. There was also little discussion of the actual duties that managers would perform on the job, which is also a further marked contrast with what was generally stated in unionized job descriptions.

Management functions beyond employment and labour relations were covered in relatively general terms in the Bell Canada training materials. The fact that new recruits were acquiring a new identity of Bell Canada manager was not explicitly stated in induction course materials, but it was nonetheless an underlying theme that no smart recruit would have ignored. Training courses also served as venues for meeting colleagues from across the company and to otherwise form a network of useful contacts. Recruits did not learn what they would do in terms of job functions as Bell managers but rather how they should think and act. As Pamela Walker Laird noted, the formation of such networks represented a form of social capital that is key to personal advancement. Knowing the right people surely helped at Bell Canada as much as it did in any large organization.[16]

The new graduate induction course was accompanied by an annual management conference that was organized every year from 1957 into the late 1960s. It was held at a resort in Ste. Marguerite, Québec, and the process of shaping and indoctrinating management occurred at it. That conference built upon the foundation established through the new graduate induction course by teaching managers how to deal with specific issues on the job. For example, the thirty-five people who attended the 1958 conference—all of them anglophone and male—were assigned into groups, and each one was assigned a lengthy case study to teach them how to deal with problem employees. A 1956 fictional case study focused on Ellis Brown, who was described as an assistant general credit manager for Enterprise Industries. He was said to have executive potential, but there was uncertainty about his ability to delegate. Brown had trouble gaining acceptance from senior executives. Bell management trainees reading that case would have been encouraged to see that the fictional Ellis Brown chose the right remedy to his dilemma:

> He could sincerely try to conform to the pattern he felt would place him in the most favorable light with top management. He could

adjust his attitudes so that he would be seen as a person who thought and acted as a top management person.[17]

A lot of the materials that were introduced at the management conferences originated at AT&T. For example, the 1958 conference used something called a "Net Change Study" that was developed in the US in 1955. The content of that study dealt with behavioural issues at work. The manner in which attitudes were formed was described, along with the action required to improve attitudes.[18] Management was advised to show empathy because "almost everyone needs somebody to talk to occasionally" and that "ideally the boss is the man to talk to."[19] They were to be confidants for the workers who reported to them, almost a parental figure to whom workers could comfortably turn to in times of trouble. This approach built on Clarence Fraser's idea of a "god-father" relationship between management and workers.

It is significant that women were involved in actually running management training courses, even though men appear to have been the only attendees in the 1950s and 1960s. Bell Canada's management training supervisor in 1956 was a woman named Peggy Evoy, and she reported to a manager named Ronald Bassett-Spiers. Rose Hart and Margaret Jeal were two of the four instructors who taught in the 1956 training program.[20] The program content provided little discretion for anyone teaching it, which helps explain why Bell staff members were instructors. They did not necessarily need the expertise to devise program content, just the ability to teach it. Bell Canada's senior management must have felt women sufficiently competent to be program instructors but not capable of actually managing in departments beyond functions like personnel. Management theory was included in the course materials distributed to Bell managers. For example, an article by Lyndall Urwick that asserted that management could be an intelligent occupation was used in the late 1950s.[21] The inclusion of academic literature was intended to add greater authority to the learning experience and to also show that management was a scientific, measurable function. The range of academic sources did not just include people like Urwick.

Bell Canada turned to academia to assess the effectiveness of its management training, and faculty from the University of Western Ontario (UWO) Business School were invited to examine the effectiveness of the training program in 1965.[22] The UWO faculty may well have produced research results that perturbed Bell's senior management. Managers attending the Bell training course reported that they either did not agree with or understand company policy and reported considerable difficulty dealing with staffing issues, despite feeling that the company had a sufficient number of workers. Indeed, managers who had gone through company leadership training were more forthcoming about the company's problems than those who had not been through training.[23] Bell Canada's senior management does not appear to have substantively responded to what the UWO Business School found, as the training course materials did not markedly change after the research results were delivered. The results of the UWO study nonetheless indicate that an emphasis on shaping common behaviour among managers was not actually helping training program attendees with their job duties. A much larger study of management training in other Bell companies from the 1950s to the late 1960s in the United States produced results that were similar to those found by the UWO Business School. New management recruits in the US were attracted to the size of the Bell system and the potential for career advancement.[24] Bell expected that half of the managers who were recruited would eventually leave for other employment, but only a sixth of recruits regretted joining Bell after eight years at the firm. The US study's authors significantly observed that new recruits had "unrealistically favourable expectations" of how life would be at Bell.[25] Their Canadian counterparts may well have had the same experience.

It is also important to consider what was not mentioned in Bell Canada's management training materials. There was little discussion of the role of corporations in relation to the state, no reference to laws regulating business activity, and absolutely no reference to workplace issues like occupational health and safety. The technical aspects of the Bell system were not even fully examined. The idea that women may have faced unique employment challenges was not referred to at a time when the vast majority of the company's office staff were female. What it would mean to have a workforce that was divided between French- and English-speaking workers, especially at a time when nationalism was appearing in Québec, was not mentioned. The content of the training materials was thus rather limited, but it was clearly what senior Bell Canada management thought was important. Many people who participated in those training programs may have also come to the same conclusion.

The Bell Canada management training programs were based on the two types of management thought that appeared prior to World War II. Concerns about planning, evaluation, and organizational structure were all emphasized by Parker-Follet, Barnard, and Fayol. The idea that management was an important "intelligent" occupation was a recurring theme in Urwick's views on organizations. Those ideas manifested themselves in internal Bell corporate training. It is important, even though Bell Canada was heavily influenced by what occurred in the American Bell system, that Clarence Fraser worked to make a Canadian contribution to the training that took place at Bell Canada and to the body of management thought that was being developed in the United States and Britain in the 1930s and 1940s. Bell Canada management thought it important to have a Canadian contribution to management theory so the company endorsed Fraser's academic activities. The company devoted substantial resources and effort to inculcating management ideology in its manage-rial staff, as did the Bell companies in the United States. The work of management theorists like Fraser, Urwick, Barnard, Fayol, and Parker-Follett shaped management training at Bell Canada—principally through Fraser—but industrial psychology was also important. Instructing a per-son on how to respond emotionally to workplace problems and making sure that there was strict adherence to company policy helped inculcate a common set of management behaviours. New Bell Canada managers were made to feel important as they were joining what was possibly the Canada's pre-eminent corporation.[26]

There was continuity in the management theories that inspired Clar-ence Fraser and the ideas that he formulated, and how it all linked to training practice at Bell Canada. Fraser and his contemporaries strongly felt that they were engaged in socially important work. Their work was mostly complementary, and they were not critical of each other and felt that they were formulating a body of theory that they hoped would be used in corporations. The various management theorists discussed here created a set of ideas that included trans-Atlantic influences, and ideas were not shaped by a specific set of national experiences. Management thinkers instead deliberately sought to integrate international perspec-tives even though their work was overwhelmingly written by men and in English. Senior management obviously felt that having a cadre of inter-nally trained managers who shared a common view on management was important to Bell's future. Andrew Pettigrew has noted that ideology is a key part of organizations that can either facilitate or impede change, and having everyone share a common management ideology was bet-ter for Bell than having people share a collection of perhaps disparate ideologies.[27]

People who participated in Bell's internal management training pro-grams may have felt disillusioned by what they were taught, but there were clearly some intrinsic benefits to having participated in training pro-grams. Attending a management training course meant that a manager was considered worthy of company investment, which would then pro-vide an advantage over managers who were not selected. Furthermore, even if the management ideology that was taught in Bell's training pro-grams limited personal discretion, familiarity with senior management's approach to problem solving represented a career advantage. People who attended the management training program were featured in inter-nal company communication. For example, the first induction course in 1956 and its participants were described in detail in the *Bell News*. A training course may not have been intellectually stimulating, but it provided useful notoriety.[28]

The Human Relations School of management, especially the idea of engaging employees, appeared at Bell Canada, but Taylorism in many ways still predominated. There was a flow chart, questionnaire, or directive for every personnel issue that senior management considered important, and being a successful manager meant being able to utilize those resources. There was little real discretion over daily managerial functions. Management was meant to be important at Bell, but it was a highly regulated occupation where efforts were made to even shape a person's emotional responses. Contentment at work meant subordinating yourself to the needs of the firm. A successful Bell Canada manager was white, male, and anglophone. That pattern was reflected in hiring and promotion practices in other organizations. As Vance Packard revealed in an early 1960s study of corporations in the US and Canada, there was a widespread preference for hiring white Anglo-Saxon Protestant (WASP) males in the 1950s and 1960s. Women, African-Americans, and workers from other minority groups were virtually absent from managerial ranks.[29] Rosabeth Moss-Kanter made similar observations about gender in her early 1970s study of a major American corporation when she noted that managerial and clerical jobs were the major sex-segregated, white collar occupations and that this division had been fostered by large corporations.[30] Other writers including Mills and Mills and McPherson have revealed how occupations in Canada such as flight attendant and nurse were also highly gendered during the interwar and post–World War II periods.[31] The gendered division of labour at Bell was thus part of a much larger pattern across North American workplaces, including the T. Eaton Company.

T. Eaton Company

The T. Eaton Company, so named for founder Timothy Eaton, was commonly called Eaton's and was a social institution in Canada as much as it was an economic one. For instance, the annual Eaton Santa Claus parade in Toronto was a holiday fixture for many decades.[32] Settlers working farms in the Canadian West usually did so with a copy of the Eaton catalogue close at hand. Successive generations of the Eaton family exercised control over the company, although their personal interest in retailing waned as decades passed. The Eaton family were adroit users of employer paternalism. Eaton employed tens of thousands of employees over its long history. The company was based in Toronto, Ontario, and had extensive retail operations across Canada. However, regardless of where they were based, long-service employees viewed themselves as Eatonians. As Patricia Phenix described in her book on Eaton's employees, former workers continued to send Eaton memorabilia to John Craig Eaton after the firm closed.[33] There is a village called Eatonia in the province of Saskatchewan and a Timothy Eaton United church in Toronto.[34] The Eaton family name is consequently part of collective Canadian memory. Eaton employees fought during both world wars with the assurance that they would be able to return to their jobs once the conflicts were over. The Canadian government sought to increase the size of the militia, or army reserve, in 1938 in preparation for anticipated hostilities in Europe. Approximately 1,500 Eatonians volunteered for militia service in 1938, and over 5,000 went on active duty when Canada entered World War II. The company permitted them to serve while securing their jobs and also supplemented their wages while they were in the military. Eaton's arranged fund-raising events for the war effort and sent gifts to company employees serving overseas.[35]

Returning veterans formed an important group within the post–World War II T. Eaton Company. The company supported an internal veterans' association, which was described as a:

> Great meeting place for all Eatonians and their friends; it would fill a long-felt need for a centre for the men's activities; it would be a great force in cementing employee and management relations; promoting customer and employee good-will; it could be a forum for the better training and education of employees that desired advancement; for the development of greater interest in the arts and gymnasium athletics; and it would stand as one more monument to the Public Spirit of the company.[36]

Participating in the veterans' association would have been a good idea for any men seeking to enter management roles. Internal groups like the veterans' association played a key role in helping with career advancement, and management levels were clearly delineated. Management was divided between in-store personnel across Canada and people working in administrative functions in the Toronto head office. All new employees in the 1950s and 1960s were provided with an orientation booklet that outlined the company's mission—"our business is selling"—and their other obligations and benefits.[37] Store managers across the country were involved in developing orientation materials before they were printed and given to new employees. For example, a Vancouver store manager was advised in 1954 about how he worded language on employee lunch breaks in case employees—in this case female clerks—took breaks in such a way that sales were interrupted.[38]

Returning veterans likely continued to be an important part of the Eaton workforce into the 1970s, when some of them would have begun to retire. Staff who had served overseas in the war—only eight had been women—were invited to a reception at the Eaton family residence north of Toronto in 1946. The Eaton family cultivated an aristocratic demeanor at a time when Canadians felt themselves more closely linked to the United Kingdom than they would in subsequent decades. The reception was a carefully planned affair, and veterans surely felt it an honour to attend a reception hosted by Lady Eaton. The influence that veterans in leadership roles had over time on the retailer is not evident in the available sources, but it is unlikely that they forgot their military experience and it probably shaped at least some of their attitudes toward dealing with staff and running the corporation.[39]

Eaton convened internal personnel management conferences in the 1950s and 1960s. The idea of hiring and promoting people through the ranks was favoured during that period. The agenda materials for a 1954 personnel management conference lamented the fact that there was still too much emphasis on filling vacant roles with people who were "the most suitable candidates at hand" and that there needed be better efforts made to "search within the house" when filling jobs. There was also considerable concern about staff turnover, despite the fact that Eaton had many long-service employees. For example, Eaton surveyed their new staff hires in Toronto in 1953 and found that, of 671 people that had been hired in the city of the preceding sixteen-month period, 504 had left the firm. This rate of turnover clearly alarmed Eaton's management, and personnel managers were advised to emphasize the generosity of the company's benefits and other programs when dealing with employees.[40]

The materials used to educate people on both front-line supervisory roles and middle-management positions were principally in paper form in the 1950s and early 1960s and stressed Eaton's role as a major Canadian retailer. It was also designed in such a way that referencing it could be part of everyday work tasks. As shown in Figure 2.1, a 1960s brochure titled "Your Career at Eaton's" was clearly meant to be slipped into the inside pocket of a suit jacket for easy reference. That brochure included information in it that would have been useful to new employees, and it conveyed what senior management thought was important for employees to know about the firm. It was also something that front-line managers would have been expected to distribute, and they would also have received it themselves when they joined the firm. The brochure advised new employees:

> As you begin your work here, you're probably wondering where you fit into this busy organization. In a few days you won't find everything so strange. Your associates will gladly help you get acquainted and if you study this booklet you will find the answers to some of the questions on your mind. It has been designed primarily to acquaint you with the personnel policies of the company and to provide you with the information that will help you feel at home. Please read it carefully and keep it handy so that you can refer to it from time to time.

The was thus served as a reassuring voice to new employees. It also discussed matters such as breaks, probation, absenteeism, overtime, and staff responsibility. Employees were told that they would have "the personal satisfaction which comes only to those who know they have done their best."[41]

Figure 2.1 Your career at Eaton's

Source: Used with permission of Sears Canada.

Eaton had national training materials in the 1950s and 1960s, such as the pocket brochure, but materials were also developed for use at specific store locations. For instance, the Eaton store in Hamilton, Ontario, in the 1950s used a short guide that discussed the need for management development. The guide noted that "the development of individuals for management has become more difficult than ever before" and further suggested "there is a growing shortage of qualified personnel for higher responsibilities in many businesses, and retailing is no exception."[42] The Eaton's Hamilton plan had four objectives:

> Improved performance on the job
> Increased reserve strength by selection of potential management material
> Improved communications up-down-across the management team
> Improved staff and management morale[43]

Eaton's senior management was obviously concerned about recruiting and retaining people who could run its operations and felt that they had to develop internal training methods to ensure that they were successful with this objective. The Eaton's Hamilton plan articulated four goals, but profitability was not one that was clearly stated. The assumption may well have been that organizational success would result from meeting the stated aims of the training plan.

Eaton's managers were reminded, particularly in the first two decades after World War II, that relations with company staff were important. A 1960 Management Guide to Personnel Policies advised managers:

> The human relationships in your department, particularly the relationship between yourself and your staff, are of prime importance for the day-to-day successful operation of the department. The level of morale and individual attitudes can contribute to or subtract from the productivity of your group . . . A successful leader makes it his business to understand staff policies and communicate them to his people. The successful application of these policies will, we feel, help you to influence job performance and build a staff with a high level of morale and productivity.[44]

There were some "basic policies" articulated to managers in that guide:

> Our guarantee, "Goods satisfactory or money refunded."

> Truth in Advertising—"Every price ticket and every advertisement must mean what it says and say what it means"

> A Square Deal for Everyone—our customers, our suppliers, our employees

Customer service that is prompt, courteous, and efficient in the Store, on the telephone, through the mails, and at the customer's door.

Progressive leadership in merchandising, customer service, good housekeeping, personnel administration, sales promotion, and community responsibility.[45]

Lastly, managers were advised that "The primary purpose of our company is to serve the community by selling at competitive prices, sufficient quantities of satisfactory merchandise and services in such a way as to afford an adequate net return."[46]

It is entirely clear from those policies that the Eaton's management also viewed the company as a social institution, in fact seeing it firstly filling that role and secondly being a profit generating enterprise. The term corporate social responsibility (CSR) was not in use in the early 1960s, but this was the main principle guiding Eaton's management.[47] Managers were advised that they should also cultivate a community profile:

The professional, social and community contacts of each member of management reflect on the integrity and standing of the Company. Each is encouraged to take part in such professional, social and community activities as will maintain desirable public relations between the Company and the community.[48]

Those instructions meant that managers bore responsibility for the company's public image and that perhaps doing things like volunteering and joining community clubs would be a good way of meeting job expectations. Managers were to adopt something like a public service ethos to be successful in their roles.

Eaton maintained contact with other companies when developing its internal printed training materials. In 1967, the company listed the titles of training materials produced by Air Canada, Bank of Montréal, Bell Telephone Company of Canada, Canadair Limited, Canadian Industries Limited, Canadian Railways, Dominion Stores, Ford Motor Company of Canada, D.H. Evan and Co. Company, J.L. Hudson Company, and Hudson's Bay Company. Giving a brochure a title like "Welcome to Eaton's" was not unusual as Air Canada had something called "You and Your Job" and Hudson's Bay utilized a document titled "Let's All Pull Together!" Of those companies, Hudson's Bay was Eaton's most direct competitor as it was also a retailer. Other companies, such as Canadian Railways and Bank of Montréal, operated in entirely different industries from Eaton. It is clear from that list of companies that thinking about orienting new workers, including new managers, was a priority for leading Canadian corporations in the 1960s.[49]

Eaton devoted time and resources to developing its own training materials from the late 1940 to the late 1960s. Engaging in practices such as convening national personnel conferences, consulting store managers on the content of training materials, and permitting the creation of training guides at both the local and national levels would have been a significant undertaking. However, Eaton's managers and other new hires, except those in senior manager roles, were apparently not enrolled in full-time training sessions that took them away from their job duties. They instead received information on company policies and procedures and relied on the Personnel Office to guide employee policy.

Eaton produced enough loyal Eatonians to ensure that the company successfully operated into the 1960s, and Eaton's training materials began to change by the late 1960s and into the early 1970s as audio-visual materials became much more commonly used. This method of training provision also continued the company's preference to integrate training into the daily tasks of supervisory staff rather than devoting a lot of dedicated work time to in-class sessions. The messages conveyed through the training materials and internal memoranda from the 1940s to the early 1960s reveal much about how management viewed the Eaton workforce. Managers were supposed to be male; there is no evidence of female managers being hired and promoted. On the other hand, it was anticipated that sales clerks would be female. Eaton's organizational structure was consequently built on a highly gendered division of labour.

The company's retail mission was emphasized throughout the new training media, with less emphasis on workplace relations that had been evident in the 1950s and 1960s along with advice on how to handle routine administrative functions. A 1974 film talked about how most of the people portrayed in Eaton commercials were in "their late twenties and early thirties, have children, and live in the suburbs" even though "not all of our customers are like that."[50] The moving images in this film and other like it featured stylishly attired actors of Western European descent and reflected little of the diversity that was increasingly evident in Canadian society. The film also emphasized the idea that women were principally consumers. The fact that Eaton's operated on a seasonal buying and selling cycle was also shown in sales promotion films, which also reinforced the company's long-standing view that it was in the sales business. An animated 1974 short training film titled "Twice Across Canada Annually" opened with a cartoon male Eaton employee in somewhat typical period garb: bell-bottom trousers, John Lennon glasses, and mustache.[51] It then cut to live action as it promoted annual sales. Whether or not any of Eaton's male employees actually dressed in the manner shown in the film was secondary to the fact that the company was trying to make itself look current in its training materials.[52]

Eaton presented its ideas about what the company's customers looked like through management and employee training materials. An early 1970s training film titled "Christmas Sales Presentation" showed footage of the Eaton's Santa Claus parade and talked of the company's success in the preceding Christmas shopping season. The actors shown in the film were attractive and white. It suggested that Eaton continued to be a successful retailer, but that its success was predicated on appealing to a specific demographic group. The advertisement was shown on television in Montréal, Toronto, Winnipeg, and Vancouver. The company relied on radio advertisements in other municipal markets.[53]

A 1974 film shown to managers and staff called "Staff Training Spring 1974" further elaborated on what senior managers thought about the company's customers. The film began as a discussion of "how women view fashion today." It then noted that most of the people in "our commercials" will be in "their late twenties and early thirties, have children, and live in the suburbs" even though "not all of our customers are like that." A "First Class Male" tag line used in a TV ad for men's wear was noted. Eaton was clearly telling its staff, including middle and front-line managers, that the objective was to attract white, suburban middle-class customers. The idea that such a strategy may have some limitations, and perhaps turn away customers with money who did not fit that demographic profile, was not considered.[54]

The 1950s to 1970s management training materials did not reference celebrity management thinkers or leadership coaches, but that trend appeared by the 1980s. Eaton's managers were shown a 1983 film titled "Managing to Win" that featured noted American college football coach Lou Holtz, who was the head coach of the University of Arkansas team at the time that the film was made. Holtz talked about the value of positive thinking and asserted that "Managing to win in football is no different than managing to win in business." He did not feel that "you can overuse the term 'motivation'" and that "pressure is what we expect out of ourselves . . . me, I thrive on pressure." This film raises important questions. How did Holtz know that managing in football is the same as managing business? Statements like those in that film presumed broad commonality across different management arenas. Did Holtz's extolling of the virtues of pressure lead Eaton's managers to believe that they had to be more punitive with the people reporting to them? The training materials from the 1950s and 1960s were much more benign in their advice on how management should interact with staff and other people with whom they came in contact as part of their duties.[55]

The films shown in the 1970s and 1980s did not reflect the challenges faced by Eaton's. For example, competition with other retailers was not discussed in much detail in internal training materials. This was a common theme from the late 1940s onward. Indeed, in the 1950s and 1960s, internal company communications could have led someone to conclude that Eaton was possibly the only retailer in Canada. The need to maintain discipline within the workforce was presented in internal communications from the personnel department, but there was little nuance on how to deal with problem employee situations or any form of conflict.

The supposition appears to have been that workers would be treated in a benignly paternalistic manner but that they would be expected to do what management wished. This included what happened when workers attempted unionization.

Eaton was not alone among major Canadian employers in its preference to remain non-union. None of the major Canadian banks, trust companies, or insurance firms had ever been unionized. Many major retailers had also avoided it, although grocery stores were unionized in the 1970s and 1980s. Canada experienced two major waves of unionization from the mid-twentieth century onward: industrial organizing from the 1930s to the 1960s, and public sector organizing from the late 1960s into the 1970s. Public sector organizing led to hundreds of thousands of women coming into the labour movement. Canadian unions, many of which were part of American parent unions and federations, actively sought to organize retail workers. However, as Eileen Sufrin has shown, Eaton's furiously resisted unionization in the late 1940s and early 1950s.[56]

A second major effort at unionization was made in the mid-1980s at several Eaton's stores in the Toronto area, and the Retail, Wholesale, and Department Store Union (RWDSU) that led the ensuing strike cooperated with a film-maker to create a documentary called *No Small Change: The Story of the Eaton Strike*. The film was highly critical of Eaton's management. Company management was described as being a "dynasty." The strikers were overwhelmingly female and ultimately were able to achieve union certification in one Toronto-area store. A copy of the film was included along with other internal training materials used by company management. There are possible reasons for this decision. One is that senior management thought that they had achieved a major victory, as the union was only able to organize one store. Alternatively, management may have viewed the film in cautionary terms and as indicative of organizational culture problems that needed to be rectified.[57]

Senior Eaton management learned some lessons as a result of the strike and unionization of one store location. The company produced a training film developed after the strike that provided direction on how to conduct meetings and suggested that meetings must be used to help motivate employees and that all concerns raised in meetings must be recorded and responded to by management.[58] This film also showed women in positions of managerial authority. The film stressed that a manager must always take meeting minutes. Another film made in the years following the strike called "One Minute Manager Excerpts" advised managers on how to set a goal in one minute, give praise in one minute, and reprimand in one minute.[59] This was all based on a book called *The One Minute Manager* by Kenneth Blanchard, which was a more popular management publication and not a work of managerial theory equal to work such as Drucker's.[60]

Events leading to the ultimate bankruptcy that Eaton's experienced are not discussed in internal training materials, but there are some signs that suggest why the firm faced challenges. The Eaton family, despite not being especially interested in the retail industry, was determined to exert direct managerial control over the company. A 1989 interview with then-company chair Fredrik Eaton revealed a senior executive who proudly carried his family's name but appeared to know little about how the company operated, although he clearly was not interested in being filmed, as a pre-introductory segment shows him visibly groaning at the prospect of participating in the event. He declared that most of the company's stores and facilities were of post–World War II construction but did not comment on the fact that forty-four years had elapsed since the end of the war. Fredrik Eaton correctly noted that the retail market was "saturated," but he also predicted that the company would expand by the year 2000. He thought that Eaton had the best credit system and that the company had thinner levels of management compared to other firms. When asked about changing ethnicity of customers, he responded that dealing with it was a challenge but that it had always been that way and that the company could change along with Canada. Fredrik Eaton thought that the company had a diverse workforce and that there were common qualities of Eaton employees such as caring about customer service. He argued that "We may have one or two bad apples, but we have barrels of good ones" among employee ranks. Fredrick Eaton did not preside over the company's bankruptcy in 1999; his brother George had succeeded before that point. Eaton's management may have agreed with Fredrik Eaton's assessment of the state of the company, but they may have also been aghast at how disconnected he appeared on screen.[61]

The content of Eaton's training films began to change by the 1990s. A 1994 video called "Eaton Credit Corporation Recruitment Video" portrayed an Eaton Credit Corporation workforce that was diverse in terms of race and gender. Eaton Credit Corporation was, as its name suggested, the retailer's credit subsidiary. As the film noted, it was at that time the largest issuer of proprietary credit cards in Canada. It also operated National Retail Credit Services, which ran credit cards for other retailers like White Rose, Holt Renfrew, Birks, and Home Hardware. The company operated an internal training program called Eaton Credit Corporation University and specifically promoted its management training program. The technological prowess of Eaton's credit subsidiary was emphasized, as were the prospects that it offered for career advancement. Computer systems were prominent in the film, which suggested that Eaton needed staff with technical and customer service skills. The presentation of a more diverse workforce was an effort to reflect what Canadian workers increasingly looked like by the 1990s.[62]

Training at Eaton's was taken seriously, but it was entirely meant to align staff with the objectives of senior management. The company was concerned with employee turnover and clearly saw Eaton's as having a socio-economic role beyond simply selling retail goods. The term corporate social responsibility was not used in internal Eaton's documents, but senior management and the Eaton family obviously felt that they were responsible for keeping the firm going as a Canadian institution. Many of the thousands of Eatonians who spent their careers at the firm seem to have agreed with them, even if some tried to organize unions. John Labatt did not have a name for its employees equivalent to the term Eatonian, but the company was also highly involved in training its management.

John Labatt Ltd

Labatt's, as the John Labatt Brewing Company became commonly known in post–World War II Canada, was different from Eaton, as it was primarily a producer of consumer products and an industrial rather than service-sector firm. London, Ontario, was the location of the Labatt head office before key functions began to move to Toronto in the 1970s. The company operated a network of breweries across Canada and produced some well-known national brands, including Labatt Blue and Labatt 50. Labatt maintained an extensive marketing function but did not directly retail beer. Labatt brewery workers were represented by the Brewery, General, and Professional Workers' Union (BGPWU), and labour relations was an important internal management function. The company also considered itself an important socio-economic part of London, and members of the Labatt family were active in philanthropy. There were additional perquisites offered to employees beyond compensation and benefit packages. For example, workers from the 1960s to the 1980s were well-known to be regularly provided with free cases of beer. The management training materials that are available from the Labatt Brewing Company Collection begin in the early 1970s and go up to the late 1990s. Audio cassette format was gradually followed by use of films and video tapes, with DVD format introduced by the mid-1990s.

The Labatt training materials used in the 1960s frequently focused on dealing with routine management difficulties. A 1975 collection of six cassette tapes focused on Management by Objectives (MBO), a management approach pioneered by Peter Drucker. It was produced by the American Management Association (AMA). The tapes advised that "the world of capitalism is breeding too many administrators and not enough managers" and warned about a "general malaise of middle management" that was inculcated by "risk free job security." Managers were beginning to think that their jobs were a "right" and that they were "not willing to fight for them." The development of management was important to the future of the organization, and the tapes suggested that there should be an emphasis "on assistance not punishment" and an effort to "bring out the full potential of each manager." Labatt managers who listened to the MBO tapes were advised that "case study method causes a manager to alter his way of thinking" and that it was "preferable to have training sessions near the job to fit schedules, nearness to work process, etc, makes training feel customized." The tapes did not talk about "her" way of thinking. Training involved incurring expenses, and training must be part of a "harmonious network of activities" that are all part of MBO. Skill development was linked to compensation, and the MBO tapes recommended that compensation for top managers should be dependent on what they contributed to the organization. The need to make management training part of the everyday work processes, be mindful of cost, and link it to compensation were all key points. Managers were cautioned from the beginning about complacency and essentially told to expect that they were not guaranteed job security. They were also being subtly told that corporations existed to make profit and that they were not firstly social institutions. This also implied disinterest in any form of social responsibility.[63]

The MBO tapes also discussed what senior management should be doing to improve an organization. Managers should be encouraged to improve on a "continuing basis."[64] It was recommended that competent managers should remain with an organization and that "managerial performance can be evaluated in quantifiable terms" without considering subjective opinions.[65] It was also recommended that an organization's structure could be reoriented on a continuous basis as necessary, with realistic objectives being set. Senior managers were encouraged to use incentives for achievement that would motivate managers to set their own objectives, as well as allowing managers to have a hand in setting their own objectives. While there was a "possibility of failure" in an incentive system, it could also create a "profound sense of accomplishment" and "drive and ambition that characterizes a successful businessman."[66] MBO was a method that "almost forces managers to talk to each other."[67] The tapes also discussed differences between line and staff management with the former described as the group that executed the primary functions of an organization, with the latter group responsible for secondary functions.[68]

The AMA tapes recommend that age and health influenced a person's potential for management and that being 55 years of age was not old for the president's office but too old for lower-level positions. Furthermore, poor health limited managers to "less pressure-packed jobs." Assessment of managerial potential was "an art, not a science" even when considering the various factors involved with the process. Training was important because it "aids the control function," and case study teaching methodology was important because it caused a manager to "alter his way of thinking."[69]

The 1975 AMA tapes conveyed somewhat contradictory messages. On one hand, they conveyed a positive message that managers should be helped to develop and not quickly punished and that MBO would make the collaborate with each other. On the other hand, the tone was decidedly Darwinistic as managers were essentially encouraged to compete against each other, even if doing so required aggressive behaviour. Someone could be deemed too old for anything but the most senior management jobs. It is difficult to see how there could be much harmony in such an environment. Management training was also to be closely tied to organizational cost considerations and individual compensation.

The earliest available training film used by Labatt was called "The Professional." It was made in the early 1970s by Dartnell Sales Training Films and starred Hollywood actor Van Johnson as a salesman facing an identity crisis when he wonders if his job actually made him a professional person. Van Johnson's character was shown at home explaining his job to his son while clearly feeling ashamed of being a salesman. At one point, a character other than Johnson's asserts, "I'm proud of me, that's what counts." The film asked if selling could not be considered the same as the medical or legal professions. Five principles of being a professional employee were introduced:

A professional is a guy who has a will to learn, and goes on learning
The need to intern
The sense to specialize
The time to fraternize (an earlier term for networking)
The desire to contribute

Toward the start, Johnson's character goes on a sales call and feels that he is being disrespected by a female receptionist. He refers to her as an "uppity little chick" and states that "if it wasn't for salesmen like me, she'd be pressing pants in Bernie's tailor shop." This dialogue was part of a song-and-dance routine. Johnson's character, along with others, is shown consuming alcohol while travelling on business. The film concludes with Johnson's character feeling reassured that he is indeed a professional. This film sent highly sexist messages to anyone viewing it, and it probably reflected attitudes prevalent among at least some management at Labatt at the time since the company used it for training. The problem of professionalization, in this case working sales, is woven throughout the film's narrative. The film's intent was clear, regardless of how problematic many aspects of it were: managers should dispel any doubt in the minds of their sales staff when it came to their importance to the company and the stature of their jobs. They also received messages in the early 1970s saying the women were not their equals.[70]

Labatt used some audio tapes in the 1980s, but videos eventually became the preferred training medium. Training materials created by other companies were sometimes used in addition to those produced internally or by video production companies. For instance, a 1984 film from Xerox discussed the need to define expectations for staff. It portrayed supervisors from a variety of industries. There was some workforce diversity evident in the film with male, female, and African-American actors shown in it. One Caucasian woman was shown in a supervisory role. Supervisors were advised of the need to set goals for subordinates, which include performance expectations. Methods such as task analysis, identifying specific procedures, establishing feedback systems, and designing checkpoints were recommended. The fact that a film showing a more diverse workforce was used by Labatt indicates that the company was itself either becoming more diverse or recognizing that it should move in that direction.[71]

New managers in the 1980s were instructed on the range of Labatt's operations in Canada. The company was diversified at that time and included ten businesses such as Catelli Pasta, Chateaugay Wines, and ownership interests in The Sports Network (TSN) and the Toronto Blue Jays baseball team. While the link to the Catelli and Chateaugay was through a wider framework of food and beverage products, the broadcasting and sports links were clearly intended to help promote Labatt's core beverage business. The Labatt's organization was described as decentralized and entrepreneurial. The company's history in the brewing industry was usually referenced in educational and promotional materials, but the Labatt family was not present except for references to founder John Labatt.[72]

The need for ongoing education and training to further career aspirations was emphasized in Labatt's training resources for management. A 1988 film called "Going Places" described the transformational impact of education on low-wage workers, especially women and people of colour. This film was also made in the United States and, like many of the training resources used by Labatt from the 1980s onward, featured much more employee diversity than had been evident in earlier materials. The film specifically described a training program for high school drop-outs. It was presumably intended to foster a learning culture within the firm, both among lower-level managerial staff and production workers.[73]

Labatt's senior management evidently felt that the firm operated in a highly competitive environment in the 1980s and 1990s and devoted resources to educating managers on the changes faced by the brewing industry. In 1996, the company convened an internal leadership conference and brought in a succession of guest speakers who described changes in the industry but also broader socio-economic change. The proceedings were filmed and disseminated across Labatt to serve as a training resource. Topics such as the coming rise of craft brewing were noted.[74] The impact of the "wired world" and enhanced micro-processing was the topic of another conference session.[75] Managers attending the 1996 conference were overall advised that their industry was changing, customers wanted more choice when it came to buying beer, and technology was rapidly advancing. It is noteworthy that Labatt paid to bring highly paid managers away from their jobs to Toronto to spend time in a conference setting, and it was likely that people in more senior management roles attended. Lower-level supervisory staff probably viewed the video proceedings at their home locations. Enhancing the skills of senior management was also thought about by Labatt's leadership. For instance, a video promoting the executive education programs offered by the business school at the University of Western Ontario was circulated internally in 1990.[76]

Internal Labatt's training sources recognized the presence of a union in the workplace, but efforts were made to promote cooperative labour relations. In the late 1970s, managers were shown a video that described a collaborative labour–management initiative that was developed in Labatt's London, Ontario, plant. It included segments quoting Canadian Labour Congress (CLC) representative Ray Murray and Peter Boffa, who was the industrial relations manager for Labatt in Ontario. Murray stated "collective bargaining is not a war game . . . it's an area where people sit down and try to solve problems." The benefits of something called single-team bargaining were extolled, as it dispensed with a bargaining table and discussions were off the record. No designated spokesperson was used for each side involved in negotiations, and nothing was written down until problems were resolved. Crossman thought that removing the bargaining table was especially significant. The joint initiative, which revolved around quality of work life (QWL), was judged a success by both labour and management. A second segment in the same film looked at a similar joint labour–management initiative at a British Columbia (BC) Forest Products Plant. BC Forest Product supervisors felt "quite a bit of relief" as they did not feel a need to deal with so many problems by themselves, although some supervisors felt anxiety because of feeling a loss of status as a result of involving the union in decision making in the plant. This film was the only example of a surviving Labatt training resource that directly dealt with labour and employment relations, which is remarkable since the company's blue-collar workforce had long been unionized.[77]

Health and safety issues were covered in a couple of the training films, which should not be surprising since Labatt was an industrial employer. A 1983 training film called "Do It Right" discussed how to successfully implement a safety training system. It was produced by a company in New Jersey and adapted by Labatt for its own use. Advice was given on how to manage people to safely perform tasks on the job. Supervisors were advised to put a person at ease during training, be patient, and keep instructions simple. Viewers were cautioned not to too "over-supervise" and to reinforce good job performance.[78]

The attitudes of at least some Labatt managers continued to reflect problematic attitudes toward women into the 1980s, even though years had passed since Van Johnson appeared on-screen and despite the company's efforts to portray a more diverse workforce in training materials. An sales film made by staff in London, Ontario, in the mid-1980s involved two beer sales representatives first visiting a park in the centre of the city to view the installation of municipal Christmas decorations, then visiting a local club where exotic dancers performed. The footage included the sales representatives talking with women who were employed to perform in the club, and the film also included sexually suggestive segments that were evidently intended to be humorous. This film was not a formal training aid, but the fact that it was made using company resources and found its way into the company's archival materials is a commentary on the type of dialogue that still appeared in the firm despite apparent efforts to make it more diverse.[79]

The Labatt training materials tended to reflect broader social change. There was greater diversity shown—both racial and gender—as decades passed. Senior management continued to be white and male, but women and people of colour were increasingly shown in roles beyond simple administrative jobs. While probably not satisfying the aspirations of people who wanted to see more diversity in Labatt's managerial ranks, the company's management training materials still reflected progress in terms of attitudes on race and gender. Labour and employee relations were the focus of a small percentage of overall training. Health and safety was discussed in some training films. The products that Labatt manufactured, and where the company would go in the future, were more frequent topics for instruction.

The Sources of Management Training

As the foregoing discussion shows, training materials came from different sources. Some of them were produced internally, such as the many films that Eaton either created themselves or repurposed for their own use. The 1950s and 1960s print materials that both Eaton and Bell used included internally developed content. Bell also incorporated content created by academics. Labatt created a comparatively limited amount of proprietary training aids and instead purchased them from other companies. Some films, like the one made by Xerox, were created by industrial employers, but most of them were acquired from production companies that specialized in training and education films.

The fact that companies spent money on training materials that were created by other firms strongly suggests that there was an industry of some scope related to management and supervisory training aids, and the volume of materials used at Bell, Eaton, and Labatt suggests that it was an industry of some breadth. Trying to ascertain the history of the corporate training media industry is a challenging undertaking, but some insights into it were provided by an industry veteran who wished to remain anonymous, but who will be referred to as John for the purposes of this discussion. John worked for a film production company that was located in London, Ontario, in the 1970s and 1980s that created training films for companies across the province. He also taught media production at Fanshawe College, which is also located in London, Ontario. John's initial post-secondary training was a Bachelor of Communication degree he earned in 1970 from the University of Windsor which, at the time he graduated, was a new program in Canada. Part of the curriculum in that program involved learning how to make films.[80]

John moved through different roles in the media industry in Canada after graduation and eventually moved to London, Ontario, where he worked for a local production company called Lockwood Films for sixteen years. He "did a lot of corporate stuff" while working at that firm and progressed into a position that involved meeting with firms that were prospective clients. When asked about where the corporate training video industry was located he replied that "a huge portion of it was in Toronto" and that "one of our selling points was that we didn't live in Toronto and have Toronto prices." Canada Trust, which later became part of TD Canada Trust, had a major corporate office in London up until the early 2000s and pioneered the introduction of automated teller machines (ATM) in Canada. The first one used by Canada Trust was called Johnnie Cash, after the famed American musician, and John shot the first commercial for it. John recalled another internal film made for Canada Trust in which an orchestra was included to show how the role of the conductor is necessary to ensure that chaos did not ensue.[81]

John emphasized that clients benefited from working with someone who "knew what they were doing" and used a project done with insurance company London Life as an example. In that case, the company had written a script and suggested that the film production crew simply follow what was presented. John pointed out several problems with the proposed script, and London Life's personnel immediately agreed to temporarily halt the production while issues were corrected. He also recalled working with Labatt in London, Ontario, and how local companies would approach Lockwood Films for assistance in the 1970s and 1980s. John shared his experience with the process used to create training videos:

> Typically this is what happened, they (the client) came to us and said we want to train these people over here how to sell our product but we want to also make this into a thing that can this product to our clients, and we said 'stop' it doesn't work that way. It's two different things. You have to have your primary market; you would have thought that they would have known about that in their marketing departments but they didn't. We had to train them to focus on who

their real single target market was . . . you need to train your people in a different way than you sell your product.

John went on to explain that when you are training someone to do a task, you have to "hit every single thing there" in terms of the steps involved.[82]

When asked about the profitability of the corporate film and video business, John indicated that "early, it was very lucrative" because Lockwood Films could do productions more cheaply that competing firms in Toronto. He said that they used a "softer" approach that was "less hard-nosed corporate" than what was created in Toronto. The industry began to change in the 1980s with the proliferation of new technologies that made it easier for new people to begin producing videos. John argued that "the trouble was that they (new competitors) didn't have the technical knowledge to have the video look good and they didn't have the business knowledge and the expertise that we had . . . so the videos came out; they missed their mark . . . they didn't deliver the message," which overall meant that there was increased competition and lower quality films being created.[83]

Lockwood Films produced twenty to thirty corporate films per year when its business was thriving, but increased competition altered the company's course. Clients increasingly made cost the primary consideration when selecting who would create a film and what would be in it, while its overall quality suffered. John described an evolution in the way that corporate training films were created and used. The fact that companies in his early years showed interest in carefully crafted productions that cost more to make illustrates that the training function was considered a good investment. However, as time progressed and cheaply made "quick and dirty" productions began to proliferate, companies were more interested in reducing costs even if it meant receiving a less compelling product.[84]

Comparing Corporate Training

There are common features, but also some differences, in the management training techniques used by Bell Canada, Eaton, and Labatt. Unlike the experience of managers at Bell Canada in the 1950s and 1960s, managers at Eaton's and Labatt did not spend much time participating in classroom training sessions of extensive duration. Instead, their training was deliberately intended to fit around their other work commitments. They were learning how to manage as they progressed with their firms. While not necessarily described as apprentices, they were nonetheless apprentice managers, although their training did not have a fixed conclusion and they were not awarded licenses confirming that they were qualified managers. They were managers because Bell, Eaton, and Labatt employed them in different managerial positions.

Labatt was clearly more concerned with maintaining at least respectful relations with the union representing its production workers, while Eaton's leadership was determined to avoid unionization. The Labatt family, though still shareholders, did not run the company. In contrast, successive members of the Eaton family led the firm until it shut down. Management in both firms was overwhelmingly male and white. This should not have perhaps been a surprise at Labatt since brewing has historically been portrayed as a male industry, and the Labatt's workforce was overwhelmingly male. Eaton's stores were full of female sales staff who were directed by male managers. This gender division was remarkably not noted in Eaton's training materials until the 1970s. The relationships that all three companies had with female employees appears to have been problematic for much of the 1945 to 1995 period. There was no overt hostility toward women in the training aids used by Bell and Eaton; the issue was that women were mostly absent from them. The situation at Labatt was more acute since there are two examples of sexualized portrayals of women in training films used by the company.

Cities like Toronto, Vancouver, and Montréal became much more multi-cultural in the post–World War II decades, but that diversity was not often reflected in Eaton's training materials. Whereas Bell Canada at least produced internal communications in both English and French, Labatt and Eaton seem to have been more Anglo-centric. Eaton notably remained wedded to its Anglo-Saxon roots. Training content used at both companies reflected a lot of American influence. This was particularly true of video sources. Many of them were distributed through Canadian firms but originated with American producers. The widespread use of video sources that began in the 1970s meant that training could be quickly conducted around other work duties. Recording events such as senior management conferences, then distributing the proceedings across an entire organization, meant that company policies and goals could be more clearly communicated than was likely possible with print resources.

A domestic English language corporate training video industry appeared in Canada, and much of it was understandably concentrated in Toronto. Neither Eaton nor Labatt retained French language training films in their archival materials, if they ever purchased films that may have been available. The industry seems to have been at its most viable in the late 1970s and early 1980s, then fragmented as new video technologies made it possible for more people to make films without necessarily having much experience with doing so. It is also evident that the corporate training film business was profitable for a long period and that companies relied on film production companies to help them craft their training programs.

Labatt's training materials reflected much more willingness to think about the challenges facing the firm, especially from other existing and emerging brewers. The content of training materials reflected differing views about how the leaderships of the two companies viewed their respective industries. The beer industry in Canada was dominated by two major firms, Labatt and Molson, until the late twentieth century but was then changed as more foreign competition arrived and craft brewing grew. Labatt recognized the growing competitiveness of their industry. Eaton did not respond quickly enough to changes in retailing. Indeed, the idea of Eaton being in competition did not appear in training materials until the 1980s. From the 1950s to the 1970s, the perception that the company dominated the Canadian retail industry was at the forefront of the messages received by anyone reading a training document or watching a film. The differing margins of brewing and retailing also surely impacted the extent of the resources devoted to training.

In contrast, a utility like Bell Canada operated in a less competitive environment during the post-war decades and would have been able to include the cost of any training programs in its regulated cost base. Bell wanted to ensure that managers and supervisors adapted to the company's organizational structure and understood their places in it. Labatt and Eaton did not routinely present organizational flow-charts to managers and supervisors, but Bell emphasized their importance. Eaton's training materials were written in a paternalistic tone, and the overall message was that a person became part of a wider Eaton family when she or he joined the firm and that the actual Eaton family sat at the top of the company. Bell's ownership structure was not discussed in its training manuals, but there was also a sense that joining the company meant more than simply joining a business organization. Bell was also paternalistic in telling its managers and supervisors that they were important, that their job was to comply with company policies and procedures, and that they should be confidants for the workers who reported to them.

Labatt sent somewhat mixed messages to its management staff. Policy and procedure were discussed within the context of complying with matters like workplace health and safety. Labatt's training materials focused on two issues: handling employee problems and the product that the company produced. Managers were not treated paternalistically, but they were expected to act in that manner. In fact, beginning in the 1970s, training materials implied that existing practices had led to lazy managers and that employment security was not something to be expected by anyone. Managers were advised that they should cooperate with each other but to also see the virtues of being under pressure.

Bell, Eaton, and Labatt devoted considerable resources to advertising, and managers were expected to be conversant with their company's public mission and persona. All three firms obviously saw benefits in spending money on management training, as they continued to do so over several decades. A direct link between profitability and training was not routinely drawn, but senior management obviously saw a link, as training was ongoing in all three instances. The companies attempted to portray themselves as being central to Canada's economy and society. Bell was the telephone services provider in Québec and Ontario and considered itself to be fundamental to Canada's progress as a country. Eaton celebrated the ongoing role that the founding family had in the company and the firm's roots and reach across Canada. Both Bell and Labatt viewed themselves as social institutions and profit-making entities. Labatt also emphasized its long history and central place in the Canadian brewing industry, and thus demonstrated at least some interest in appearing like a social institution but became more focused on competition in the 1970s. The message was clear: being a manager at one of these firms meant working somewhere important. There was never any suggestion that managers were learning skills and gaining experience on the job that would enable them to develop their careers at other companies. It may have been counter-productive for Bell, Eaton, or Labatt to provide training that would facilitate movement to another firm. However, training was also meant to further tie someone to the firm. Managers were to participate in training sessions and programs, then go back and use what they learned on the job.

Managers at the three companies were also expected to align their personal career objectives with those of their firms, and not being a "company man" was not acceptable. Many Eaton's employees were willing to devote themselves to the firm and proudly called themselves Eatonians. It is unclear if offering training made a substantial difference over time to the comparative success of the three firms, even though money continued to be spent on it. Labatt did not go into bankruptcy but, as Matthew Bellamy has discussed, it was one of the major Canadian brewing firms that were subsumed into larger multinational corporations. Managers who participated in internal training of any type were not involved in major decisions about company policy and planning, and nobody participating in management training at Bell, Eaton, or Labatt was encouraged to believe that they would be involved in making strategic decisions about the future directions of their firms.[85]

Both Eaton's and Labatt's senior leaders sought to create management identities and beliefs that were specific to their firms. Doing so would ensure that the people actually overseeing daily operations would adhere to overall policies. Both firms surely had expectations about desired performance among managers and sought to promote it. The training materials used by both firms did not extensively refer to management theory. Management thinkers like Peter Drucker were noted through the use of such methods as Management by Objectives, but in a practical rather than theoretical way. Management was presented as an applied function. Bell, Eaton and Labatt senior management obviously saw value in providing management training, as they devoted resources to it in the post-war decades. The archives are silent on what lower-level managers who participated in training thought of the experience. If nothing else, it helped them form internal networks, and the experience of going through training, even of a tertiary manner, meant that a manager represented an investment for an employer. The training that they experienced aligned them with the broader objectives of their firms. Management, as shown at these three firms, was a vocation practiced within specific organizational spheres. This vocational approach would also be prevalent at community colleges.

Notes

1　Lawrence Surtees, *Pa Bell: A Jean de Grandpré and the Meteoric Rise of Bell Canada* (Toronto: Random House, 1992), 47.
2　Surtees, *Pa Bell*, 87.
3　Douglas W. Bray, Richard J. Campbell, and Donald L. Grant, *Formative Years: A Long-Term AT&T Study of Managerial Lives* (New York: Wiley-Interscience 1974), 4.
4　Bell Canada Archive (hereafter BC), "University Graduates' Induction Course 1955", catalogue number 21119–1, 1.
5　BC, "University Graduates' Induction Course 1955, the Company Organization", 6.
6　BC, "University Graduates' Induction Course 1955, Company Responsibility for Service", 3.
7　BC, "University Graduates' Induction Course 1955, Address by R.H. Keefler, Vice-President, Public Relations", 1.
8　BC, "University Graduates' Induction Course 1955, the Company Organization", 6.
9　BC, "University Graduates' Induction Course 1955, Employee Relations Program", 4.
10　BC, "University Graduates' Induction Course 1955, Labour Relations With Our Employees", 3.
11　BC, "University Graduates' Induction Course 1955, Labour Relations With Our Employees", 2.
12　BC, "University Graduates' Induction Course 1955, Labour Relations With Our Employees", 5.
13　BC, "Supervisor's Course on Employee Relations—Conference, May 1940", catalogue number 25449.
14　BC, "Supervisor's Course on Employee Relations—Conference, May 1940", catalogue number 25449.
15　BC, "Supervisor's Course on Employee Relations—Conference, May 1940", catalogue number 25449.
16　Pamela Walker Laird, *Pull: Networking and Success Since Benjamin Franklin* (Cambridge, MA: Harvard University Press, 2006), 2.
17　BC, "Management Conference, Alpine Inn, 1958", catalogue number 26159.
18　BC, "Management Conference, Alpine Inn, 1958, Net Change Study 1955", catalogue number 26159, 13.
19　BC, "Management Conference, Alpine Inn, 1958, Group Leadership and Communications", catalogue number 26159, 5.
20　BC, *Bell News*, 30 May 1956, 8.
21　BC, "Management Conference, Alpine Inn, 1958", catalogue number 26159, Urwick, "Management *Can* be an Intelligent Occupation".
22　BC, "Industrial Effectiveness Through Team Action", letter from W.M. Rankin, vice-president, to program participants, 8 March 1965.

23 Bernard Portis, "Management Training Through Organization Development", *Business Quarterly* (Summer 1965), pp. 44–55, 51.

24 Bray, Campbell, and Grant, *Formative Years: A Long-Term AT&T Study of Managerial Lives*, 14.

25 Bray, Campbell, and Grant, 154–156.

26 BC, "Management Conference, Alpine Inn, 1958, Management *Can* Be an Intelligent Occupation", catalogue number 26159.

27 Andrew Pettigrew, "Context and Action in the Transformation of the Firm", *Journal of Management Studies* 24, 6 (November 1987), pp. 649–670.

28 BC, *Bell News*, 30 May 1956, 8.

29 Packard, 39.

30 Moss Kanter, *Men and Women of the Corporation*, 18.

31 Albert J. Mills and Jean Helms Mills, "When Plausibility Fails: Towards a Critical Sensemaking Approach to Resistance", Robyn Thomas, Albert J. Mills, and Jean Helms-Mills, ed., *Identity Politics at Work: Resisting Gender, Gendering Resistance* (Abingdon: Routledge, 2004), pp. 141–157.

32 On the significance of the Eaton's Santa Claus parade see Steve Penfold, *A Mile of Make-Believe: A History of the Eaton's Santa Claus Parade* (Toronto: University of Toronto Press, 2016).

33 Patricia Phenix, *Eatonians: The Story of the Family Behind the Family* (Toronto: McClelland and Stewart, 2002), 3.

34 See Eatonia and Timothy Eaton United Church, accessed 17 August 2016, www.eatonia.ca/and www.temc.ca/.

35 Archive of Ontario (hereafter AO), T. Eaton Fonds, F229–170, B253184, File: Procedure Military Service Record: Second Great War, 1939–1945.

36 AO, T. Eaton Fonds, B253184, File F229–170, File: Employee Participation—Eaton Veterans' Association, 1938 to 1958, Eaton Veterans' Association Club Building.

37 AO, T. Eaton Fonds, F229–170, B253182, "E Service", 1954.

38 AO, T. Eaton Fonds, F229–170, B253182, Loose binder Welcome to Eaton's, 1950 to 1964.letter to F.G. Peskett, 15 October 1954.

39 AO, T. Eaton Fonds, F229–170, B253184, Military Service—Employee Participation, Military Service Summary, 1939 to 1948.

40 AO, T. Eaton Fonds, F229–170, B25318, Personnel Managers' Conference, November 1954.

41 AO, T. Eaton Fonds, B253182, F229–170, File: Welcome to Eaton's, 1964 to 1969, Welcome to Eaton's.

42 AO, T. Eaton Fonds, B253182, F229–170, File: Toy Inspector Manual, Management Development Plan: Eaton's of Hamilton, 4.

43 AO, T. Eaton Fonds, B253182, F229–170, File: Toy Inspector Manual, Management Development Plan: Eaton's of Hamilton, 6.

44 AO, T. Eaton Fonds, B253182, F229–170, File: Handbooks, Management Guides to Personnel Policies, Management Guide to Personnel Policies, 1.

45 AO, T. Eaton Fonds, B253182, F229–170, File: Handbooks, Management Guides to Personnel Policies, Management Guide to Personnel Policies, 2.

46 AO, T. Eaton Fonds, B253182, F229–170, File: Handbooks, Management Guides to Personnel Policies, Management Guide to Personnel Policies, 2.

47 For an overview of the history of Corporate Social Responsibility see Douglas M. Eichar, *The Rise and Fall of Corporate Social Responsibility* (Abingdon: Routledge, 2015).

48 AO, T. Eaton Fonds, B253182, F229–170, File: Handbooks, Management Guides to Personnel Policies, Management Guide to Personnel Policies, 5.

49 AO, T. Eaton Fonds, box B253182, F229–170, File: Welcome to Eaton's 1964–1969, Various Companies.

50 AO, T. Eaton Fonds, F229–403–0–89, "Staff Training Spring 1974".

51 AO, T. Eaton Fonds, F229–403–0–84, "Twice Across Canada Annually".
52 AO, T. Eaton Fonds, F229–403–0–84, "Twice Across Canada Annually".
53 AO, T. Eaton Fonds, F229–403–0–88, "Christmas Sales Presentation".
54 AO, T. Eaton Fonds, F229–403–0–88, "Staff Training Spring 1974".
55 AO, T. Eaton Fonds, F229–403–0–88, "Managing to Win".
56 Eileen Sufrin, *The Eaton Drive: The Campaign to Organize Canada's Largest Department Store, 1948 to 1952* (Toronto: Fitzhenry and Whiteside, 1982).
57 AO, T. Eaton Fonds, F229–421,"No Small Change: The Story of the Eaton Strike", DVD 24.
58 AO, T. Eaton Fonds, "Meetings: Taking the Minutes", F229–417, DVD 657.
59 AO, T. Eaton Fonds, "One Minute Manager Excerpts", F229–417, DVD 660.
60 Kenneth Blanchard and Spencer Johnson, *The One Minute Manager* (New York: Berkley, 1983).
61 AO, T. Eaton Fonds, "Corporate Culture: Tape 1 (Fred Eaton—Part 1) 1989", F229–421, B381930, DVD 664, approximately 20 minute run time.
62 AO, T. Eaton Fonds, "Eaton Credit Corporation Recruitment Video", F229–417, B381933, DVD 666, approximately 15 minute run time.
63 ARCC, Labatt Brewing Company Collection, AFC-101, "Managing by Objectives" (Unit One) LA00920.
64 ARCC, Labatt Brewing Company Collection, AFC-101, "Managing by Objectives" (Unit Two) LA00920.
65 ARCC, Labatt Brewing Company Collection, AFC-101, "Managing by Objectives" (Unit Two) LA00920.
66 ARCC, Labatt Brewing Company Collection, AFC-101, "Managing by Objectives" (Unit Two) LA00920.
67 ARCC, Labatt Brewing Company Collection, AFC-101, "Managing by Objectives" (Unit Two) LA00920.
68 ARCC, Labatt Brewing Company Collection, AFC-101, "Managing by Objectives" (Unit Five) LA00920.
69 ARCC, Labatt Brewing Company Collection, AFC-101, "Managing by Objectives" (Unit Eight) LA00920.
70 ARCC, Labatt Brewing Company Collection, AFC-101, "The Professional", CC00460.
71 ARCC, Labatt Brewing Company Collection, CC00550, "Defining Performance Expectations".
72 ARCC, Labatt Brewing Company Collection AFC-101, "John Labatt Limited Orientation"—VHS, LA01986.
73 ARCC, Labatt Brewing Company Collection AFC-101, "Going Places"—VHS, CC01142.
74 ARCC, Labatt Brewing Company Collection, AFC-101, "Labatt Breweries of Canada: Jake McCall, Ross Taylor PhD, 'The Past and Future of Beer—Product Focus'", CC01340.
75 ARCC, Labatt Brewing Company Collection, AFC-101, "Labatt Breweries of Canada: Jeff Hallett, 'The Corporation in the 21st Century'", CC01336.
76 ARCC, Labatt Brewing Company Collection, AFC-101, "The Western Executive Experience"—VHS, LA00898.
77 ARCC, Labatt Brewing Company Collection, AFC-101, "Quality of Working Life", CC01762.
78 ARCC, Labatt Brewing Company Collection, AFC-101, CC00557.
79 ARCC, Labatt Brewing Company Collection, AFC-101, Marketing Video, CC00163 11 minute run time.
80 Anonymous (John) interview, 6 September 2016.
81 Anonymous (John) interview, 6 September 2016.
82 Anonymous (John) interview, 6 September 2016.

83 Anonymous (John) interview, 6 September 2016.
84 Anonymous (John) interview, 6 September 2016.
85 Matthew Bellamy, "I Was Canadian: The Globalization of the Canadian Brewing Industry", in Dimitry Anastakis and Andrew Smith, ed., *Smart Globalization: The Canadian Business and Economic History Experience* (Toronto: University of Toronto Press, 2014), pp. 206–230.

3 Community Colleges

Community colleges became key providers of management and supervisory education in Canada in the post–World War II decades. Those institutions were intended to be distinct from universities and were meant to provide applied training that would enable students to readily enter the workforce. Three institutions are the subject of the analysis: Vancouver Community College in British Columbia (VCC), Niagara College in Ontario, and Collège Ahuntsic in Québec. Materials from George Brown College, which is also in Ontario, will be referenced to help further explain the importance of a specific program offered by community colleges across Ontario. VCC, Niagara, and Ahuntsic were chosen to provide insights into how community college management programs developed across Canada. They were also chosen for a more fundamental reason: all three had available archival materials.

One of the remarkable aspects of attempting to study community college programs of any type across Canada is the challenge of finding archival sources. Colleges retain records, but most do not do so in an accessible manner. Community colleges in Québec—known as Collège d'enseignement général et professionnel (CEGEP)—are legally required to deposit some materials at Bibliothèque et Archives nationales du Québec (BAnQ). There is no similar requirement imposed upon Ontario and British Columbia colleges. Indeed, of the twenty-four community colleges in Ontario, only two have organized archives: George Brown and Canadore. Niagara College is part of this analysis because, even though their records are not organized into an established archive, they were nonetheless willing to provide access to their library's records room. The Niagara holdings, while not organized by an archivist, are the most comprehensive community college records cited in this analysis. Langara College (formerly part of VCC) also holds some materials in their library. The way in which community colleges store and provide access to their historical records is in marked contrast to the practices of Canadian universities. However, the colleges should really not be blamed for their lack of formal archival systems. Even the ones that have organized archives are pleasantly surprised to learn that someone wants to come and view their holdings. The archival materials used for this analysis mainly include program guides and, in the case of Niagara College, course information sheets (syllabi), other internal college documents, and an oral interview with a former employee.

Community colleges played a key role in the overall management and supervisory education process in Canada and, as this analysis will show, that role may be unexpected for vocational institutions. This chapter is going to address some key issues including the types of management programs community colleges offered and their content. Community college management education, which often fell under the broad category of business education, conveyed certain ideas about what it meant to be a manager. This leads to another issue that this chapter will address: what did community college management programs say about what it meant to be a manager in terms of both individual and wider societal expectations, and were graduates of those programs able to assume managerial roles and oversee business functions? This analysis will show that community colleges exerted considerable influence over how managers were trained and on the meaning of management in post–World War II Canada.

Canadian Community Colleges in Perspective

Community college education, like other forms of higher education in Canada, emerged in somewhat different forms across Canada. The key common feature of all community colleges in Canada is how and when they emerged. Their origin was rooted firmly in the baby boom generation. As Doug Owram showed, Canada had one of largest post-war baby booms in the world.[1] Community colleges were formed in the 1960s, most often for the purpose of preparing young people for the workforce. There were important differences in the way that they were established in English and French Canada. In the latter instance, the CEGEPs were a transition between secondary school and university, although they would also offer education options that led directly to the workforce. In contrast, colleges in neighboring Ontario were not initially intended to be a pathway to university. The Catholic Church influenced the creation of the CEGEPs, while community colleges in other provinces were shaped more by economic interests. Québec colleges were also distinct based on language. Ahuntsic was formed with the intent that it would offer programs taught in French, although it would also offer specific courses in English. In contrast, a place like Dawson College in Montréal was founded as an English-language institution.

The emergence of colleges in Ontario most dramatically illustrates the speed with which community colleges emerged in Canada. Mid-1960s Ontario was governed by a Progressive Conservative government led by Premier John Robarts, and the provincial education minister—Bill Davis—developed a plan to create a new network of community colleges across the province.

Canada experienced enormous economic growth in the 1960s, and public policy makers were concerned about ensuring ongoing prosperity and with shaping the country's workforce to meet the needs of new and emerging industries. Helping people to secure rewarding employment was also considered important. In Ontario's case, some existing vocational institutions became community colleges. As Figure 3.1 shows, community colleges grew at a rapid rate following their founding, and programs were sometimes taught in temporary facilities.

British Columbia community colleges were slightly different from their eastern Canadian counterparts. The need to prepare people for jobs in the province's growing economy was a priority, as it was in Québec and Ontario, but subsequent analysis will show that the impetus for creating colleges often originated at a local rather than provincial level. As with many other public policy matters in Canada, geography surely loomed over the formation of British Columbia community colleges. Policy makers did not just want to provide baby boom students with practical workplace skills, but to also acquire such skills in their home province rather than somewhere else in the country. The need to create new post-secondary institutions would have been evident in the 1950s. As Owram has noted, there was a huge expansion of public schools in the 1950s, both in terms of facilities and teaching staff. The students would eventually graduate from secondary school and need somewhere to go.[2]

Canadian community colleges came after their American counterparts and differed from them in significant ways. Canadian colleges were not initially founded as degree-granting institutions. They instead began

Figure 3.1 A 1967 image of an outdoor classroom used by Niagara College in advance of building construction

Source: Used with permission of Niagara College.

offering certificate and diploma programs. In contrast, American colleges awarded associate degrees that could potentially lead to a bachelor's degree. Canada has post-secondary institutions that include the names of provinces, such as the University of New Brunswick and the University of Alberta, but does not have institutions that are comparable to American state university systems such as the State University of New York (SUNY) system. In that latter example, community colleges were part of the same broad administrative structure as four-year comprehensive colleges and university research centres. The community colleges in such a system formed a pathway to further higher education accomplishment and perhaps the hope of upward class mobility. Canadian community colleges, because of their distinct and separate status compared to universities, were working-class institutions that were intended to help people enjoy more prosperity within their own social class. In this sense, they were similar to further education (FE) colleges in the United Kingdom, which also expanded in the post–World War II years to provide vocational learning to Britain's baby boom.[3]

Community colleges in Canada thus share common features, but also some key differences. A desire to provide more education to baby boom students in the 1960s was a broad policy objective across Canada, as was a strong interest in ensuring that this would lead to more prosperity at the provincial level. Canadian community colleges were, as the term suggested, rooted in specific communities. They were not created to recruit students from across their respective provinces, never mind from across Canada. They were initially meant to serve certain geographic areas. VCC was formed to educate high school graduates in Vancouver. Ahuntsic was meant to serve francophone students in Montréal, and Niagara College was to educate young people from across the many communities found in the Niagara Peninsula. Those institutions were representative of the wider community college experience in Canada, but they also rapidly moved beyond their seemingly narrow missions and grew in importance to their communities and students.

Vancouver Community College (Langara)

VCC's origins are found in a 1962 British Columbia report titled *Higher Education in British Columbia and a Plan for the Future*. It was chaired by John B. MacDonald and became known as the MacDonald Commission. MacDonald visited many communities across BC and also consulted a range of studies on higher education in the United States, United Kingdom, Australia, and New Zealand.[4] MacDonald recommended expansion of higher education in the province and emphasized BC's rapid population growth as a primary reason for doing so.[5] The existing post-secondary education system, which mainly consisted of the University of British Columbia and Victoria College, were taking as many students as could be accommodated. MacDonald did not expressly use the term "community college" in his report, but he did stress the need for two types of institution in BC: degree-granting universities and four-year colleges, and two-year colleges offering one- and two-year programs after completion of grade twelve in secondary school.[6] The two-year college would be something new for BC, and they would offer a path to university, "technological and semi-professional courses," and adult education.[7] It is clear that MacDonald must have had community or junior colleges in mind as they were already common in the United States in the early 1960s. VCC's Langara campus was situated in the south side of Vancouver, near the Fraser River and across from the city of Richmond. Vancouver was Canada's third-largest city in the mid-1960s and dominated British Columbia both economically and demographically. 1960s Vancouver had some demographic diversity when VCC was founded, but not nearly as much as it would have by the late 1990s. Efforts were made to foster support for the new college. For instance, presentations were made to school board trustees asking them to support the new college.[8]

VCC began offering programs at its King Edward Centre (which would later be called Langara) in 1965. VCC itself was listed in the first course guide as being a product of the Vancouver School Board and was the result of amalgamating three preceding schools: the Vancouver School of Art, the Vancouver Vocational Institute, and the King Edward Senior Matriculation and Continuing Education Centre.[9] VCC enrollment was open to Vancouver residents, although non-residents could enroll and pay an additional fee.[10] The tuition fees were modest, with the most expensive option being $20 per term to a maximum of $100 in the first two terms.[11] The cost went up slightly to a maximum of $125 in the third and fourth terms of a program, with technical programs not being more than $75 per term.

The initial mid-1960s offerings were modest and included four Business Administration programs that were listed as technical in nature: Accounting, Finance and Investment, Salesmanship, and Executive Secretary. These programs did not include the terms "manager" or "supervisor" in their titles, but there were nonetheless courses that did include them. Accounting, Finance and Investment and Salesmanship both required students to take Management Policy and Practice. The former program also required a course called Supervisory Training. The Executive Secretary program did not include any management or supervisory courses. Indeed, there were quite gendered implications in the way that two of the programs were structured. Working in sales was for men and, while the Executive Secretary program did not say that it was expressly meant for women, secretarial work in the 1960s was widely known to be overwhelmingly female.[12]

The Accounting, Finance and Investment program was the most obvious choice for someone thinking of entering a management or supervisory role. It was described as preparing students for "careers in investments, insurance, trust companies, banks, and related businesses in this field." The importance of Vancouver as a western Canadian financial centre was also emphasized. The program required these courses:

Communication Skills
Oral Communications
Economics
The Pacific Trading Company
Accounting
Business Procedures
Introduction to Promotional Techniques
Mathematics for Finance
Psychology for Business and Industry
Data Processing Equipment Orientation
Investments and Investment Institutions
Government Fiscal and Monetary Policies
Consumer Credit
Personnel Administration
Life Insurance
General Insurance
Business Trends and Forecasting
Practical Banking
Supervisory Training
Economic Development of British Columbia
Management Policy and Practices
Business Law

This was a lot of ground to cover in a two-year program. The workload, although it was intended to be applied rather than theoretical, would have kept students busy. The content of the Accounting, Finance and Investment program reveals what VCC thought was important for young people to know about business. The program emphasized economics, including economic development in British Columbia, and the legal environment in which businesses functioned. It also would have taught students graduating in 1967, when the first cohort would have completed the program, that they knew something about supervising and managing people.[13]

VCC's offerings continued to expand from the late 1960s into the mid-1970s. By 1976, the King Edward Centre was known as Langara. The campus was organized into a department structure that included Business Administration, Arts and Applied Arts, Community Services, Nursing, and Physical Education and Recreation. Early course guides did not include images, but black and white photographs were printed by the mid-1970s. The 1976 course guide showed young students pursuing a range of academic and extra-curricular activities and in a way that illustrated gender and racial diversity. VCC was a community-based institution, and it wanted to send a message that it wanted to attract students from the increasingly diverse Vancouver metropolitan area.[14]

1976 was also an important year at the Langara campus because that was when a program titled Business Management was first offered. This program shared a core group of courses with the campuses other Business program:

Accounting
Business Law
Communications
Marketing
Mathematics
Psychology
Geography

The Business Management program also required:

Data Processing
Fundamentals of Finance
Industrial Engineering
Managerial Accounting
Purchasing
Office Management and Procedures
Management Policies and Practices
Personnel Management[15]

Course descriptions reveal what students should have learned about management. For example, the description for Personnel Management said that it was:

> Essentially a course in human relations with emphasis on the various processes and techniques of establishing and maintaining an efficient working force through high morale and effective public relations. The more technical aspects of personnel management are studied only in sufficient depth to give a reasonable understanding of their nature and purpose.[16]

Students presumably learned how to influence workers and perhaps heard something about workplace motivation. They were taught enough to motivate people without becoming too burdened with theory. Students enrolled in Management Policy and Procedure were taught about implementing workplace policy and how it related to personnel issues.[17] In contrast, students taking Accounting were introduced to fundamental practices and procedures that pertained to the subject.[18] Maintaining effective control over business functions, including personnel, was a common theme in the Business Management program.

The term "management" began appearing in new VCC program titles offered at Langara by the mid-1980s. A Pacific Rim Management program was first offered in 1984, and Recreation Facilities Management was introduced in 1986. The Pacific Rim program was, as its name suggested, intended for students who wanted to work in businesses involved in trade with other countries on the Pacific Ocean. It included the same usual courses found in the college's other management programs, but also included liberal arts content. Students were required to take courses in History, Religious Studies, and a language spoken in the Pacific Rim area. Personnel Management and Management Policy and Practice were listed as electives. The addition of courses such as Religious Studies and Pacific Rim Language implies that VCC felt that learning about the technical aspects of running a business was not sufficient training if working in a business that operated beyond Canada. The language course was open in terms of which language would actually be learned.[19]

The Recreation Facilities Management program was a post-diploma certificate program, whereas the other management programs awarded diplomas. Recreation Facilities Management included a series of Recreation courses and others such as Physics, Accounting, and Personnel Management. The latter course was not an elective as it was in Pacific Rim Management, which raises the question of why knowing something about dealing with personnel issues was core to running recreational facilities but not to conducting business with other Pacific Rim countries. The possible answer is that someone working in recreational facility management presumably was going to deal with people more than someone employed in something seemingly less labour intensive.[20]

VCC's Langara offerings grew further by the latter 1990s. While the management programs increasingly dealt with personnel issues as electives topics, the college also introduced a Labour Studies program in 1993. The college offered over fifty programs at Langara in 1996, and twenty-one of them were in business topics. Enrollment statistics for Langara were not printed in the course calendars, but it is quite evident that business education was central to the college's operations. The Labour Studies diploma program perhaps not surprisingly focused more personnel issues than the comparable business programs. It required completion of ten courses:

Canadian Studies
Three in Economics
English
Geography
History

Political Science
Two in Sociology[21]

The Canadian Studies course was called Work in Canadian Society and was described as incorporating an interdisciplinary approach to the subject.[22] In contrast, students in the Business, Finance, and Investment Management program were advised that they would learn about the "interdependence of business and other social and political actors" but were not expressly told that their program would help them deal with people in the workplace.[23] They also could not take courses in other programs such as Labour Studies that would provide that crucial insight. On the other hand, the management programs offered by VCC at Langara likely prepared students to find employment in the BC economy. The college's program offerings expanded considerably from the late 1960s to the 1990s, and business education became a major part of the college's overall programming. This suggests that, while enrollment figures are not available for that three-decade period, there were growing numbers of students who wanted to study business-related subjects and saw VCC as a good place to do so.

Collège Ahuntsic

Québec community colleges occupy a unique place in higher education in Canada. The CEGEP system was created in 1967, which was during the same period that community colleges were founded in English Canada. However, the CEGEP represented a stage between secondary school and post-secondary education through which all Québec students would progress. The existence of university and vocational streams meant that CEGEPs were not solely applied learning institutions. As with community colleges in British Columbia, the CEGEP system was also the result of a provincial commission on higher education. The Parent Commission—formally known as the Royal Commission of Inquiry on Education in the Province of Québec—was established in 1961 by the provincial Liberal government led by Jean Lesage. The commission was led by a Catholic priest named Alphonse-Marie Parent.[24]

The election of Lesage in 1960 is widely recognized in Canada as the start of the Quiet Revolution (Révolution tranquille) in Québec. The role of virtually every public institution in the province was reconsidered, especially the role of the Catholic Church. Improving the social, cultural, and economic circumstance of the francophone majority in the province was a main priority for the Lesage government. Economic growth and improving educational opportunities for Québecois youth was an objective of the Parent Commission, but within the wider context of the Quiet Revolution. The Parent Commission met from 1961 to 1966, and the report that it produced dwarfed the MacDonald Commission report in

BC in terms of size and scope. As Claude Corbo has noted, the Parent Commission's recommendation of the creation of the CEGEP marked a break from existing practice in Québec. It moved away from classical education, addressed the existing vocational programs that existed across the province, and reflected a broader North American trend of creating colleges of different types. CEGEPs were also crucially different from their counterparts in English Canada, as Québec students would pass through them on their way to university. It was within that framework that Collège Ahuntsic began offering programs.[25]

Ahuntsic was, like Vancouver Community College, an amalgamation of three existing schools: L'Institut des Arts Graphiques, Le Collège Saint-Ignace, and L'Institute de Technologie Laval. The college experienced some initial challenges in its first two years, but a 1969 annual report indicated that its founding objectives were being realized.[26] Ahuntsic had 4,000 students enrolled in Health Sciences, Pure and Applied Science, Social Science, Administrative Science, and General Arts by 1974.[27] The description for the Administrative Science program was quite brief in 1974 and did not provide course descriptions or a detailed program outline. The prospectus specified that it would be useful for working in manufacturing, commercial and financial business, and government and para-governmental organizations.[28] The 1974 prospectus did not provide much detail about the nature of Ahuntsic's student body, other than the number of people who attended.

Ahuntsic expanded by the mid-1980s in terms of programming and the number of students attending. The college had a core liberal arts curriculum regardless of the concentration that students would eventually pursue. Students were required to take four courses in French, four in Philosophy, and four in Physical Education whether they were in the two-year university stream or three-year professional program stream.[29] They could choose from forty-two different programs between the university and professional streams, although the former option was much more focused on liberal arts subjects. The professional stream included three options under Administrative Studies (Techniques), including Industrial Management.[30] Students entering Industrial Management were advised that they should have the following traits in order to seek employment in that field:

Analytical spirit
Strong personality
Sense of organization
Aptitude for mathematics
Be dynamic and have initiative
Interpersonal skills, tact, finesse
Resourcefulness
Show maturity and leadership[31]

The obvious message was that taking Industrial Management at Ahunt-sic would impart these traits and abilities. Students would learn how to identify and solve operational problems while increasing productivity and decreasing costs.[32] The program required completion of fourteen courses, and they would have required quantitative aptitude since they included Statistics, Industrial Production, and Quality Control.[33] Only one course—Collective Bargaining—involved dealing directly with people.

Ahuntsic's offerings continued to develop through the 1990s, but only two of them—Administrative Studies and Finance—pertained to business or management. Students interested in the Administrative Studies program were advised that they would become familiar with the national and international environments in which businesses operated, understand main legal concepts and how they related to the principal functions of business, and understand work relations between individuals and groups in an organization. The program was oriented toward quantitative analysis despite its description indicating that it would cover a range of business-related topics. It required completion of twenty-five courses over six terms, and fifteen of them pertained to topics like finance, mathematics, costs, information systems, statistics, and taxation. There was only one offering that focused on human relations at work:

Global Economics	International Economic Relations
Introduction to Business Organization	Management
Business Law	Costs and Systems
Accounting I	Financial Planning
Accounting II	Statistics
Operations Management	Human Resource Management
Marketing	Office Organization
Introduction to Information Management	Information Systems
	Quality and Control
Mathematics	Financial Quantitative Methods
Management Accounting	Sales
Management of Supplies and Services	Finance Internship
Financial Accounting	Taxation
Finance I	

A student studying that program may have thought that s/he had learned about managing people but had really learned about manipulating and analyzing numbers. It is also significant that, outside of the two economics courses and one on business law, the broader social context in which business operated was not the focus of even one course.[34]

Ahuntsic students were not featured in the 1995 prospectus, but they were frequently presented in the college's internal newsletters. The first edition of *Communications Ahuntsic* published in 1986 illustrated that the college had a racially and ethnically homogeneous staff and student body. The college's close relations with industry were noted.[35] The college promoted the notion of CEGEPs being entrepreneurial.[36] The overarching view being conveyed was that Collège Ahuntsic was a rewarding place to pursue learning that would readily enable someone to obtain skilled work in the Québec labour market.

Niagara College

The Ontario community college system was devised in a political milieu that was more similar to the one found in British Columbia than in Québec. Ontario had been governed by a Progressive Conservative government for twenty-two years when education minister Bill Davis released a statement in the legislature on community colleges in May, 1965. He introduced Bill 153 to amend the Department of Education Act. His statement, which ran to thirty-nine pages, explained the government's rationale for creating the province's community college system. Davis told the legislature that "a considerable number of (Canadian) companies are experiencing a scarcity of managerial, scientific, and technical personnel" and further noted that "there has long been a deficiency in our education system in regard to the training of technical personnel beyond the high school level but short of the university level." Community colleges would remedy that deficiency.[37]

The term community college became the popular way of describing the new colleges, but they were formally called Colleges of Applied Arts and Technology (CAAT).[38] The principle underlying their founding was that they would offer both full-time and part-time study and "meet the relevant needs of all adults within a community, at all socio-economic levels, of all kinds of interests and aptitudes, and at all stages of educational achievement."[39] The formation of the colleges was considered essential by Davis if Ontario hoped "to continue to compete for markets on even terms at home and abroad."[40] His statements revealed much about how colleges like Niagara would develop in subsequent years. They were ostensibly open to people from all social classes, but in practice they would be much more working class than middle class in composition. Community colleges, including Niagara College, would align their programs with the needs of business to help ensure Ontario's future prosperity.

Niagara College was founded in 1967, and it was as much a product of the Niagara Region as it was of provincial government policy. The first campus was located in Welland, Ontario. In the late 1960s, it was a small industrial city that the Welland Canal passed through. It was in some ways an odd location for a new college campus as it was not especially close to other larger communities that it would serve, such as

St. Catharines and Niagara Falls. Each of the fourteen new community colleges were intended to draw students from specific areas in Ontario. Niagara College broadly served students from across twenty-six communities in the broader Regional Municipality of Niagara. Niagara College offered thirty-six programs in 1968, with thirteen in the Business Division. Those business programs further included five in secretarial work which, like the secretarial programs offered at Vancouver Community College, were clearly meant for women rather than men. Niagara's calendar listed five programs with "management" in their titles: Data Processing Management, Financial Management, Marketing Management, Personnel Management and Industrial Relations, and Production Management. The college also offered a range of applied programs in subjects like horticulture, engineering technology, graphic arts, and drafting.[41]

Niagara was not unique in offering management courses from the time that it opened. The Ontario government believed that management and supervisory education needed to be offered by community colleges, and Niagara complied. It is noteworthy that the college offered Personnel Management and Industrial Relations. The Niagara Region was heavily industrialized and unionized in the late 1960s, and it was widely known as the home of large private sector employers including Ontario Paper, Domtar, Hayes-Dana, Norton Industries, Ford Glass, General Motors, and Thompson Products. Offering Personnel Management and Industrial Relations must have seemed appropriate in these circumstances, and the program required that students complete forty courses over six semesters. Of those forty courses—there were only three electives—students took nine courses that directly pertained to personnel and industrial relations topics:

Industrial and Personnel Relations
Applied Psychology
Industrial Sociology
Wage and Salary Administration
Labour and Industrial Relations
Psychology of Industrial Relations
Labour Economics and Labour Relations
Employment Psychology: the Interview
Collective Bargaining

The balance of the program was heavily weighted toward quantitative topics such as accounting and statistics. Other core business functions like marketing and taxation were also required in the Personnel Management and Industrial Relations program. It was consequently not really a program that focused specifically on the terms in its title and was instead more of a general management program with a selection of personnel management courses included in it.[42]

The increasingly quantitative nature of the Personnel and Industrial Relations program was even evident in the courses that should perhaps have been more qualitative in content. For instance, the Psychology of Industrial Relations course description said:

> A study of psychology as it relates to industrial relations. The topics to be studied are: social needs, conditions for security, motives, causes of industrial content, surveys, interviewing, employee selection, supervisions, complaints and grievances, counselling, fatigue related to working conditions, incentives, organization and communications, relations between employees, management and employee relations, relations with union organizations.[43]

Someone taking this course may have rightly anticipated learning how to handle employee problems just like other production issues. Students may have heard the term "human relations" or the name Elton Mayo from their course instructor but, even if they did not, the course surely reflected a strong human relations orientation. The Industrial and Personnel Relations course description also implied that human relations and scientific management shaped what would be learned:

> A study of the theory and problems related to industrial and personnel relations. The topics to be studied are: background of modern manpower management, statistical tools, job analysis and descriptions, employee sources and recruitment, selection, training, efficiency rating, wage and wage policies, wage and salary administration, promotion and transfer, employee services, collective bargaining, personnel records and reports, labour legislation.[44]

Management, as described in these courses, principally involved using methods to measure and monitor employee performance and to channel workplaces issues through bureaucratic processes.

Community colleges in Ontario followed the provincial government's directive to provide part-time studies in parallel with full-time programs. Niagara College offered management and supervisory programs shortly after the college opened. Those programs were often founded in conjunction with external organizations. For instance, a 1968 Supervisory Management program was offered through evening classes at the Welland campus in conjunction with the Industrial Management Clubs of Canada, and the courses were essentially the same as those offered during the day. They included Human Relations in Industry, Industrial Relations, and Industrial Psychology.[45] The initial part-time evening programs tended to include less quantitative content than was found in the full-time day programs. Most importantly, these evening management and supervisory programs demonstrated a great eagerness by the college's administration to closely align their offerings with the needs and interests of the region's business community. Evening programs were also crucially different from their daytime counterparts because they permitted people working full-time to pursue college-level study. What people would learn in such programs would thus complement what they did at work, rather than necessarily provide a foundation before they entered the workforce. Students had to apply for admission to the Supervisory Management program, but a minimum 60 percent average on a Junior Matriculation Grade 12 diploma was the requirement.[46] The courses were not especially expensive as the 1968 continuing education calendar showed that courses like Industrial Economics, Psychology, and Labour Relations cost $18 for a fifteen-week term in 1970.[47]

Niagara's offerings continued to expand into the late 1970s. The college expanded business programs, but also offered a certificate in Labour Studies through an Institute of Labour and Labour-Management Studies. This was where non-quantitative courses on workplace issues were found. The Labour Studies certificate program was intended to help address a "serious shortage of personnel" who understood industrial relations. It was not framed as being specifically for either people aspiring to managerial roles or union members and was instead described as meeting the needs of workers in "the plant or office."[48] This certificate included core and elective courses, and many of the titles were completely unlike anything listed in Niagara's other business programs. They included Social Psychology for Trade Unionists, Public Relations at the Local Level, The Effective Use of Leisure, The White-Collar Unionist: A Specialist Approach, and the Role of Women in Canadian Trade Unions.[49] This program was unique and, as former college faculty member Sherri Rosen remembered, it was the first community college program of its kind in Canada.[50] While the Labour Studies certificate objectives and course titles seem oriented more toward union activists, the program dealt with issues that impacted management. For instance, the catalogue description for The Effective Use of Leisure stated: "the trend toward the shorter working week will be examined; also the work ethic and whether changes in styles of living must take place if workers are to use their leisure in a manner useful both to them and to society."[51] The idea of workers having more leisure time may have been anathema to Niagara College's partners in the local business community but would have been a management issue in the late 1970s, otherwise it would not have been included in a program curriculum.

In contrast to the Labour Studies certificate offered in 1978, the Personnel Management and Industrial Relations curriculum still emphasized a quantitative approach to recognizing workplace issues. Courses on Effective Supervision and Motivation, Personnel Management by Objectives, Management Training, and Management of Human Resources had been added and replaced previous parts of the program.[52] The term "human resources" was beginning to supplant "personnel management," but the program still framed workplace issues essentially within the confines of a given organization rather than within a broader social context. The college's range of programs reflected changes in the Niagara Region's economy even if their individual focus was not broad. In 1979, the college began offering a diploma in Hotel and Restaurant Administration, which was a decision influenced by the growing importance of tourism and hospitality to the region's economy. The requirements of the Hotel and Restaurant Administration program meant that it was a management program, but it was shaped by service industry expectations, whereas earlier college programs were influenced by manufacturing. The program catalogue advised that:

> It takes a special kind of person to thrive in the hotel and restaurant industry. Some of the personal qualities required would include ambition, good personal appearance, strength of character and an interest and desire to be hospitable.[53]

This program incorporated forty-one courses, including many that reflected specific aspects of working in the hospitality industry such as Wines and Beverages I, Hospitality Management Accounting, and Hospitality Dynamics. There was only one course related to human resource management: Staff Planning and Personnel Relations.[54] A largely quantitative approach was as prevalent in this program as in the other management programs offered at Niagara. The program also implied that good emotional control was required of people who wished to succeed in hospitality. As Arlie Russell Hochschild has revealed, this was an aspect of work that became more prevalent as the service sector became more central to the modern labour market.[55]

Niagara College programs were intended to initially give students a broad overview of how business functioned, then move them into more specialized topics. The Introduction to Business I course required in the late 1980s Retail Management program revealed what the college thought was essential to first learn about business:

> An introduction into business with emphasis placed on business within the Canadian economic system. Forms of business ownership, management, organization, personnel management and production/operations management.[56]

The course was then divided into nine sections:

Canada's Business System
Sole Proprietorship and Partnership
The Corporation

Long Term Financing
Business Management
Modern Manufacturing
Inventory, Purchasing, and Quality
Labour Relations and Collective Bargaining
Final Review and Testing

Dealing with matters pertaining to people in the workplace was the focus of the Business Management and Labour Relations and Collective Bargaining sections. There was one required textbook in the course, *An Introduction to Canadian Business* by Maurice Archer, and it covered different aspects of business operations:

Canada's Business System
Forms of Business Ownership
Business Management
Production Management
Marketing Management
Financial Management
Human Resources
Small Business
International Business
Electronic Data Processing[57]

Students who used this textbook were told that "Business management is the art of using human and material resources to produce and market goods and services" and were furthermore advised that "What is particularly significant about business management is that it is a wealth-creating activity."[58] Archer then went on to describe the roles and functions of top management, middle management, and supervisory management and noted that the latter group supervised the bulk of a corporation's employees.[59] The textbook did not promise career greatness, and its contents aligned with the key points covered in the course.

Niagara College's continuing education department offered more non-quantitative management options in the late 1970s, although technological change in business was clearly shaping the introduction of computer-related courses. For example, the college offered courses on Computer Applications, Computer Operations, Fortran programming and Cobol programming in the Winter 1979 term.[60] It also offered ten courses that pertained to management and supervisory skills, including one called Management Skills for Women Supervisors.[61] This last offering is noteworthy because it would have reflected the fact that women were increasingly assuming supervisory roles in organizations. It was briefly described as providing instruction for "women who have recently been promoted, or are working toward promotion, in supervisory positions."[62]

There are two ways of viewing a course such as that one. On one hand, its title suggested that being a woman supervisor was much different than being a man in such a role. On the other hand, the course also acknowledged that women may have faced unique challenges when working in supervisory roles. As with Niagara's other part-time courses, a student taking that ten-week course would have only paid $33.[63]

The influence of technological change in the workplace was further evident in Niagara College's mid to late 1980s programs. The college offered a three-year diploma in Data Processing Management in 1985 to 1987. A diploma in Industrial Management was offered, as were others in Business Marketing, Accounting, and Personnel Management and Industrial Relations. The curriculum in the latter program had changed little since the late 1960s. It did not include courses on topics such as challenges facing women in management. It is also noteworthy that occupational health and safety was not included in the full-time personnel management program despite the fact that Ontario's Occupational Health and Safety Act had been passed in 1978.[64]

Niagara College's part-time offerings were a major part of its overall programming by the mid-1990s. They included a large variety of courses that were perhaps taken by themselves or part of wider programs and were intended to help current or aspiring managers make sense of what their jobs entailed. A 1994 continuing education course called The Complete Manager was presented as:

> A primary goal of professional managers is to get quality work done through people. This course presents the opportunity for individuals to pursue this goal by understanding the various roles managers play throughout their careers. Areas discussed include all management areas from communications, motivation, interviewing and conflict resolution to planning and problem solving. The course examines how the qualities of the professional manager can be used in such areas as training, delegating, goal setting and performance evaluation.

That course was twenty-one hours in duration, and the course information sheet (CIS) for it did not list any required readings. It did show that the college recognized the need for managers to learn to deal with people in the workplace. This had been a consistent message since the college began offering part-time courses.[65]

Niagara College formed partnerships of different types, but its partnership with the Ontario government on a part-time program called the Ontario Management Development Program (OMDP) was particularly important. Vancouver Community College offered nothing similar at its Langara campus, nor did Collège Ahuntsic. OMDP was initiated by the provincial government and offered at community colleges across Ontario. The program ultimately illustrates the extent to which governments across Canada felt that management development was central to the country's economic growth economic growth, and the role that community colleges would play in providing that training. The Federal Business Development Bank (FBDB) convened a conference in Montréal in February 1976 that focused on the seemingly mundane topic of "owner-manager courses."[66] Representatives from government agencies in each province attended, including someone from Ontario's Ministry of Colleges and Universities.[67]

An FBDB representative attending the conference noted that the agency became interested in management courses in the three years preceding the conference largely because it had a long history of providing small business loans.[68] The FBDB felt that education courses for small business owners and managers needed to focus on three things: people, ideas, and money.[69] The bank additionally argued that providing education and counselling to small business managers and owners was as important as giving them funding to start and run new enterprises.[70] This concern with improving the skills of small business managers was not entirely altruistic. Conference attendees from the FBDB noted that there were 300,000 businesses in Canada in 1976 employing less than ten people, and that many were owned and managed by one person.[71] There were also between 200 and 300 business bankruptcies every month.[72] The FBDB clearly had an interest in mitigating the frequency of small business loan defaults. Conference attendees were advised that the FBDB identified four functional areas with which small business owner/managers needed to be conversant: financial management, business administration, marketing, and personnel administration.[73] Attendees from provincial departments of education would have been especially pleased to learn that the FBDB would provide funding for "owner-manager courses used for continuing education."[74]

The 1976 FBDB conference had been preceded by other similar gatherings, and it was from events such as this one that Niagara College's involvement with the OMDP program developed. The Ontario Ministry of Colleges and Universities coordinated the program in order to ensure that course content was common across all community colleges. That management program may have been the only one offered by Ontario colleges that had a province-wide curriculum, regardless of the subject matter, and was sponsored by government. Furthermore, participating in this program was advantageous for colleges for two reasons: it gave them the opportunity to attract more students, and it also provided additional revenue as colleges were paid to develop courses that would be used across Ontario. Each course was based on materials contained in a binder, and instructors were provided with a separate binder that included teaching notes. No external texts or readings were assigned. This meant that a college could find someone on fairly short notice to teach a course, provided that the person hired had sufficient credentials.[75]

OMDP would be a source of revenue for colleges because they could offer them to students, but also because the provincial government would compensate them for developing new courses that would be offered across Ontario. For instance, development of seven new courses was divided between four colleges.[76] Sales revenues from the courses were carefully tracked.[77] Student interests were reflected in those statistics, with the OMDP Human Relations course as the most popular between 1989 and 1992.[78] The OMDP program very clearly showed the management education had become a business.

Niagara College began listing the OMDP program in its continuing education calendars in the Fall 1991 term. There were eighteen courses divided into five groups:

Business Management—General

Effective Business Communication
Management by Objectives
Principles of Supervision
Team Dynamics

Financial Control

Bookkeeping for Small Business
Practical Financial Management
Financial Planning for Profits

Marketing

Marketing for Small Business
The ABC's of Selling
How to Start a Small Business
Advertising and Promotion

Production

Supervision—Administration
Supervision—Production
Job Enrichment—Production

Personnel Management and Labour Relations

Supervision—Communications
Supervision—Human Relations
People Management Techniques
Skills in Personnel Selection[79]

Ontario community colleges refer to their course syllabi as course information sheets (CIS), and the CISs for the OMDP program reveal that it was strongly oriented toward practical aspects of running a business, including dealing with people issues. The CIS for Job Enrichment—Production is representative of what a student could expect in courses in the OMDP program. The course was described as:

> This Ontario Management Development (OMDP) course is designed to enhance the supervisor's ability to improve his/her organization's productivity. The supervisor can discover the techniques of recognizing the achievements of individual employees while effectively

integrating the individual accomplishments of all employees. Participants will be provided with an insight into the motivational concepts underlying job enrichment and will study the importance of communications and effective delegation.[80]

The course was thirty hours long and required students to attend 80 percent of classes. Students would earn a C if they attended and participated, a B if they also did one project and one presentation, and an A if they completed two projects and two presentations. The OMDP course manual was the only required reading.

The OMDP clearly had expanded since its early outlines were discussed almost twenty years earlier at the FBDB conference in Montréal. Small business was still an important part of OMDP offerings, but courses like Team Dynamics and Job Enrichment may have been viewed with some skepticism by small business owners and managers looking for a night school program that would help them to better run their organizations. The OMDP curriculum instead looked like it would prove useful to students working in larger organizations. The program was additionally focused more on topics like human relations and communication. The quantitative component was comparatively small in scope.

OMDP graduation statistics were gathered by the province and reviewed by the program standards committee. The program may not have led to large enrollments at each individual community college campus, but the province-wide enrollment numbers were substantial. For example, there were 9,638 course packages produced between April 1991 and March 1992 and 1,320 certificates issued.[81] The manner in which the Ministry of Education and Training monitored the health of the OMDP program reflects that it was a business program that was also viewed as a business. Enrollments were not monitored by the number of students who enrolled but rather by course sales. The Human Relations course was the most popular one sold in 1993, with Management for Results having the least appeal. The program standards committee, which included representatives from ten colleges and one from the Federal Business Development Bank, routinely reviewed the program to change courses in an effort to expand enrollments.[82]

The OMDP program continued to be offered by Niagara College through the end of the 1990s. It was part of a large range of management and supervisory programs that the college mainly offered part-time on evenings and weekends. There were eighty-one different full-time programs offered in 1998.[83] There were ten in the Business area including:

Business—Accounting (Academic and Co-op)
Business Administration—Accounting (Academic and Co-op)
Business Administration—Human Resources (Co-op)
Business Administration—Marketing (Co-op)

Business Administration—Operations Management (Co-op)
Business—Retail Management
Business—Sales

Business related programming was consistently offered through to the end of the 1990s, but Niagara was equally interested in areas like Health and Community services and Apprenticeship. Part-time business programs and courses were one of fourteen program areas offered through continuing education. There were twenty-one OMDP courses offered by the Fall 1998 term, which indicates the amount of interest that the program generated among potential students.[84] The college promoted programs that were offered in conjunction with external organizations. OMDP was one example, and a partnership with the Canadian Institute of Management (CIM) was another one.[85] The CIM was a professional association created in 1942 to provide training and set professional standards for managers in Canada.[86] The acronym OMDP was not something that program graduates would necessarily put after their names, but CIM encouraged the use of its designation in that manner.

Niagara College's business and management programs, regardless of their form, attracted many students. As an example, there were 3,607 students in the college's full-time post-secondary programs as of the Fall 1984 term, and 1,191 were in business programs including those in management. They represented a third of the college's overall enrollments, and business programs had grown by 10.6 percent over the preceding year. Hotel and restaurant management had the largest number of students, with 125 in it. Taking business and management programs at a community college like Niagara College was clearly a popular option and an important part of the college's overall operations.[87]

Niagara College's programs grew significantly in the thirty years since it had been founded, and business and management programs grew along with everything else that was offered. The college provided student testimonials in its programs guides and, while students who liked the college were obviously chosen to be quoted, those short profiles revealed much about who enrolled in Niagara College's programs and what they hoped to achieve as a result of having done so. For instance, the college profiled a husband and wife named Don and Sharon Svob in its Fall 1991 Continuing Education guide. The Svobs were both enrolled in the OMDP program. Don was a millwright at General Motors, and Sharon was an administrative assistant at a social service agency called Port Cares. They told the college:

> We are both in the OMDP program and believe these Continuing Education courses will help provide job security and advancement. With knowledgeable instructors and student interaction you get "real life" management and business experience, not just the textbook variety.

Another student named Kevin Smith, who worked as a project manager at a company called Howard C.L. Joe Ltd., was profiled. He had taken a range of continuing education courses and stated:

> I have found the applied technology programs I have taken at Niagara College to be an asset to my career. Continuing Education's instructors are both professional and experienced, and I plan to take additional courses, whether for upgrading or just plain fun.

Taking something like the OMDP course or the other part-time offerings at the college was about learning some applied management skills that would help with overall employability. The people that Niagara College profiled in Fall 1991 were not interested in climbing corporate management ladders. They were instead interested in being lower- and middle-level managers. They were also attending a college that placed considerable emphasis on dealing with human issues in the workplace, including dealing with workers who had joined unions.[88]

Management as an Applied Vocation

There are some common aspects in the programs offered by Vancouver Community College, Collège Ahuntsic, and Niagara College. Each college was the product of deliberate government policy. Public policy commissions of various types are ubiquitous in Canadian history, and the provincial commissions that led to the foundation of VCC and Ahuntsic are part of that tradition. The Ontario government of the 1960s engaged in other major infrastructure projects and pursued an interventionist role in the province's economy. It was therefore not surprising that Bill Davis was able to promote the creation of Ontario's community college system. The community colleges and CEGEPs were provincial creations, but they developed at the same time and essentially on a national basis. Their creation, while not yet the subject of considerable scrutiny by Canadian historians, can be considered a defining aspect of 1960s Canada and reinforces the remarkable demographic impact of the baby boom generation.

Public policy makers in British Columbia, Ontario, and Québec felt that management and supervisory education as important. BC community and Québec CEGEPs offered vocational and university streams to provide a pathway to further post-secondary study. However, as Michael Skolnik has noted, Ontario was the only Canadian province that created a community college system that did not provide a path to university. The CAAT system was founded with the intent of providing terminal qualifications in a manner distinct from universities. That training was intended to be applied, as the Applied Arts and Technology part of CAAT indicated. However, the decision to mandate that colleges teach business programs meant that they would overlap somewhat with university programs even if they were supposed to teach such programs from a more applied perspective.[89]

In terms of who was encouraged to attend community colleges and pursue vocational training, the Ontario government encouraged colleges to enroll men and women, albeit in gendered program streams. For example, a 1973 pamphlet produced by the Ontario Ministry of Labour Women's Directorate described how women could work in jobs such as forester, graphic designer, government expenditure analyst, archaeologist, flying instructor, interior designer, and town planner. Management was not described as a career vocation in this case. Colleges did not have archaeology programs, but they did offer programs in the other occupational areas mentioned. Increasing and improving the province's workforce was a clear public policy priority.[90]

There are some characteristics that can be inferred about the students at the three colleges discussed here based on their historical records, even though specific enrollment statistics are not available. Vancouver Community College drew a diverse group of students in terms of gender, race, and ethnicity and this was to be expected considering the demographics of the city in which it was located. Collège Ahuntsic had a student population that reflected gender diversity, but its programs were offered entirely in French, and images of students show that most of them were of European descent. Niagara College's program calendars also showed gender diversity, but little in terms of race. Niagara interestingly offered some courses that were taught in French, and this was surely due to the existence of a francophone community in Welland, Ontario. Overall, students coming out of management and supervisory courses at Ahuntsic and Niagara could have been male or female, but they also were likely to have been white.

There are some other key features shared by the management and supervisory programs offered at these three colleges, despite differences in student diversity. The programs were inexpensive during the decades that are the focus of this analysis. Working-class students could have aspired to graduate from one of the programs or courses discussed here without likely having a lot of anxiety about cost. Community colleges were furthermore intended to be readily accessible, and attending one would have not necessarily have required students to move away from home. Indeed, there was no reference to residency lodging in the Ahuntsic, Niagara, and VCC program calendars. A student could graduate, live at home, pay reasonable tuition fees, and earn a diploma that was supposed to prepare him or herself for management and dealing with workers.

The reality is that colleges, especially those in Ontario, were established as vocational institutions. As Rakesh Khurana and others have noted, there was a widespread effort in North American to professionalize management in the post–World War II decades. The decision to include management and supervisory training in the mandates of community colleges can be viewed as diverging from the professionalization path. The Ontario experience is especially noteworthy as that province eventually had twenty-one colleges of applied arts and technology (CAAT) and twenty-four universities. Each college would follow the provincial mandate to offer management courses and programs and arguably did so to a greater extent than in Ontario universities. Community colleges became major providers of various forms of business education, including for current and aspiring managers and supervisors. In all likelihood, they made management in Canada into more of an applied vocation than a profession. Community colleges also contributed to credentialization as they formed partnerships with organizations like the CIM, the Ontario government's OMDP program, and other groups in order to provide specific designations that were intended to connote managerial prowess. The fact that colleges like Niagara offered a wide range of part-time management and supervisory programs, often with external partner organizations, meant that there was demand for them. The practice of offering evening and weekend in-class programs as a complement to workplace experience is a common feature of vocational programs.

Niagara offered Labour Studies programs that were also intended for non-union and managerial workers. As Larry Savage and Carmela Patrias have shown, the Niagara Region historically had a strong labour movement, and it is not surprising that its influence was felt through Niagara College program decisions.[91] Moreover, as Jeff Taylor revealed, Labour Studies started at the college with a teaching staff of seasoned union activists.[92] However, as time progressed, the labour movement's influence over college programs diminished. The faculty at the college were represented by the Ontario Public Service Employees Union (OPSEU) and, while the union would have liked to have always had representation on the Niagara College governing board, this objective was not always a bargaining priority. Sherri Rosen, who was also a former president of the Ontario Public Service Employee's Union (OPSEU) academic employee local union at the college in the 1980s, recalled:

> Yes, it was an objective but not necessarily at the local level. It was more at the policy level . . . it was up to each local how aggressive they wanted to be. The colleges got smarter as the went along . . . it was always a hired mouthpiece lawyer doing the talking . . . none of the decision makers from the colleges were on the other side of the (bargaining) table. The colleges started acting together on things . . . we had won the right to have one faculty member and one support (member) on governance, but it wasn't limited to union members.[93]

Ontario community colleges did not have a shared governance model that gave faculty major influence in shaping college policy and curriculum and pursued a labour relations strategy that would maintain that situation.

Maintaining ties to the region's business community, and seeking input on programming, was always a priority for the college. Rosen's observations about the nature of Niagara College's board of governors can be seen in the composition of the 1994 board. There were sixteen members that year, with two of them appointed on an ex-officio basis. There were six women, one student representative, and one each from support staff and faculty. The college was careful to ensure that the board of governors included representation from across the Niagara Region with five people from St. Catharines, two from Niagara Falls, one from Welland, and a person from Pelham. The first city was the most populous one in the college's area of operation, with the other communities having representation also clearly apportioned by population size. The board of governors were obviously considered important as their names were listed on the first page of the full-time program guide, just below a photo and profile of the college president.[94]

There is a key question, as with other forms of management and supervisory education, of whether or not graduates of community college management programs were actually trained to manage and assume the role of manager. Students in full-time programs at all three colleges were mainly educated in quantitative skills such as finance, accounting, and statistics. The availability of part-time calendars from Niagara College reveals that those offerings, which were meant for students working during the day, were much more focused on employee issues in the workplace. The OMDP program, which essentially permitted students to audit courses, was certainly accessible if not especially rigorous. The term manager, fraught with meaning in the context of undergraduate and graduate programs, was similarly difficult to reconcile in the context of community college education. It was used in the context of programs including Operations, Recreation, Hotel and Restaurant, and Personnel/Human Resources. It really connoted the idea that a person had been trained in a common core of business functions, with some additional courses pertaining to a given program title, and would hopefully be able to interpret and oversee them in an organization.

Community colleges programs were generally taught by people with university degrees or professional designations, but experience working in a related field was especially valued. This approach was congruent with the overall applied nature of the programs being offered. Full-time programs were taught by permanent full-time faculty, but part-time programs were generally taught by instructors who were paid on a per course basis. They were not tenured university professors with publications and research agendas. The manner in which the latter instructional group was recruited was not always especially sophisticated. For example, the 1982 Niagara College part-time calendar for all three terms included a notice for potential future instructors that said:

> Continuing Education Services, Niagara College, is interested in receiving applications from individuals who wish to teach part-time, either day or evening. Applicants should have three years related work experience, preferably combined with supervisory and/or instructional training.[95]

What is important about this job notice is that it was included in a publication intended for students. This meant that Niagara was hiring its own continuing education graduates to teach part time. However, as Sherri Rosen noted, it was also not unusual in the 1980s for full-time day faculty to teach in evening part-time programs for extra money.[96]

The management and supervisory training that students at Canadian community colleges such as Niagara College, Collège Ahuntsic, and Vancouver Community College met the objectives that were mandated for them. The provinces of British Columbia, Québec, and Ontario ultimately got what they wanted from their community colleges when it came to management education and training programs. The colleges made them foundational parts of their curriculums. There is some irony as government promoted business programs, yet the content of those programs did not frequently include content that pertained to how business related to government or wider Canadian society. The students who entered those programs may well have felt that they had climbed the Canadian social ladder, especially if they were able to secure managerial jobs after graduating. They became part of a different stratum of the managerial class than the one occupied by university business graduates if they chose a terminal diploma at VCC or Ahuntsic. The learning stream was even more well-defined for Niagara graduates. They were vocational managers and supervisors who would occupy front-line and middle management roles. Students graduating into such roles doubtless felt themselves fortunate, and they had reason to feel that way. Their provincial governments had created a vast network of new institutions to educate them, and deliberate policy decisions helped shape Canada's economy and post-secondary landscape from the late 1960s onward. Their learning experience was different from what occurred in undergraduate university business and management programs.

Notes

1 See Douglas Owram, *Born at The Right Time: A History of the Baby Boom Generation* (Toronto: University of Toronto Press, 1996).
2 Owram, *Born at the Right Time*, 119.

3 For information on the founding and development of further education colleges in the United Kingdom see University of Exeter, accessed 3 February 2018, http://elac.ex.ac.uk/fecolleges/index.php.

4 John B. MacDonald, *Higher Education in British Columbia and a Plan for the Future* (Vancouver: University of British Columbia Press, 1962), 3.

5 MacDonald, *Higher Education*, 6.

6 MacDonald, *Higher Education*, 62.

7 MacDonald, *Higher Education*, 63.

8 Langara College Library (hereafter LCL), Box 2, File: 80–213 VCC History, Statement Prepared by Dr. D.E. Wales for the Board of School Trustees, 7 October 1966.

9 LCL, Box 1, File: VCC King Edward Centre Catalogue, 1965 to 1966, 5.

10 LCL, Box 1, File: VCC King Edward Centre Catalogue, 1965 to 1966, 9.

11 LCL, Box 1, File: VCC King Edward Centre Catalogue, 1965 to 1966, 12.

12 LCL, Box 1, File: VCC King Edward Centre Catalogue, 1965 to 1966, 18–19.

13 LCL, Box 1, File: VCC King Edward Centre Catalogue, 1965 to 1966, 18–19.

14 LCL, Box 1, File: VCC King Edward Centre Catalogue, 1976 to 1977, 14.

15 LCL, Box 1, File: VCC King Edward Centre Catalogue, 1976 to 1977, 14.

16 LCL, Box 1, File: VCC Langara Catalogue, 1976 to 1977, 81.

17 LCL, Box 1, File: VCC Langara Catalogue, 1976 to 1977, 80.

18 LCL, Box 1, File: VCC Langara Catalogue, 1976 to 1977, 75.

19 LCL, Box 1, File: VCC Langara Catalogue, 1984 to 1985, 57.

20 LCL, Box 1, File: VCC Langara Catalogue, 1988 to 1989, 116–117.

21 LCL, Box 1, File: VCC Langara Catalogue, 1996 to 1997, 34.

22 LCL, Box 1, File: VCC Langara Catalogue, 1996 to 1997, 126.

23 LCL, Box 1, File: VCC Langara Catalogue, 1996 to 1997, 51.

24 Parent Commission report, accessed 30 December 2017. http://classiques. uqac.ca/contemporains/Québec_commission_parent/commission_parent. html.

25 Claude Corbo, *L'education pour nous: une anthologie du Rapport Parent* (Montréal: Presses de l'Université de Montréal, 2002), 207.

26 Bibliothèque et Archives nationales du Québec (Hereafter BAnQ), Rapport annuel / Collège Ahuntsic, Box PER Z-4555, Rapport du Director General Au Conseil D'Administration Pour L'Annee Finissant Le 30 Juin 1969, 2.

27 BAnQ, Tableau des programmes / Collège Ahuntsic, Box PER Z-4565 CON 1974–75 and 1976–77, Collège Ahuntsic Prospectus, 1974–75, 13.

28 BAnQ, Tableau des programmes / Collège Ahuntsic, Box PER Z-4565 CON 1974–75 and 1976–77, Collège Ahuntsic Prospectus, 1974–75, 15.

29 BAnQ, Tableau des programmes / Collège Ahuntsic, Box C-1484, Collège Ahuntsic Prospectus, 1986, 10.

30 BAnQ, Tableau des programmes / Collège Ahuntsic, Box C-1484, Collège Ahuntsic Prospectus, 1986, 12.

31 BAnQ, Tableau des programmes / Collège Ahuntsic, Box C-1484, Collège Ahuntsic Prospectus, 1986, 31.

32 BAnQ, Tableau des programmes / Collège Ahuntsic, Box C-1484, Collège Ahuntsic Prospectus, 1986, 31.

33 BAnQ, Tableau des programmes / Collège Ahuntsic, Box C-1484, Collège Ahuntsic Prospectus, 1986, 31.

34 BAnQ, Tableau des programmes / Collège Ahuntsic, Box C-1484, Collège Ahuntsic Prospectus, 1999, 42.

35 BAnQ, Communications Ahuntsic, Box C-1484, vol. 1, no. 1, 3.

36 BAnQ, Communications Ahuntsic, Box C-1484, vol. 4, no. 3, 3.

37 *Colleges of Applied Arts and Technology: Basic Statements, June 1967* (Toronto: Ontario Department of Education, 1967), 5.

38 *Colleges of Applied Arts and Technology: Basic Statements, June 1967* (Toronto: Ontario Department of Education, 1967), 7.

39 *Colleges of Applied Arts and Technology: Basic Statements, June 1967* (Toronto: Ontario Department of Education, 1967), 8.

40 *Colleges of Applied Arts and Technology: Basic Statements, June 1967* (Toronto: Ontario Department of Education, 1967), 9.

41 Niagara College Archive Room (hereafter NCAR), Full-Time Calendars, 1968–1969, 2.

42 NCAR, Full-Time Calendars, 1968–1969, 44–45.

43 NCAR, Full-Time Calendars, 1968–1969, 104.

44 NCAR, Full-Time Calendars, 1968–1969, 104.

45 NCAR, Part-Time Calendars, 1968–1969, 101–102.

46 NCAR, Part-Time Calendars, 1968–1969, 11.

47 NCAR, Part-Time Calendars, 1970–1971, 22.

48 NCAR, Full-Time Calendars, 1978–1979, B33.

49 NCAR, Full-Time Calendars, 1978–1979, B34.

50 Sherri Rosen interview, 11 October 2016.

51 NCAR, Full-Time Calendars, 1978–1979, G90.

52 NCAR, Full-Time Calendars, 1978–1979, G90.

53 NCAR, Full-Time Calendars, 1978–1979, D19.

54 NCAR, Full-Time Calendars, 1978–1979, D20.

55 See Arlie Russell Hochschild, *The Managed Heart: Commercialization of Human Feeling* (Berkeley: University of California Press, 1983).

56 Niagara College Library (hereafter NCL), Course Information Documents, Introduction to Business I, 1988/0/13.

57 Maurice Archer, *An Introduction to Canadian Business, fifth edition* (Toronto: McGraw-Hill Ryerson, 1986).

58 Archer, *An Introduction to Canadian Business*, 122–123.

59 Archer, *An Introduction to Canadian Business*, 124–125.

60 NCAR, Part-Time Calendars, Winter 1979, 13–14.

61 NCAR, Part-Time Calendars, Winter 1979, 14–15.

62 NCAR, Part-Time Calendars, Winter 1979, 15.

63 NCAR, Part-Time Calendars, Winter 1979, 15.

64 NCAR, Full-Time Calendars, 1985–1987, School of Business.

65 Niagara College Library (hereafter NCL), Course Information Documents, The Complete Manager, 1994/08/03.

66 George Brown Archive (hereafter GBA), Business and Industry Training Administration and Program Records 1967–1991, Box 92–50 21, File 5, *Transcript of the FBDB/Provincial Conference Held on the Continuity of Owner-Manager Courses.*

67 GBA, Business and Industry Training Administration and Program Records 1967–1991, Box 92–50 21, File 5, *Transcript of the FBDB/Provincial Conference Held on the Continuity of Owner-Manager Courses.*

68 GBA, Business and Industry Training Administration and Program Records 1967–1991, Box 92–50 21, File 5, *Transcript of the FBDB/Provincial Conference Held on the Continuity of Owner-Manager Courses*, 2.

69 GBA, Business and Industry Training Administration and Program Records 1967–1991, Box 92–50 21, File 5, *Transcript of the FBDB/Provincial Conference Held on the Continuity of Owner-Manager Courses*, 4.

70 GBA, Business and Industry Training Administration and Program Records 1967–1991, Box 92–50 21, File 5, *Transcript of the FBDB/Provincial Conference Held on the Continuity of Owner-Manager Courses*, 5.

71 GBA, Business and Industry Training Administration and Program Records 1967–1991, Box 92–50 21, File 5, *Transcript of the FBDB/Provincial Conference Held on the Continuity of Owner-Manager Courses*, 6.

72 GBA, Business and Industry Training Administration and Program Records 1967–1991, Box 92–50 21, File 5, *Transcript of the FBDB/Provincial Conference Held on the Continuity of Owner-Manager Courses*, 6.

73 GBA, Business and Industry Training Administration and Program Records 1967–1991, Box 92–50 21, File 5, *Transcript of the FBDB/Provincial Conference Held on the Continuity of Owner-Manager Courses*, transparency 4.

74 GBA, Business and Industry Training Administration and Program Records 1967–1991, Box 92–50 21, File 5, *Transcript of the FBDB/Provincial Conference Held on the Continuity of Owner-Manager Courses*, 14.

75 The author had some experience teaching in the OMDP program at Fanshawe College in the mid-2000s, before it was discontinued, and used the required teaching materials. The format in which OMDP materials were presented is also evident in archival records, particularly at the Archives of Ontario.

76 AO, OMPD, Box B852440, File: OMDP General, 1992 to 1993, Harold Best to Trudy Heffernan, 8 October 1992.

77 AO, OMPD, Box B852440, File: OMDP General, 1992 to 1993, Sales Statistics 1989 to 1992.

78 AO, OMPD, Box B852440, File: OMDP General, 1992 to 1993, Sales Statistics 1989 to 1992.

79 NCAR, Part-Time Calendars, Fall 1991, 41.

80 Niagara College Library, Course Information Documents, Job Enrichment—Production, 1993/01/29.

81 AO, RG32–92, Box 852440, File: OMDP General, 1992 to 1993, OMDP Standards Committee Meeting 16 April 1993.

82 AO, RG32–92, Box 852440, File: OMDP General, 1992 to 1993, OMDP Standards Committee Meeting 30 June 1993.

83 NCAR, Full-Time Calendars, 1998–1999, 2.

84 NCAR, Part-Time Calendars, Fall 1998, 18.

85 NCAR, Part-Time Calendars, Fall 1998, 17.

86 Canadian Institute of Management. 30 December 2017. www.cim.ca/organization/about-cim-chartered-managers-canada.

87 NCAR, Niagara College Board of Governors, 1985 Report, 15–16.

88 NCAR, Part-Time Calendars, Fall 1991, 1.

89 Michael Skolnik, "A Look Back at the Decision on the Transfer Function at the Founding of Ontario's Colleges of Applied Arts and Technology", *Canadian Journal of Higher Education*, vol. 40, no. 2 (2010), pp. 1–17.

90 GBA, Business and Industry Program Training Records, 1967 to 1991, Box 92–50 (117), File 13, Ontario Ministry of Labour Women's Directorate pamphlet 1973.

91 See Carmela Patrias and Larry Savage, *Union Power: Solidarity and Struggle in Niagara* (Edmonton: Athabasca University Press, 2012).

92 Jeffrey Taylor, *Union Learning: Canadian Labour Education in the Twentieth Century* (Toronto: Thompson Educational Publishing, 2001), 182.

93 Sherri Rosen interview, 11 October 2016.

94 NCAR, Full-time calendars, 1994–1995, 1.

95 NCAR, Part-Time Calendars, Fall/Winter/Spring 1982, 8.

96 Sherri Rosen interview.

4 Universities and Undergraduate Management Education

Undergraduate business and management education preceded all other forms of university and college education, and it helped to shape the programs offered at the graduate and college levels in Canada. This chapter examines the development of undergraduate business and management programs at three universities: the University of British Columbia (UBC), the University of Western Ontario (UWO), and École des hautes études commerciales de Montréal (HEC). Those institutions were founded in different social and geographic contexts, with UBC established in 1908, UWO in 1878, and HEC in 1907. Business and management education would become one of many undergraduate concentrations available at UBC and UWO, but HEC was founded for the purpose of providing commerce education, although it would become affiliated with the Université de Montréal. Canada's original universities, such as UWO and the University of Toronto (U of T), were rooted in the education of clergy and were thus linked to organized religion. UBC represented a departure from this pattern, as it was not founded by religious organizations but did incorporate colleges that had been founded with the help of churches. This chapter addresses several key issues, including what was taught in the undergraduate business and management programs at these three universities, how students were prepared to become managers or execute managerial functions, and whether there were significant differences in the curriculums of the three institutions. Undergraduate business education became ubiquitous in Canada from the 1940s to the 1990s, and it had a significant impact on higher education. Students who enrolled in business and management programs learned about the different aspects of a large business, but there were limits to what they learned about actually being managers.

Undergraduate degree programs are commonly recognized to be the main form of education offered at universities in North America and the United Kingdom, mainly because undergraduate students are far more numerous at most institutions. Canadian universities are distinct from their American counterparts because the overwhelming majority of them are public rather than private in nature. There is also a key difference in nomenclature between Canadian and American schools as, in the latter case, the term "college" is ubiquitously used to describe undergraduate education. Canadians draw careful distinctions between "college" and "university" because the former term is often associated with vocational training, while the latter is used to describe four-year schools that award bachelor's degrees. In terms of organization, the first Canadian universities— such as the University of Toronto and the University of Western Ontario—were intentionally modelled on universities in the United Kingdom like Oxford and Cambridge, with students assigned to individual colleges within a wider structure. Undergraduate business education began in Canadian universities by the early twentieth century, and it consequently preceded credential-granting community college and graduate programs. As with all the forms of education in Canada, language and geography exerted considerable influence over how universities and programs developed. The first universities in the country were founded in Ontario and Québec, and other provinces gradually followed. The number of Canadian universities increased markedly in the post– World War II decades because of the influx of students from the baby boom generation. This chapter is based on archival materials found at the UBC, HEC, and UWO archives. The availability of records at these three institutions means that there will be slightly more emphasis in this chapter on UBC and HEC. There are similarities between how undergraduate education developed at the three schools but also crucial differences that were influenced by region, language, culture, and economics. This discussion will describe how the undergraduate programs at these institutions developed from the late 1940s to the late 1990s, with somewhat more emphasis on the 1970s onward due to the nature of the sources used.

The University of British Columbia

UBC was founded in 1915 because of a decision by the British Columbia government that the province needed a university.[1] McGill University, which was based in Montréal, had offered programs in BC, but the need for a new institution was identified by the provincial government. BC had become a province in 1871, and Canada's universities were still largely concentrated in Ontario and Québec by the turn of the twentieth century. Initial programs in Commerce were offered shortly after the university was founded. UBC's programs across all departments grew in the decades up to the 1940s, and growth then accelerated after World War II. This was particularly true of the business and management offerings. The curriculum of a university degree reflects what the institution offering it thought should be covered in a given subject area. A four-year Bachelor of Arts (BA) degree was the usual credential earned at the undergraduate level, and what UBC thought should be part of an undergrad degree in commerce changed over time. In 1945, UBC was divided into three faculties: Arts and Science, Applied Science, and Agriculture. The fee for an Arts and Science degree was $176 per year.[2] The Commerce program was part of Arts and Science, and students interested in pursuing this degree were required to complete the following courses:

First Year: A course in First Year Arts and Science or Equivalent

Second Year: English 2 or English 3 and 4

Mathematics 2 or 3
Economics 1
Elective

Third Year: Economics 4

Economics 12
Commerce 6
Commerce 1

Fourth Year: Economics 6

Commerce 4
Commerce 9[3]

Students could choose from slightly over twenty elective options. The 1945 UBC course calendar did not provide descriptions for the core Commerce program courses but did provide them for elective courses. Prospective students were advised that Commercial Geography was:

A broad survey of the economic and geographic factors which lie behind the structure of business, with particular emphasis upon the North American continent. Reports are required of students.[4]

There was one required textbook: *Introductory Economic Geography, second edition*. This text was an interesting choice for a Commerce program course. It was written by faculty at the Wharton School of Finance and Commerce at the University of Pennsylvania (later the Wharton School of Business). It was an example of a business text from the United States being used in Canadian undergraduate courses. Its contents in many ways reflected the staples approach to political economy pioneered by Harold Adams Innis. Lester E. Klimm, Otis P. Starkey, and Norman F. Hall divided *Introductory Economic Geography* into five parts: Introductory; The Physical Environment; Foods, Raw Materials, and Fuels; Commerce and Manufacturing; and Regional Geography.[5] There were further subsections in each of the parts. For example, in one subsection, petroleum was described as a "disappearing resource."[6] Readers were advised that "the world has produced and consumed more mineral resources since 1900 than in all the countless ages which have gone before."[7] Some resources, such as coal or copper, would last for centuries to come, but the "point of exhaustion is in sight" for others like petroleum.[8] The authors were clearly making this assertion before the enormous post–World War II development of Middle East and off-shore petroleum reserves, but their views on natural resources were still important as they showed that resource exploitation was not necessarily infinite.

The section of *Introductory Economic Geography* devoted to commerce and manufacturing was the briefest of the five found in the book. Klimm, Starkey, and Hall focused on the importance of transportation to commercial activity. They considered many global factors that could have potentially shaped commerce. The importance of climate was noted, although racist observations were made of the "wantlessness of tropical people" although disinterest among people in tropical areas in consumer consumption was not ascribed to "lower intelligence or general quality."[9] The "problem of tropical development" would simply be solved if the inhabitants of such areas would just "want all the things which the civilization of the cooler lands has to offer."[10] Klimm, Starkey, and Hall than suggested that slavery was still prevalent in "warm lands" because of "the common inability to arouse the natives' desire to consume."[11] The authors discussed transportation routes in different regions of the world in considerable detail including rivers in Asia and Africa.[12] Manufacturing was portrayed as a predominantly North American and European activity.[13] The idea that perhaps consuming was not a preferred mode of living was not considered. The message was that there was something fundamentally wrong with people who did not like capitalism. The overall message that UBC Commerce students would have received from Klimm, Starkey, and Hall was that geography was an important consideration when engaging in business. The term globalization was not used when their book was published, but they nonetheless saw commercial activity in global terms. The authors worked in a country, the United States, that did not assemble an extensive physical overseas empire but would nonetheless have been well aware of the nature of imperial economic systems. They exhibited a belief in Western cultural superiority and racially biased views of non-white people.

Another course in the Commerce program—Industrial Management—was described as:

> A study of the organization and management of manufacturing concerns from the standpoint of control of raw materials, plant and equipment, operations, labour, etc. Class discussion will be based on cases taken from actual business. Field work comprising visits to

factories and written reports form a part of this course. To qualify for the final examination a student is required to submit 75 percent of the written assignments and to take in 75 percent of the assigned factory visits.[14]

There was one required text for this course and one reference volume. The text was *Introduction to Industrial Management* by Franklin E. Folts, who was a professor of Industrial Management at Harvard Business School (HBS). This book was a collection of teaching cases that examined various aspects of business management including specialization of labour, standardization, materials supply, plant location, and personnel organization.[15] The centrality of the business case to Harvard Business School teaching has been described by a range of authors including Carter and McDonald.[16] Folts' use of cases was thus in keeping with his usual teaching and research practice. The purpose of his text was "to develop a sound point of view for the business manager by analyzing industrial problems and businessmen's solutions to industrial problems."[17]

Introduction to Industrial Management was intended to impart practical rather than theoretical knowledge and to otherwise essentially teach students by example. The cases presented in it also reveal what Folts thought that managers should think about at work and, by extension, what the creators of the Industrial Management course thought was central to the manager's job. For instance, cases on the specialization of labour—such as one on the Mellon Company—argued that specialization in production was preferred.[18] Personnel matters were discussed in cases such as the Jute Bag Company. In that case, readers were advised that:

> Personnel work is very necessary. It is hard to overestimate its importance in any scheme of scientific management. Personnel devices must, however, be used with discretion. In and of themselves, they neither advance the cause of management nor further the welfare of employees. When, however, they are used intelligently and in conjunction with other sound production devices, they are very powerful aids making for effective management.[19]

The Jute Bag Company case did not incorporate the term welfare capitalism, but it nonetheless argued in favour of it. It emphasized the virtues of using management devices such as operating a company cafeteria and offering employee stock ownership in order to provide security against unemployment.[20] Managers were advised to employ such management methods because they increased productivity and profits.[21] The Jute Bag Company case stressed the value of having an employment department in a firm that would handle matters such as maintaining labour supply, adjusting disputes between "workers and overseers," terminating employment when it was in the firm's best interests, maintaining employment records, summarizing statistics, and coordinating with other departments.[22]

The cases found in *Introduction to Industrial Management* emphasized the need for organizational structure, control processes, and the importance of personnel practices. This book complemented *Introductory Economic Geography,* as both volumes portrayed management as an important practice that required careful judgement and stewardship of company resources. The primacy of management in organizational decision making was clear in both books, as managers would make decisions about what was best for the firm. As Nancy Harding has argued, management textbooks are intended to legitimize a body of knowledge related to business. The Commerce program texts used at UBC in 1945 were not as overtly oriented toward specific management functions, but they nonetheless conveyed specific themes about working in business. Commerce was portrayed as a serious pursuit that required the astute application of practical knowledge.[23]

There is little available information about the demographics of the students in the Commerce program in the 1940s, but there are some insights available on the nature of the faculty. There were only three professors in the program in 1945: Ellis H. Morrow, Archibald W. Currie, and Frederick Field. Morrow was the department head and had earned an MBA at Harvard. Currie held MBA and Doctor of Commercial Science degrees from Harvard. Field was a Chartered Accountant. The importance of Morrow and Currie having earned degrees at Harvard and the nature of commerce education at UBC cannot be underestimated because, as has been noted previously in this analysis, the Harvard Business School had an enormous impact on the nature of business and management education across North America. That influence also reached into UBC.[24]

The Commerce program expanded through the balance of the 1940s and into the 1950s. By 1955, UBC added a Faculty of Law, Faculty of Pharmacy, Faculty of Medicine, Faculty of Forestry, and Faculty of Graduate Studies. The university was clearly growing in the immediate postwar decade. The fee for an Arts and Science degree had increased to $240 per year.[25] The Bachelor of Commerce Degree (BComm) was now offered by a School of Commerce that was housed within the broader Arts and Science faculty. Students had expanded degree options, including a combined BComm and Bachelor of Laws (LL.B) and a BComm leading to a Chartered Accountancy (CA) designation, from which to choose. UBC's Commerce options were markedly expanded since 1945, with thirteen possible areas of specialization other than law and accounting:

Marketing
Production
Finance
Transportation and Utilities

Commerce and Economics
Commerce and Public Administration
Commerce and Actuarial Science
Commerce and Teaching
Commerce and Forestry
Commerce and Agricultural Science
Commerce and Hospital Administration
Commerce and Agricultural Economics

This wide variety of study options suggests that the School of Commerce was clearly thinking about providing students with a range of career options. It is also significant that academic links were drawn between business study and public-sector areas like administration, health care, and teaching. Agreements were concluded with provincial associations to help smooth the transition between university and employment. For example, UBC and the BC Institute of Chartered Accountants agreed that BComm graduates were exempt from having to write the institute's primary examination and were eligible for a reduced articling period and able to write the Final Uniform Examination a year after graduating with their degrees. Graduates with the degrees in Commerce and Teaching were recommended to the Department of Education of British Columbia for a provincial academic certificate.[26]

Commerce undergraduates at UBC continued to be required to take a range of social science courses including economics, geography, and psychology and could also choose from humanities subjects such as language, history, and philosophy. Required core Commerce courses in the mid-1950s concentrated on fundamental influences on business management. Commercial Law was one of those courses and required students to read two volumes of legal cases. Industrial Relations was a required course in some Commerce streams including Production and Marketing, and an elective choice in other streams.[27] This course asked students to read one text published in 1938 titled *Personnel Management and Industrial Relations* by Dale Yoder.[28] UBC used the third edition of the book, which is now not accessible, but it likely did not differ substantially from the second edition published in 1945 that is referenced here. The influence of Elton Mayo and Frederick Winslow Taylor was found throughout Yoder's work. He argued that employee morale was an important feature of the production process, and Mayo would have fully agreed.[29] On the other hand, his text was filled with many graphs and other statistical evaluation methods that would have garnered the approval of Taylor. For instance, Yoder advocated the use of careful quantitative methods in wage plans.[30] Collective bargaining and employee representation, which had become legal with the passage of the National Labour Relations Act in 1935, were also covered by Yoder.[31] He essentially suggested that management should not avoid collective bargaining and that managers could indeed make gains through that process.[32] Managing, in this analysis, involved quantitative methods while being mindful of the need to cooperate with workers.

Who enrolled in the UBC School of Commerce in 1955 is not clear, but the composition of the faculty had markedly changed since 1955. There were twenty professors and lecturers and an additional seven people with the title of honourary lecturer. Sixteen of the Commerce program faculty had completed at least one credential—usually a bachelor's degree—at UBC. There were several instructors with Chartered Accountant designations, but nobody with a Ph.D. in 1955. The MBA or a professional designation like a CA were evidently considered sufficient qualifications to teach at the university level.[33]

The UBC Commerce program continued to evolve into the mid-1960s, and the 1965 UBC calendar provided a revealing rationale for the Commerce program:

> It is hoped that students who obtain the Bachelor of Commerce degree will on the one hand be familiar with the principles and techniques of those who are dealing most successfully with the varied problems of business—organization, development, control, and social responsibilities and, on the other hand, have the intellectual and cultural background to enable them to deal constructively as business men and citizens with the social, political, and legal problems of their times and environment. The Faculty does not attempt to prepare graduates in the skills and techniques of individual industries or services. It does not expect its graduates to assume immediate managerial responsibilities. It does assume that that its graduates will be well trained in general techniques of business and will be ready to adopt these principles and practices to specific problems. It expects its graduates to display well-disciplined minds and sound work habits. In accordance with this philosophy the curriculum is organized to ensure a proper blending of regular arts or science courses, business courses, and specialized courses in particular fields in commerce and business administration. No particular programme of studies is in the secondary school is necessary in preparation for admission to the Faculty except that students must take Mathematics to the Grade 12 level (Mathematics 91). In Grade 13 the full five-course programme must include English 100/1 and Mathematics 101 or 120.[34]

Commerce was portrayed in this passage as a generalist degree that did not necessarily ensure that graduates could be certain to enter managerial roles, and at no point was the Commerce program described as a professional degree. The importance of arts and sciences courses in the overall degree program was stressed, and students coming out of high school need not have possessed advanced quantitative skills. The Commerce degree at that time was not highly quantitative in nature. Students could still apply to combined programs such as Law and Commerce.[35] Furthermore, they could undertake studies in the Commerce program at the relatively inexpensive cost of $401 dollars in their first year of studies and $451 in subsequent years.[36]

There were fourteen different Commerce concentrations in 1965. The number of concentration areas had thus not considerably expanded since 1945. The number of courses had expanded within those concentrations. For instance, whereas there had only been one Industrial Relations course for several years, that subject had now become a degree concentration and included new offerings such as Collective Bargaining and Management of Human Resources.[37] The course descriptions no longer included assigned readings, but still revealed much about what students would learn. The use of the term human resources in the Commerce program reflects a shift away from the use of the previously ubiquitous term personnel management. The Human Resources course would teach students:

> The examination of decisions, plans and policies formulated to ensure maximum development and utilization of human resources. Special attention will be given to problems of motivation and morale associated with changing technology. Materials will be drawn from a wide spectrum to provide a detailed understanding of diverse approaches to problems of manpower management.[38]

While UBC portrayed their Commerce program as a broadly generalist degree that did not require a lot of prior mathematics preparation, the course calendar nonetheless reflected some quantitative orientation in offerings like Marketing Analysis, Research Methods, and Business Logistics.[39]

The composition of the Commerce program faculty becomes much clearer in 1960s archival sources. A 1960 yearbook called the *Ledger* included images of students and revealed what they studied and the extracurricular activities in which they engaged. There were 124 graduating from the program in 1960. Three of them were women, and three were men of Asian descent. The rest—118 students—were all white men. While these students were surely proud of their academic accomplishments, it is also possible that the very few women and non-white students who graduated would have viewed themselves as outsiders even though everyone had been engaged in the study of business and management subjects. The place of women in Commerce was perhaps best illustrated by the selection of a Commerce Queen in 1960. A Commerce King was not similarly designated. Women may have aspired to study business and management, but they were not viewed as entirely equal with their male peers.[40]

There were additional changes to Commerce program as it grew through the 1970s. Tuition fees had not grown significantly since the mid-1960s, with students paying $462 in the first year and $540 in subsequent years.[41] Most notably, UBC published statistics on enrollments across different faculties in the 1975 calendar. The university had total enrollments of 23,185, which included undergraduate and graduate students and those in professional programs.[42] Of that total, 47 percent were men and 53 percent were women.[43] The Faculty of Commerce and Business Administration enrolled 1,373 students, and 90 percent were men.[44] There was an obvious gender disparity in business and management programs, but this reflected wider trends found across the university that were hidden within the overall enrollment numbers. Women were instead concentrated in the Faculty of Education and the Faculty of Arts.[45]

The actual Commerce undergraduate degree of the 1970s still reflected some elements that were included in 1965. The composition of the student body reflected marginal demographic changes since the 1960s. There were 1,373 students in the faculty in 1975, but women still only comprised 13 percent of enrollments.[46] Commerce and Business undergraduate students represented 5 percent of UBC's overall enrollment of 28,728.[47] There was a significant change in the student body by the mid-1970s as students of colour—all Asian and South Asian—were enrolling in growing numbers. A 1976 guide to Bachelor of Commerce graduates listed biographies of 156 graduating students, and thirty-one of them were non-white.[48] Most notably, nine of them were women of Chinese descent, and they outnumbered the seven other female graduates.

Students took a core set of required courses in the first two years of the undergraduate program, with eight possible degree concentrations. The focus of the concentration areas had also changed since the 1960s. For example, the Industrial Relations stream now included Organizational Behaviour in its title.[49] The scope of the faculty's offerings was considerable by 1975. There were 155 different Commerce courses listed in the UBC calendar that were open to undergraduate students. They would not have all been offered every term, but time and effort had been devoted to developing and listing them. The course titles evidenced an increased emphasis on numeric literacy and quantitative analysis such as seminars in Stochastic Models and Computer Applications in Business.[50] Possessing more than basic secondary school mathematics training would have been required for anyone coming into this program. The description for Topics from Management Science quite clearly revealed the program's emphasis:

> A study of the methods of management science as applied to problems involving randomness or uncertainty. Particular attention will be given to statistical problems which arise in problem formulation and to decision making under uncertainty. Stochastic models of inventory, queueing, and allocation will be considered. The techniques of dynamic programming and simulation will be discussed in

relation to the above models. Case studies will be used to illustrate the applications of the models.[51]

The liberal arts aspect of the program that was so evident in the 1940s and 1950s was mostly gone by the 1970s with the exception of specific areas of study. Program streams that dealt with human issues in the workplace, like Industrial Relations Management, continued to be available, and students were encouraged to take electives in Political Science and Sociology.[52] Issues relating to people and organizations continued to be a focus of Commerce and Business at UBC because, as an internal early 1970s development plan argued, business schools were facing challenging new trends:

An ambiguous socio-political environment
Organizations were become more diffuse and complex
Increased job and organizational mobility
Increasing employee expectations[53]

The Faculty of Commerce and Business also offered several professional and diploma programs:

Certified General Accountants: a five-year program that met the CGA licensing requirements in British Columbia
Chartered Accounts: a three-year program that met the academic requirements for membership in the Institute of Chartered Accountants of British Columbia
Registered Industrial Accounts: a five-year program that met the academic requirements for the RIA certificate
Junior Management: a three-year program
Real Estate and Appraisal: a four-year program
Sales Management: a three-year program[54]

These programs would have linked with undergrad degrees and provided the opportunity for further education to people with bachelor's degrees and others seeking their first post-secondary credential. As with other UBC business and management programs, they were offered in traditional learning formats such as lectures and correspondence. The university did not include enrollment numbers for each faculty in the 1975 calendar, but the marked increase in Commerce and Business Administration faculty certainly suggested that many more students wished to study management and business.

The 1980s were a decade of remarkable growth for the Faculty of Commerce and Business Administration. There were 1,670 students enrolled in the faculty's programs.[55] Most notably, women comprised 39 percent of Commerce and Business students. This was an enormous increase since the mid-1970s that reflected increased interest in business and management education among women coming out of secondary school. The number of faculty affiliated with the Faculty of Commerce and Business Administration had grown to 102, although only two of them were women.[56] The influence of the Harvard Business School in terms of faculty backgrounds had waned, as faculty received their doctorates at universities across North American and beyond. Commerce and Business was organized into nine divisions:

Accounting and Information Systems
Finance
Industrial Relations Management
Law
Management Science
Marketing
Policy Analysis
Transportation
Urban Land Economics

Accounting and Management Information Systems had the largest concentration of faculty, with nineteen members.[57] The Division of Industrial Relations Management, still concerned focused with the human side of business, had grown to fourteen faculty members.[58]

The undergraduate Commerce degree was five years in duration in 1985, with the first year being preparatory. The pre-Commerce year also required completion of two Mathematics courses.[59] This was indeed a marked change from the early years of the Commerce program, when one secondary school Mathematics course was considered sufficient for admission. There were ten areas of concentration in the degree, with Computer Science being the major addition since the 1970s.[60] The number of Commerce and Business courses listed grew to 197 by 1985.[61] There were significantly more courses on various aspects of the use of information technology in business, but the course titles did not especially reflect changes in the backgrounds of the students. For instance, a course called Manpower Planning was still listed even though close to 40 percent of the students in it could have been women.[62]

The UBC undergraduate Commerce program moved in new directions in the 1990s. There were 46,128 students at the university in the 1994–1995 academic year, and 1,247 of them were in the Faculty of Commerce and Business.[63] The gender composition of the Commerce student body had undergone major change, as slightly over half of the students—53 percent—were women.[64] Students enrolling in Commerce were also a remarkably diverse group. The 1996 Bachelor of Commerce graduates included 191 students, with 54 of them being women of Chinese or other Asian and South Asian descent.[65] There were 34 men graduating with similar backgrounds. Women clearly felt that pursuing a business and management degree was a good educational choice and decided to enroll in greater numbers than their male peers. The cost of a Commerce degree continued to gradually increase, with students paying between $2,295 and $2,751 per year depending on the number of credits in which they enrolled.[66]

There are two particularly interesting student stories in the UBC Faculty of Commerce archival materials that merit attention, as they illustrate the extent to which pursuing a degree that focused on business and management was perceived by students as a vehicle for personal advancement. The first case involved a woman named Edna Winram. She was born in 1921 and entered the UBC Bachelor of Commerce program in 1939. Winram expressed interest in either working in a civil service position or for an insurance company. She was a Vancouver resident and indicated under religious affiliation that she was Anglican. UBC rated students based on seven personality traits, from below average to outstanding: mental (intellectual ability), reliability (consistency, dependability), application (industry, attention to detail), social (willingness to cooperate with others), initiative (independence of thought), personality (personality strength), and judgment (accuracy of conclusion). Winram was rated above average on the first five criteria, and average on the last two[67]

Winram successfully completed the Bachelor of Commerce program in 1943. Her intellectual ability was such that she scored 99 out of 100 in one Mathematics course and 50 out of 50 in a second one, and she was rated "outstanding" in terms of academic attainment.[68] Winram won two scholarships and a gold medal for achievement and attended the University of California at Berkeley to complete a Master of Business Administration (MBA) degree.[69] She excelled at Berkeley and wrote to Dean Ellis Morrow in 1944 to tell him that she had earned As in all of her graduate courses.[70] Winram was clearly a gifted student but, as she said to Earle MacPhee in 1954, she married in early 1945 after completing her MBA and spent the next nine years "as a housewife."[71] This obviously reflected the social mores of the late 1940s, but Winram surely felt that her career had been abruptly halted, and she asked MacPhee if he would provide her with a reference for part-time teaching positions.[72] MacPhee, even though he also likely believed that women should be home raising children if they had them, may well have observed that a promising career had been regrettably put on hold.

The second notable case of a student with a particularly interesting life story involves an Ethiopian man named Taffara Deguefé. He was born in 1926 and worked for the State Bank of Ethiopia in Addis Ababa when he expressed interest in attending UBC in 1947.[73] As Figure 4.1 shows, he was young and enthusiastic about attending UBC. Deguefé was sponsored by people in Canada, and they attempted to find him employment

Figure 4.1 1947 student photo of Taffara Degeufé
Source: Used with permission of the University of British Columbia Archive.

at a bank. The Bank of Montréal indicated that they could not employ him and instead offered to have him visit its offices in Montréal for a month.[74] UBC initially did not know how to respond to Deguefé's interest in attending the university, with correspondence indicating that they had "no adequate measure of the work that he has done already" but ultimately decided to admit him as a special student.[75]

Deguefé was sent to UBC by G.A. Blowers, who was the governor of the State Bank of Ethiopia. Ellis Morrow described him as Blowers' "protegé" in an August, 1947, letter outlining plans that had been made for Deguefé. Blowers was advised that arrangements had been made for the young man to spend two years in Vancouver, including summer work at the Barclay's Bank office in the city, and that he would benefit from two additional years at the London School of Economics and Political Science.[76] Deguefé's time at UBC was short, but he went on to a distinguished career. By 1970, he was the general manager of the Commercial Bank of Ethiopia.[77] He was awarded an honourary degree by UBC in 1974 with the Governor-General of Canada in attendance.[78] The UBC Faculty of Commerce and Business Administration valued the fact that Deguefé was one of its graduates. There was political upheaval in Ethiopia in the mid-1970s, and Deguefé was put in detention by the country's military government. A letter was composed by the Faculty of Commerce and Business Administration to United Nations Secretary General Kurt Waldheim asking that efforts be made to secure his release.[79] Deguefé eventually went into political exile and chose to spend his remaining years in Vancouver.[80] It would not have been common for a young man, even one with financial resources, to travel from Ethiopia to western Canada in the late 1940s, and Deguefé exhibited great courage by doing so. He commented in 1969 on his experience visiting the United States as a young student within the context of growing African American responses to racial prejudice and wrote:

> As a student in the early '50s in America I recall we African students were looked down as uncouth savages and at that time no one had the desire to be identified with Africa in any way. How things have changed with time![81]

He obviously felt that UBC and Vancouver treated him well at a time when African students travelling abroad were not always welcome.

There may have been some diversity among the undergraduate students in the Faculty of Commerce and Business Administration, but much less so among the faculty members. There were 103 faculty affiliated with Commerce and Business in 1995 and, while the undergraduate student body was highly diverse, the faculty was still overwhelmingly male.[82] Only five women were appointed as professors: three as associates and two at full rank. There were some faculty of colour, but the names listed in the 1995 calendar were predominantly European in origin. They taught in eleven different divisions:

Accounting
Finance
Industrial Relations Management
Law
Management Information Systems
Management Science
Marketing
Policy Analysis
Transportation, Logistics, Public Utilities
Urban Land Economics
General

Students thus had access to a range of learning options. Issues pertaining to people in the workplace, including labour–management relations, continued to be a potential area of concentration. Faculty in that particular area, such as Brian Bemmels, published research from both labour and management perspectives.[83] The number of divisions had fluctuated somewhat since the 1960s, and there was clearly an effort to have the program reflect emerging trends and practices in business. The program, however, stopped being a generalist degree. It evolved into one requiring skills in quantitative analysis. The 1995 UBC calendar listed 110 courses at the 100 to 400 levels that were open to undergraduate students, and courses such as Decision Analysis I and II that were essentially mathematics-based were common.[84] As with prior years, not all of the courses in the catalogue would have been offered in every term or even yearly, but they illustrated the focus of business and management studies at UBC in the 1990s. The overall message was clear: business and management problems were quantifiable.

École des Hautes Études Commerciales de Montréal (HEC)

École des hautes études commerciales de Montréal (HEC) was founded for reasons somewhat similar to those behind the creation of UBC and its business and management programs. HEC was unique compared to the other business schools and commerce faculties that emerged across Canada in the twentieth century for a key reason: it was founded to provide business education in French. This may seem like a small detail to people unfamiliar with Canadian history and society, but it is important because of Canada's origins as a bi-lingual country. The history of HEC from 1926 to 1970 was the subject of a lengthy official history written by Pierre Harvey, and this chapter will not summarize all of what he wrote.[85] He provided some key insights into HEC and noted the importance of Montréal as a commercial centre in Canada in the early twentieth century, as it was arguably the country's leading financial centre at that time.[86] Harvey also stressed that HEC was initially shaped by European management education influences, especially Belgian, rather than by early developments in the United States.[87] The commercial importance of Montréal and the fact that Québec had a population that was predominantly francophone helped spur the founding of HEC in 1907. This meant that HEC would be first and foremost a francophone school for students from Québec. It was also not founded in affiliation with an established university, which made it markedly different from its counterparts in English Canada.

HEC was well-established in Montréal by the late 1940 and drew students from across Québec, although there appear to have been few from outside of the province. The first available HEC program guides begin in 1957. An undergraduate degree was its main offering at that time, but the school also offered a range of other business programs, with many of them intended for people pursuing part-time studies. Students could enroll in diploma programs in Commerce or Accounting that were offered in the evening.[88] There were also programs in Business Correspondence offered in French and English.[89] Students could complete language programs in Spanish, Italian, or German.[90] Part-time programs in Financial Analysis and Personnel Administration was also available at HEC.[91] There were no programs dealing with international or comparative business, or with manufacturing. The absence of the latter option is noteworthy since Montréal was widely known to have a substantial manufacturing sector, along with other industries like pulp and paper operating across Québec.

The part-time Personnel Administration program curriculum revealed something about the teaching and research orientation of HEC in the late 1950s. There were ten courses:

Planning
Hiring
Task Evaluation
Assessment of Competence
Employee Training
Salary Administration
Medical Services
Intelligence Services
Collective Labour Agreement Negotiation
The Collective Agreement[92]

The focus of these courses was communicated fairly clearly by their titles, perhaps with the exception of Intelligence Services. That particular offering had a comparatively brief description that simply stated that the nature and objective of these services would be discussed. It was more likely a course on business information services. Collective bargaining was central to this Personnel Management program, with two courses on labour relations included in the curriculum. However, planning and measurement were also clearly considered to be key personnel management functions. For instance, the description for the course on competence assessment indicated that students would:

Learn the use and limits of such evaluation. Determination of the relative value of employees. Establishment of a plan to evaluate competence.[93]

The course on labour negotiation would cover:

> The nature and value of a collective agreement system. Preparation for negotiation. The art and science of negotiation.[94]

The readings for the various courses were not listed, but the descriptions suggest that the personnel program was more focused on methods reflecting scientific management rather than human relations. Systems and techniques for measuring, quantifying, and evaluating were emphasized in this program. HEC would have chosen to offer programs with content like personnel management because of marketability and also because of available teaching expertise. The courses were taught on different days, with some being held twice a week. The cost per course ranged from $30 to $40.[95] They were clearly intended for people who wanted to further their careers, and someone who was perhaps already working in an entry-level or middle management role would have found the price to be acceptable.

The names of the instructors were listed at the front of the HEC brochure. There is a key common aspect to all of them: only four of thirty-four were not francophone. Three of the instructors taught English, Italian, or German language courses while a fourth non-francophone taught Accounting. Some instructors taught across different subject areas. For instance, Edward Levins taught a business writing course in English and also one on English language. Enrollments numbers for 1957 were not indicated in the brochure, but the number of instructors assigned to each subject area implies what most attracted students. There were ten instructors teaching accounting courses, while only one taught in each of subjects like personnel administration, political economy, or financial mathematics. The part-time programs, in the late 1950s, thus likely attracted students who had more quantitative than qualitative learning interests. The list of instructors also shows that HEC was able to fill part-time teaching posts with francophone instructors.[96]

The undergraduate program offered by HEC was central to the school's programming, and the need to make the program accessible to working adults was a policy priority. The Bachelor of Science in Commerce (B.Sc. Comm) was first offered in 1966 in an evening format, and it had a liberal arts emphasis. The first year of the program required completion of courses in:

Accounting
Geography
History
Initiation to Intellectual Work
Introduction to World Affairs
French Language
Mathematics

The second year of the program continued with a liberal arts emphasis:

Accounting
Geography
History
English Language
French Language and Report Writing
French Literature
Mathematics
Business Organization

Content more focused on business subjects began to appear in year three:

Marketing
General and Industrial Accounting
Finance
English Language
Financial Mathematics and Statistics
Personnel and Industrial Relations
Philosophy
Production
Report Writing

However, liberal arts were again emphasized in the fourth year:

Professional Ethics
Finance
English Language
Major Currents of Thought
Phenomenology of Religion
Psychology[97]

This program provided a well-rounded education: everything from religion to statistics. However, it looks more like a general liberal arts degree that included a business concentration rather than a business degree with a lot of humanities and social science electives. This surely reflected a pedagogical belief at HEC that having liberal arts content was important to the study of business and management. The curriculum would continue to reflect this interest in subsequent years.

HEC's undergraduate program became a Bachelor's of Administrative Affairs (BAA) and continued to develop into the mid-1970s. This was also when HEC would have been accepting students who had first attended a CEGEP. The school was still entirely led by francophone faculty, with 111 different professors and instructors involved with teaching the undergraduate program. HEC appears to have chosen to list the names of all of the instructors affiliated with the institution, which is a notable difference from schools in English Canada. For instance, the names of professors and instructors at all ranks were listed, as were the visiting faculty. There were sixty-three faculty members who were at or above the rank of assistant professor, which indicates that the majority of faculty were either tenured or on tenure-track appointment. There were only seven women included in the faculty ranks, and principally in non-tenure stream appointments. While making definitive conclusions about the ethnic makeup of the faculty is difficult, there was only person—Van The Nhut—who did not have a European name.[98]

The professional backgrounds of the various faculty were diverse if their gender and ethnic makeup was not. Many faculty had earned at least one graduate degree from an American university. There were six faculty who had earned either an MBA or DBA at Harvard, but other universities such as Columbia and Berkeley were represented. There were also nine faculty members who earned terminal degrees at French universities. HEC additionally hired faculty who had earned one or more degrees at the school or at another francophone university in Québec. Language would have played a role in hiring decisions, but the decision to hire HEC graduates reflected a belief by HEC's leadership that the school graduated capable people who would be good instructors.[99]

The number of faculty had increased by the mid-1970s, and the undergraduate curriculum altered from the 1960s. This may have been due to changes in faculty composition but was surely also due to greater overall interest at HEC in teaching a more overtly business-oriented curriculum. The first year of the BAA required:

Introduction to Administration
Fundamentals of Organizational Psychology
Organizational Sociology
Mathematics[100]

The 1970s course guides were more detailed than their 1960s predecessors and provided course descriptions, such as this one for Introduction to Administration:

> The administrator's characteristic activities: planning, organization, control, decision making. Basic concepts of techniques useful for administration: analysis of break-even point; the critical path method; the decision tree. Situations in the administrative processes of marketing, finance, control, human resources management, etc. Studied by the case method with appropriate texts. Perspective: develop a systematic approach to situations using relevant concepts.[101]

The case method again appeared in an undergraduate business program in this particular offering. The course would inform students of the basic functions of the administrator's role. The idea that using situational analysis in the form of case studies and the integration of specific decision-making methods was also a key part of the learning process. Being an administrator was a systematic process in that course description. The second-year curriculum further expanded on the ideas found in the first introductory administration course. Students would study:

Marketing
Finance
Organizational Behaviour
Production
Elements of Statistics
Elements of Operational Research
Two sections of Economics
Management Accounting[102]

Humanities subjects were gone from the curriculum, with a modicum of social science content remaining. The year-three curriculum provided considerable choice for students, with concentrations in Human Resource Management, Public Accounting, Governmental and Institutional Accounting, Control, Quantitative Management Methods, Applied Economics, and Production.[103] The concentration areas were, however, also quantitative in nature while also reflecting emerging trends in business practice. The Control concentration exemplified the program's overall emphasis, as it obliged students to take:

Industrial Accounting
Taxation
Information Systems
Cost Analysis
Internal Verification and Control

The purpose of the concentration was to "prepare administrators responsible for exercising functions connected to accounting, internal verification and control in industry and commerce."[104] The Human Resource Management concentration stressed somewhat less quantitative analysis and more social science content:

Personnel II
Compensation Management
Labour Relations
Industrial Psychology
General Administrative Policies[105]

There were four electives in this stream:

Research Methods
Sociology of Work
Human Problems in Organizations
Labour Economics[106]

The social and economic context of work would have been covered in the Human Resources concentration.

Cost was one area where the HEC program did not alter significantly from the mid-1960s. The tuition fee in 1975 was $380, which was actually cheaper on a per-course basis than what had been charged in 1965.[107] The 1980s undergraduate program showed further changes from what was offered in the 1960s. The faculty were not listed in that year's course guide, but new courses and program emphases were evident. The purpose of the first two years was described as providing an introduction to the diverse functions in a business. The third year provided opportunity for specialization in "one or two areas of management."[108] The first year required:

Introduction to Administration
Foundations of Organizational Psychology
Organizational Sociology
Statistical Methods I
Statistical Methods II
Microeconomics
Macroeconomics
General Accounting

The second year included:

Marketing
Finance
Personnel Administration
Labour Relations
Production
Introduction to Information Systems
Elements of Operational Research
Problems and Political Economy
Management Accounting[109]

The second-year electives were divided into three blocks, with nine electives spread across them. The objective of the third year, learning more deeply about two areas of management, would be accomplished by selecting from among eighteen different courses.[110]

The emphasis of the 1985 program still included some social science content, as students were required to take labour relations and could also enroll in Sociology of Work. The overall thrust of the program was toward quantitative analysis in years two and three. This was particularly evident in the third-year course choices, as six of them clearly required advanced ability with using mathematic analysis. Those courses included Quantitative Techniques in Marketing, Quantitative Techniques in Finance, and Quantitative Techniques in Accounting and Verification. The social science electives that were available were also more focused on numbers, such as Labour Economics, and Micro and Macroeconomics.[111]

Students who did choose to take one of the social science electives in the mid to late-1980s, for example Sociology of Work, may have been surprised at the syllabus that they encountered. The objective of the 1987 version of Sociology of Work was presented as:

> The course of labor sociology aims to highlight the dynamics of the process as well as the main structural and cultural characteristics of work and forms of work organization in contemporary societies in general and in Québec in particular.[112]

The course was based on a range of readings rather than a textbook. The assigned works were written in French but occasionally referenced well-known authors who had been published in English or German. Max Weber, Frederick W. Taylor, and Harry Braverman were discussed in articles and book chapters.[113] The readings also focused on union and non-union workers. A section of the course focused exclusively on work in Québec, and the assigned literature discussed private sector unionization in the province, worker cooperatives, and professionalization, among other topics.[114] Professions and professional work and technology were the focus of the third part of Sociology of Work. An article by Laval University sociologist Gilles Dussault was representative of the course readings. In that article, "L'analyse sociologique du professionnalisme au Québec," Dussault discussed the rise of professional jobs in Québec and the different types of them.[115] He also emphasized the importance of professionalism in organizations. This was surely an article that would have resonated with students who aspired to be considered professionals.

Sociology of Work appears to have been an engaging offering that would have interested students, but the description for Quantitative Techniques in Marketing probably more accurately reflected the type of content that students saw during their time at HEC:

> Hypotheses tests. Parametric and non-parametic tests. Cochran test. Kolmogorov-Smirnov test. Mann and Whitney test. Kruskal-Wallis

tests. Friedman tests. Spearman and Kendall non-parametic correlation. Multiple regression. Variance analysis of one and many correlating factors. Covariance analysis. Analysis of variance in a Latin square and a Greco-Latin square.[116]

This was a remarkably opaque course description, but it nonetheless described various methods for testing and verifying in marketing. The context in which these testing tools would be used was not enunciated. Students presumably would deduce what would transpire in the course from daunting nature of the description. The Cochran test is described by the National Institute of Standards and Technology as:

> The Cochran test is a non-parametric test for analyzing randomized complete block designs where the response variable is a binary variable (i.e., there are only two possible outcomes, which are coded as 0 and 1).[117]

The other tests were similar in nature to Cochran, and substantial mathematic ability would have been required for anyone enrolling in Quantitative Techniques in Marketing and anything else with the term quantitative in the title. The program calendar did not indicate that students would need advanced mathematics skills in order to succeed in the program. It simply stated that "to be admitted to the baccalaureate program, the candidate must have obtained a diploma of collegial studies comprising the courses of a suitable program or equivalence structure and meet the other requirements set by the school."[118] HEC students continued to pay reasonable tuition fees for their undergrad degree, even if the program was more mathematic in nature with every passing decade. The yearly tuition fee was $1,710, with foreign students paying $26,100.[119] HEC did not indicate how many foreign students enrolled in its programs, but the far higher fee charged to such students must have help cover the cost of the much lower and subsidized amount assessed to domestic students. The fact that HEC could contemplate charging such a high fee to foreign students in the mid-1980s also reflected the school's reputation and stature as a place to study business and management.

HEC's mid-1990s BAA represented an ongoing program evolution. The school had 173 faculty members, with forty-three at the rank of professor and eighty-one associate professors by that time. Most of the instruction was handled by full-time faculty, as there were only thirty-six adjuncts listed in the 1995 course syllabus. The other faculty were in roles such as visiting professor. The number of women had increased since the 1970s, although they were still a minority of thirty-five. The influence of American graduate programs on HEC had considerably lessened since the 1970s. There were only two faculty members who had at least one degree from Harvard, but forty-seven who had earned at least one from HEC itself. That included thirteen full professors. English Canadian graduate programs also had a significant role in educating HEC faculty, as several faculty had earned degrees in graduate programs at institutions like the University of Toronto and the University of Western Ontario. For example, there were two Ph.D. graduates from the University of Western Ontario business school.[120]

The bachelor's program had altered since the mid-1980s, and the purpose of the program was presented as:

> The BAA program aims to convey knowledge and develop the skills necessary for the conduct of human organizations, and more specifically those of business organizations. It is by learning the languages used in these organizations, by understanding the behaviors that prevail in them, by examining the functions that compose them, by analyzing the environment in which they are situated, and by development of expertise in one or other of the practical fields of the manager . . . to prepare the candidates best able to contribute to the orientation and the development of the organizations to which they will integrate.

The human aspect of organizations was first mentioned, followed closely by the business aspect of them. This description, while appearing holistic, was still rather vague before moving to a practically oriented conclusion. The description also implied that student would learn to participate in organizations and to also run them. The program curriculum indicated that being a manager would be an even more quantitative undertaking than it was in the 1980s.[121]

There were further changes ten years later, as the first year of the 1995 BAA program required students to take ten courses:

Foundations of Organizational Psychology
Organizational Sociology
Administrative Processes
Managers and Organizations
Statistical Methods I
Statistical Methods II
or
Quantitative Methods I (or Mathematics)
Quantitative Methods II
Microeconomic Analysis (or Mathematics)
Macroeconomic Analysis
Presentation of Accounting Information[122]

The only choice was whether or not to take two statistics courses or two quantitative methods courses. The first-year emphasis was heavily weighted toward mathematical analyses of different types. The social science courses that were present did not represent the core of the introductory curriculum even if they were required. The second year was focused on quantitative methodology. The third year of the program afforded students a wide range of concentrations:

Professional Management
Applied Economics
Entrepreneurship
Finance
Operations and Production Management
Human Resource Management
International Management
Marketing
Quantitative Management Methods
Information Systems
Mixed Option[123]

The list of possible courses within each stream was quite lengthy, with the Mixed Option concentration being representative with eighteen different choices. The title of this stream suggests that it represented what general management meant at HEC. It included three courses focused on quantitative methodologies, one mathematics course, another on stochastic and probabilistic management methods, and one on deterministic models in operational research. There was a course on management theory, another on the sociology of work, and three on economics. Even the social science content, in the form of economics offerings, was highly quantitative in nature.

The core of management, in this instance, was entirely about understanding how to use numbers. There was some content that examined what it meant to be a manager. For example, HEC offered a course called Managers and Management Practice in 1995. That description for the course was intended for anyone who wanted to become a manager. It emphasized the importance of understanding leadership personality and the overall role of personality in management. This course did not emphasize quantitative management methodology and the role of human behaviour in shaping management decisions. It could well have been a welcome break for students who were interested in social sciences rather than using numbers.[124]

HEC also offered courses on important subjects like law. The 1995 Business Law course had two learning objectives: the role of law in a business, and the role of law in the management process and on the manager.[125] The course was coordinated and taught by Gaston Meloche, who was an associate professor with training in law.[126] Two other instructors—Michèle Larose and Jean Lorrain—also taught sections of the course, but their backgrounds are unclear. This course required students to write two exams, one at the middle of the term and one at the end, and the readings were based on materials on library reserve. The assigned reading was largely comprised of legal decisions, and protection of resources of matters such as intellectual property was the focus of one section of the course.[127] Laws on the founding, operation, and ending of corporations were examined in another part of it.[128] Other key aspects of law such as property and contracts were discussed.[129] The section on legal responsibilities described the perils facing management in terms of criminal and civil penalties.[130] It also described contractual and non-contractual obligations and faults and damages. The course concluded by examining the employment contract, including reciprocal obligations and termination.[131]

The syllabus for Business Law, like the majority of the HEC program's content, did not always expressly delineate who managers were as individuals. Courses like Managers and Management Practice were exceptions to this overall trend. The program instead taught what managers did at work and the methods that they should have used to execute their responsibilities. The program taught students how to use statistical and other quantitative methods to run organizations. Furthermore, the program focus was principally on for-profit corporations rather on public non-profit entities. Students were explicitly advised, by the late 1990s, that HEC trained managers with solid professional qualities.[132]

The faculty who taught in the program changed somewhat over time. They became far more numerous, and they increasingly received their educations in graduate programs based in Québec. They were overwhelmingly francophone, and a few women gradually joined the faculty ranks. The influence of American business schools gradually lessened as Québec-based institutions graduated more doctoral students of their own. Indeed, HEC produced many of its own faculty. There was some diversity within the francophone faculty. As with most business schools, there were significant numbers of adjunct instructors used by the school by the mid-1990s. The HEC faculty were nonetheless mostly associate or full professors.

The nature of the student population at HEC from the 1950s to the 1990s is evident from promotional materials. Even images from program guides from the mid to late 1990s, when the school resumed inclusion of numerous photo images after several years of not using them, show a predominantly white male student body.[133] HEC, because of the fact that program instruction was in French, was principally attempting to recruit students in order to train a class of managers who would expand free enterprise in the province. Students were active in extra-curricular pastimes, such as helping run the HEC Co-Operative that had been founded in 1944. The alumni network had grown to 33,000 by 1997. The fact that the school continued to grow over time, in terms of size of faculty and diversity of program offerings, suggests that there were ever more students who thought that pursuing a business degree in Montréal was a good academic choice. HEC played a leading role in Québec higher education by the end of the 1990s and was a leading choice for French-language business education. The situation in English Canada was different as there were more competing institutions, including the business school at the University of Western Ontario.[134]

The University of Western Ontario

Undergraduate management education was taught at different Ontario universities by the beginning of the 1950s, and the University of Western Ontario Business School endeavoured to be at the forefront of new program expansion.[135] The university was founded in 1878 so, unlike HEC, the UWO Business School's relationship to its home institution was like the one UBC's commerce programs and business school had with the wider university. A program in Commercial Economics was first offered at UWO in 1922, and the school of business was established in 1950.[136] The UWO Business School was heavily influenced by practices developed at Harvard Business School (HBS). The first dean of the school, Lloyd Sipherd, was an HBS graduate, as were other key members of the early faculty including Walter Thompson.[137] The case teaching method, which was first widely used in business education by HBS, was adopted by UWO.[138] The school's origins were rooted in some key imperatives. UWO, unlike UBC and HEC, was not located in one of Canada's major cities. London, Ontario, was a mid-sized city in 1950 with a diversified economy that included financial firms like London Life and manufacturing firms such as John Labatt Ltd., along with several American-based firms such as General Motors Diesel. There was interest in London, both within the city's business leaders and the university leadership, in developing UWO's stature. W. Sherwood Fox was Dean of Arts and Science at UWO when the Bachelor of Commerce program—forerunner of the business school—was founded in 1919. Fox and others at the university were concerned that commerce was growing in popularity as a subject of study, and that UWO was losing potential students to other institutions that offered it.[139] The case method was chosen as the preferred one as an HBS graduate, Ellis H. Morrow, was chosen as the first director of the new Commerce department. As prior analysis shows, he would go on to UBC.[140]

The program that had developed into a formal business school by 1950 offered a range of programs in undergraduate, graduate, and professional education. 1950 was also an important year as this was the first year of the program under the auspices of the business school rather than a department. Potential students were advised that they were joining a program where "for nearly thirty years men had been educated for business at the University of Western Ontario." The school had been founded for four reasons:

> Canada needed, and would continue to need, capable administrators. That this need could in large part be met by assuring an adequate supply of young men college-trained for business. That this training should feature a broad background in the arts and sciences, coupled with a thinking attitude toward business problems and a sure knowledge of the basic skills; and that the elements of business administration could best be learned in a School whose place in educational circles was well-defined and whose professional status was unmistakably clear.

Furthermore, it was clear that students were training to be business leaders:

> The purpose of the School is to provide an opportunity for young men to prepare themselves for responsibilities in the business world. The business administrator, broadly speaking, is one who determines and executes policies.

The school did not guarantee that students were guaranteed of enjoying prestigious careers after graduating, but there was a clear implication that students joining the program were becoming involved with an institution that had a clear national mission and that the education received would be broad yet comprehensive. They were assured that they would be capable of running businesses after thy graduated. It was also very clear that management was considered an important male occupation.[141]

The UWO Business School faculty was composed of fourteen people, only two of whom had Ph.Ds. The bulk of them either had Master of Arts (MA) or Master of Business Administration (MBA) degrees. Having an MA was obviously sufficient preparation to teach in the various programs offered by the school in 1950. The faculty was mostly male, although there were two women members. The school's registrar was also a woman with an MA. The school's links to Canadian business were essentially put on display for prospective students. The administration committee, or advisory board, had thirteen members, and many represented major firms like Dominion Stores (grocery), London Life (insurance), Ford Motor Company of Canada (automotive), and Imperial Oil (petroleum). The academic advisory committee, which had influence on curricular matters, included seventeen members. All of them were corporate executives, and companies such as Firestone Tire and Rubber of Canada (tires), John Labatt (brewing), Dominion Securities (investing), and Canadian General Electric (industrial products) were represented.

Corporate leaders vastly outnumbered the faculty when it came to shaping and governing the school when it was initially founded.[142]

The 1950 program in Business Administration was four years in duration and was to provide a "general arts background" in the first two years with the final years concentrating on "general administrative and executive skills applicable to all businesses."[143] Students were required to take the following subjects in their first year:

English
Library Science
Mathematics
Physical Education
Business
Economics
Psychology
Biological, Physical, or Geological Science
Three of: French, German, Latin, Hebrew, Russian, Spanish, Geography, Zoology[144]

The second year consisted of:

English
Physical Education
Business
Any six of: English, French, History, Philosophy, Psychology, Spanish
Six credits from Economics (seven course choices)[145]

Year three required:

Four business courses (including Marketing, Business Finance, and Production Management)
Three approved credits from Humanities or Social Sciences[146]

In the final year, students had to complete one third-year course with a mark of at least a 66 percent and an overall average of 60 percent. The fourth-year courses were:

Nine Business credits from fourteen full and half courses (including Personnel Administration, Financial Management, Production Management, Advertising, Market Analysis)
Six credits from the Humanities and Social Sciences[147]

The program had a significant social science and humanities component that was evident throughout its duration. It was structured to provide a broad generalist education that was promised in the program description. The curriculum suggested that being a successful manager meant knowing something about languages, history, and other subjects along with business. The course descriptions in 1950 were broad and reflected a generalist approach to business education. For instance, Introduction to Business was presented as:

> This introductory course in business is designed to acquaint the student with the widest possible range of business problems from the point of view of the business manager. It assumes little or no business knowledge on the part of the student.[148]

Even courses such as Business Mathematics, Fundamentals of Accounting, and Marketing did not specify that any prior knowledge was required.

The type of students who attended the UWO School of Business Administration in 1950 is not depicted in the program guide, but the guide's language emphasizing the training of men makes it clear that most if not all were male. Attending the UWO School of Business Administration in 1950 did not represent an enormous financial commitment as students paid $250 per year in tuition.[149] There were several scholarships available, financial assistance, and also a job placement program for graduates.[150] The school thus not only provided what appeared from the program guide to be a well-rounded business education but also made efforts to make it accessible while also ensuring that graduates enjoyed a promising entry into the workforce. Indeed, careful entry into the job market was considered crucial, as "A year or two in the right job is not only an apprenticeship for top level jobs; it is a continuation of the graduate's training."[151] The use of the term "apprenticeship" is noteworthy because it suggested that, at least in 1950, management was considered a vocation.

The UWO undergrad program grew by 1960. The School of Business Administration faculty had expanded to twenty-one members. Only one faculty member, Donald Thain, had a Doctor in Business Administration (DBA) degree. Thain indicated that he was the first faculty member at the business school to have that degree.[152] There was one other faculty member who held a Doctor of Commercial Studies (DCS) degree from Harvard. Thain and his colleague with the DCS were two of eight Harvard graduates teaching at the business school, with the other six having Master of Business Administration degrees (MBA) as their terminal credential.[153] There was only one woman on the school's faculty, and she held a BA and was listed as a Report Grader.[154] What is striking about the 1960 faculty is that a majority of them—twelve people—had earned their MBAs at UWO. The impact of Harvard Business School practices was as evident in the UWO School of Business Administration's personnel practices as much as they were in pedagogical methods. As Duff McDonald has suggested, Harvard Business School has long preferred to bring its own best graduates into faculty positions, and UWO followed the same path.[155]

The undergraduate program structure had altered somewhat since 1950. The school clearly indicated that the business program would comprise years three and four of an undergraduate degree. The first two years were intended to provide "a broad education in the humanities as well as the social and natural sciences." However, the school also included a caveat in the description of program objectives when it noted, "Because of this general foundation, if the student later finds that he has mistaken his aptitudes or tastes he may transfer with little loss of time to another course." This surely indicated that the school had admitted students who were not as inclined to business and management studies as they originally thought and that there was a way of continuing with another degree choice if need be.[156]

The program 1950 consisted of twenty-four courses, including six required arts and science courses:

Economics
Two in English
Foreign Language
Mathematics
Psychology[157]

The remaining electives were:

One of: Botany, Chemistry, Geology, Physics, Zoology
One of: Choice of four History courses, Philosophy, and Politics[158]

The third-year business curriculum required students to take:

Introduction to Business
Fundamentals of Accounting
Marketing
Finance
Production
Control
Administrative Practices
Executive Problems[159]

The required courses in the third year of the program were largely focused on statistical analysis, since subjects like accounting, finance, and control were emphasized. The electives included options like Sales Management, Personnel Administration, Investment Management, International Business Management, and Probability Statistics for Business Decisions.[160] The fourth year involved taking one core course, another in the arts or sciences, and four business electives.[161]

The 1960 curriculum appeared to further promise that students were being prepared for senior leadership roles. The description for Executive Problems stated:

> The course on Executive Problems will focus on business problems faced by executives at the top of administrative levels of business organization. In most cases these will be presidents' problems.

The course description did not make reference to front-line or middle management responsibilities, nor was there another course available in the program that examined the roles of managers at those levels. Although the 1960 program was intended for undergraduate students who had only recently graduated from high school, the program description reassured anyone entering it that they could look forward to rapid career advancement and important roles in business. Images from the UWO School of Business Administration brochures show a homogeneous group of students in 1960, and it would be several years before the school's gender demographics began to alter. Their demographics were likely the same as in 1950, but the cost of the undergraduate program had increased, as students paid $425 in each of their first and second years and $450 in each of their final two years. That was almost 60 percent more than the cost in 1950.[162]

1969 is the last year for which there is an especially detailed description available for the UWO undergraduate business program, although there is sufficient information to also describe how the program evolved into the 1990s. In 1969, the School of Business Administration had fifty-five faculty members. This was over twice as many who were appointed there in 1960. There were twenty faculty with either Ph.D. or DBA degrees, which was far more than six years earlier. Twenty-four of the school's faculty had earned at least one degree at UWO, usually an MBA, and two of them had completed their Ph.Ds. at the school. The impact of Harvard Business School was still quite evident in 1969, as ten faculty members had earned their DBAs at that school. There were no women faculty members listed in the 1969 program guide, and nobody without a surname of European origin.[163]

The overall undergrad program themes and objectives had not significantly changed since 1960. Reference to students being able to change their minds about a business concentration were still there in 1969. However, the opening sentence of the program description had altered somewhat when it said that "The program leading to the degree of Bachelor of Arts in Honors Business Administration has three objectives: to contribute to the liberal education of the student, to help the student acquire an administrative point of view, to acquaint the student with the modern body of knowledge and techniques for management." The idea of business and management education being a form of liberal arts education continued to be important for the school and was considered similarly important for students.[164]

The requirements for the first two years of the program had changed since 1960. First year students were advised that "any General Program of the University of Western Ontario" was sufficient background to apply for the honors business program, provided that students had taken one introductory Mathematics course and one in Economics.[165] Students in their second year at the university could continue with their initial program concentration, but also had to take a Business course as a pre-requisite to apply to the honours business program.[166] The only required course—Fundamentals of Accounting—was "designed as a preparation for entry to the Business School."[167] It focused on three areas: economic accounting, financial accounting, and the uses of published reports.[168] The course description further noted that "quantitative and economic areas" would be referenced in terms of relevance to the study of accounting.[169] Requiring an accounting course as the sole pre-requisite indicated that potential students needed to understand that having strong facility with numbers was important to success in the honours business program.

The second year of the program required:

Marketing
Finance
Production
Management Science
Control
Administrative Practices[170]

Students enrolled in one required course—Executive Problems—in their final year in the program along with four electives from the business school, or two business electives and two senior courses offered by other departments in the university.[171] This last point was crucial because it meant that it could be possible for a student to complete a degree in which liberal arts courses were half of the overall content. Students who came from humanities and social science concentrations would nonetheless have faced a significant educational transition when they were admitted to the business school and had to make more use of numbers than they had during their preceding two years at the university. For instance, Management Science was described as:

> The course in Management Science covers the main mathematical and statistical techniques available to the administrator. It is designed to provide a level of understanding which will help the student follow developments in his own field of specialization and to make use of the techniques in his analysis of business problems. The emphasis throughout the course is on the use of quantitative methods of

analysis as an aid to executive decision making. A portion of the class time is devoted to teaching the student the use of the computer.[172]

This course not only required well-developed numeracy skills, but it would also probably have introduced students to using a computer for the first time. Computers were appearing in business school curricula by the late 1960s, and UWO business students had the option of taking an elective half course called Computers and Information Systems if they found the using new technology useful.[173] The cost of the undergraduate program had increased to $540 per year, which was an approximately 20 percent increase since 1960. The program was becoming more expensive, but the range of student learning options, in terms of electives and the technology that students could use, had also expanded.[174]

There were new changes to the UWO undergraduate business program in the 1970s. The business school's faculty included seventy faculty by the mid part of that decade.[175] Fifty-one were in tenured or tenure-track positions. Their gender was not specifically evident from the university program calendar, but it can be concluded that they were mostly male. The 1976 program description was broad while also providing some specifics about what students would study:

> The focus of Western's Undergraduate Program in Business Administration is somewhat unique. Whereas most programs prepare students for distinct functional duties, Western is concerned with the preparation of generalists; individuals who are prepared to launch into their immediate environment and, at the same time, are building a foundation to become managers in top executive positions. While most of Western's graduates enter business careers, a significant number are attracted to positions in non-profit-oriented operations such as governments, labour unions, health and charitable organizations, colleges and universities.[176]

The program learning objectives were the same as in 1969. Potential students were assured that "The successful managers must know people, see events in perspective, and develop flexibility in thinking; in short, he requires a general education."[177] The degree continued to require that applicants first complete two years in another program. The calendar specifically indicated that students should take ten courses, and four of them needed to include:

An introductory university Mathematics half course or one Ontario Grade 13 Mathematics course

One of five introductory Mathematics courses (including three that had last been offered in 1975), a combination of three Mathematics half courses, one of two Computer Science courses, or two Computer Science half courses

An introductory second-year business course
One of two introductory Economics courses[178]

The course requirements for the third year were similar to those in 1969:

Marketing
Business Finance
Operations Management
Management Science
Planning Information and Control Systems
Managing Human Resources[179]

The fourth year mandated five courses, one of which had to be Business Policy, and two could be from Arts, Science, or Social Science.[180] The school also emphasized the importance of its undergraduate placement program.[181] Tuition fees had again increased since 1969, and students in 1976 to 1977 paid $662.50 per year at the business school.[182] That was the same fee charged in the faculties of Arts, Science, Social Science, and Physical Education.

There are some key points that can be derived from the 1976 program information. The emphasis on generalist education continued to endure from its original presentation in 1950. Liberal arts education was still a significant component of the overall undergraduate business degree. However, it was also clear that possessing quantitative skills was necessary if a student wanted to have a chance of succeeding in the business program. The use of computers became more central to the learning experience. While the UWO Business School argued that it wanted graduates to become managers who understood people, the majority of business courses were not focused on people issues in the workplace. Only one required course focused on human resource management. The Business Policy course examined:

> Policy making and administration integrated with other fourth year courses. The approach is from the level of top management in order that management problems may be studied from an overall, rather than from a departmental point of view in many different industries and types of companies. Mandatory in fourth year Business Program.

The implication from this course description, indeed from the entire 1976 program literature, was that graduates were learning not just to manage but to do so at senior levels in organizations.[183]

The UWO undergraduate business program altered somewhat by 1986, but its direction was the essentially the same as it had been in 1976. The pre-requisite requirements for the first two years were essentially the same—a combination of mathematics, computer science, and economics courses—but the third-year course requirements had importantly changed:

Marketing
Management Communications
Finance
Operations Management
Management Science
Managerial Accounting and Control
Management Behaviour[184]

Human Resource Management was no longer a required course. Business Policy and The Political Environment of Canadian Business were again both required courses in the fourth year.[185] The mode of learning was "based on individual study and preparation, group discussion and projects, classroom discussion, lectures, use of audio-visual aids, report writing, field trips, and in most courses considerable emphasis on the use of case studies as a means of acquiring management decision-making skills and attitudes" and the development of communication skills was stressed in the first year of the business program.[186] Students were assured that they would be videotaped while presenting in class and could use the footage for self-evaluation and improvement.[187]

Students continued to have a considerable choice of elective courses in the mid-1980s, but there was an emphasis on quantitative analysis rather than dealing with issues pertaining to people. There were sixty-two different full and half-courses offered in the School of Business Administration, all of which would not be offered every year, and there were some such as two industrial relations courses that obviously pertained to personnel matters in the workplace.[188] A course such as The Political Environment of Canadian Business was however still taught using cases without any apparent comprehensive analysis of the historical development of business in Canada and its links to the country's political system:

> This course provides students the opportunity to practice devising a constructive response to political and social pressures in the environments. The course uses a series of case studies which involve a business enterprise caught up in a political or social crisis. Mandatory in fourth year Honours Business Program, half course.[189]

There is no mention of political theory, the role of capital and the state, or other topics that are usually examined in a course on politics. This description instead implies that students will be taught in one term how to maneuver a company out of social and political trouble. The importance of the undergraduate job placement program continued to be stressed in the mid-1980s.[190] Undergraduate Business students in the late 1980s paid $1,422 per year in tuition, which was still the same amount paid by students in Arts, Science, Social Science, and Physical Education.[191] They surely felt that they were getting good value for their money. The business school was closely linked to the Canadian business community, and students were assured that substantial efforts would be made to place them in rewarding careers upon graduation. Those trends would continue into the 1990s.

The UWO School of Business undergraduate program had significantly developed by 1995 into a program that specialized in many ways, even if it still claimed to provide a broad education. The undergraduate program description now explained a program that was far more international in scope than it had been in prior years:

> The Western Business School is positioned among the world's leaders in international business education. The program's global perspective results from an increasingly multinational student population, a large exchange program, faculty with extensive international experience, and an increased global perspective in core courses. Gaining and sustaining an advantage in today's globally competitive environment requires close cooperation among the different functions in an organization. Students will develop a working knowledge of each of the major functions, so that they can work effectively with fellow managers. Accordingly, the first two years of the 4-year program provide students with a general education in the arts, social or natural sciences. During the second two years, students study each of the major business fields.[192]

Prospective students who had completed two years of study in another program may have thought that they were ready to apply to the business school, but would have needed to contemplate the requirements when first entering the university. The business school required mid-1990s applicants to have completed one Mathematics course, a half course in Computer Science, another half course in Statistics, a course in Economics, and one Business course.[193] The Business course was a second-year offering, with the other were chosen from among first-year courses. Successfully completing the minimum requirements essentially meant devoting a year's worth of study to the specified subjects, since a typical full-time yearly course load comprised five courses.

The undergraduate business degree was thus really one year of liberal arts education combined with three years of what the business school expected, provided that someone who completed the pre-requisite courses actually made it into the program. The third year of the program varied somewhat from what was mandated in the mid-1980s:

Marketing
Management Communications

Finance
Operations Management
Managerial Accounting and Control
Management Behaviour
Management Science
Information Systems[194]

Students in their fourth year were encouraged to "design a personal program of study best suited to their individual needs" but that included taking Business Policy with the option of also taking one course in the faculties of Arts, Science, Social Science, or Law.[195] The importance of understanding the role information technology was confirmed by the fact that a course in that subject was now a required part of the actual business curriculum, not simply something that was studied at the introductory level in the first two years as an undergraduate student. This was a further evolution in learning requirements from students who had been advised in the 1960s that they would receive an orientation on how to use a computer if they were interested. There was also a key change in the fees charged by the business school. Whereas the school's fees had long been in line with the tuition charged for Arts, Social Science, and Science degrees, a slight differential appeared between 1994 and 1995. The undergraduate business program cost $2,780 per year, which was the same as the Faculty of Kinesiology, while liberal arts programs were $2,680.[196] This was a seemingly small price difference, but it meant that the value of the business degree was leading to increased costs. It also meant, even with a hundred-dollar price difference, that students may have thought twice about pursuing a business degree if they did not have sufficient financial resources.

The UWO School of Business Administration's undergraduate program changed markedly from 1950 to the mid-1990s. The program was always framed as a general degree that would prepare graduates to assume positions of senior authority within organizations, principally corporations. It was a program that was intended for aspiring corporate executives; there were no courses offered on small business during that forty-five-year period. It did not include specific specializations, as it was intended to cover all functions of a business, but students would have been able to focus on one area of business in their final year in the program. The business school grew over four and a half decades, with the number of faculty members increasing over time. The faculty were initially shaped by attendance at American business schools, especially Harvard, but they were eventually trained at Canadian schools, with UWO itself training its own faculty. The students, while not described in detail in program outlines, were mostly male. One key indicator that women were enrolling in the school by the mid-1980s was the absence in the program description of management as essentially a male occupation.

Three Undergraduate Programs

UBC, HEC, and UWO all developed undergraduate business programs that changed and expanded over time. Each school sought to teach a program with some liberal arts content while also providing an overview of the many functions found in large business organizations. The programs were founded in response to wider social and economic considerations. Business became more important in the post–World War II decades, and all three schools began offering undergraduate business and management education long before the war in response to perceived needs to train more people in that field. Two of the schools—UBC and HEC—were driven by similar imperatives as they were concerned with training managers to work in businesses in specific regions of Canada. HEC was especially unique because it offered business and management education in French, and within the context of students first attending a CEGEP from the late 1960s onward. UWO was different because its business school aspired to train managers to meet national business needs. Both its students and UBC's would have largely come directly from high school.

Differentiation between the programs is found in how they proceeded to educate students. UBC and HEC offered specialization options that expanded as decades progressed, while UWO never offered defined streams or concentrations. The programs were taught by faculty who at first were trained at American business schools but who more often earned their terminal degrees at Canadian schools as time passed. This trend was most evident at HEC and UWO, as faculty at those institutions had often earned their degrees at them. For HEC, offering business and management education in French additionally meant having faculty who could speak it so hiring HEC graduates was a logical choice. The HEC faculty produced scholarship written in French, which in turn could have been used in course curricula while adding to the existing business and management literature.

The impact of American management education was felt throughout the post-war decades, even if faculty were being trained at Canadian schools. The case teaching method was found at UBC, HEC, and UWO. The latter school embraced that pedagogical method with the fullest commitment. This leads to the issue of what students learned in these three undergraduate business programs. They were taught that they needed to have some liberal arts background in order to situate their business learning within a broader context. The importance of liberal arts and social science content in business and management degrees lessened at all three schools beginning in the 1970s and accelerated in the 1980s. Students needed to have substantial mathematics and quantitative analysis skills by the late 1980s. Computer systems had gone from being somewhat of a new aspect of business education to a core required subject of study. This meant that, while prospective students were encouraged to have a liberal arts background, they needed to begin shaping their program choices basically upon entry into university or CEGEP if they ultimately wished to enter a business school and management program.

The curriculums that formed the bases of the three undergraduate programs lead to another salient question: did these programs train people to manage or act as manager? Students at all three schools were assured, either implicitly or explicitly, that they were going to be trained to execute managerial functions. UWO's program descriptions would have increasingly led graduates to believe that they would enjoy an expeditious path to executive offices. Nothing in the descriptions of the programs indicated that students may well have only been ready to assume relatively modest entry-level work. The successive descriptions of the three programs argued to different degrees that understanding people was key to effective management. The programs all included significant content that pertained to personnel issues in their early years, such as the inclusion of personnel management courses as core requirements, but it waned in importance as topics such as finance, control, information systems, and accounting eventually became dominant. Even marketing, as shown at HEC, was a course that used statistics. The message conveyed by the content of these programs was that dealing with people meant managing and interpreting numbers. This approach, while seeming to actually diminish rather than accentuate the human aspect of business, must have been successful for UBC, HEC, and UWO because it grew in prominence from the 1950s to the 1990s. It would also become key to their respective graduate business programs.

Notes

1 Earle D. MacPhee, *History of the Faculty of Business Administration at the University of British Columbia* (Vancouver: University of British Columbia Press, 1976), 3.

2 University of British Columbia Archive (hereafter UBC), [Unknown]. 1945. "The University of British Columbia Calendar." P. UBC Calendars. Vancouver: University of British Columbia Press. August 30. doi:http://dx.doi.org/10.14288/1.0169865, 35.

3 [Unknown]. 1945. "The University of British Columbia Calendar." P. UBC Calendars. Vancouver: University of British Columbia. August 30. doi:http://dx.doi.org/10.14288/1.0169865,100.

4 [Unknown]. 1945. "The University of British Columbia Calendar." P. UBC Calendars. Vancouver: University of British Columbia. August 30. doi:http://dx.doi.org/10.14288/1.0169865, 143.

5 Lester F. Klimm, Otis P. Starkey, Norman F. Hall, *Introductory Economic Geography* (New York: Harcourt, Brace and Company, 1937), vii–viii.

6 Klimm, Starkey, Hall, *Introductory Economic Geography*, 231.

7 Klimm, Starkey, Hall, *Introductory Economic Geography*, 231.

8 Klimm, Starkey, Hall, *Introductory Economic Geography*, 231.

9 Klimm, Starkey, Hall, *Introductory Economic Geography*, 271.

10 Klimm, Starkey, Hall, *Introductory Economic Geography*, 271.

11 Klimm, Starkey, Hall, *Introductory Economic Geography*, 271.
12 Klimm, Starkey, Hall, *Introductory Economic Geography*, 287.
13 Klimm, Starkey, Hall, *Introductory Economic Geography*, 297–303.
14 [Unknown]. 1945. "The University of British Columbia Calendar." P. UBC Calendars. Vancouver: University of British Columbia. August 30. doi:http://dx.doi.org/10.14288/1.0169865, 143.
15 Frankin E. Folts, *Introduction to Industrial Management: Texts, Cases, and Problems* (New York: McGraw-Hill, 1949).
16 See Daniel, *MBA: The First Century* and Duff McDonald, *The Golden Passport*.
17 Folts, *Introduction to Industrial Management*, 8.
18 Folts, *Introduction to Industrial Management*, 38–40.
19 Folts, *Introduction to Industrial Management*, 447.
20 Folts, *Introduction to Industrial Management*, 441.
21 Folts, *Introduction to Industrial Management*, 441.
22 Folts, *Introduction to Industrial Management*, 444–445.
23 Harding, *The Social Construction of Management*.
24 [Unknown]. 1955. "The University of British Columbia Calendar." P. UBC Calendars. Vancouver: University of British Columbia. August 30. doi:http://dx.doi.org/10.14288/1.0170146, 11.
25 [Unknown]. 1955. "The University of British Columbia Calendar." P. UBC Calendars. Vancouver: University of British Columbia. August 30. doi:http://dx.doi.org/10.14288/1.0170146, 59.
26 [Unknown]. 1955. "The University of British Columbia Calendar." P. UBC Calendars. Vancouver: University of British Columbia. August 30. doi:http://dx.doi.org/10.14288/1.0170146, 135.
27 [Unknown]. 1955. "The University of British Columbia Calendar." P. UBC Calendars. Vancouver: University of British Columbia. August 30. doi:http://dx.doi.org/10.14288/1.0170146, 137–140.
28 [Unknown]. 1955. "The University of British Columbia Calendar." P. UBC Calendars. Vancouver: University of British Columbia. August 30. doi:http://dx.doi.org/10.14288/1.0170146, 143.
29 Dale Yoder, *Personnel Management and Industrial Relations* (New York: Prentice-Hall, 1945), 516.
30 Yoder, *Personnel Management*, 373–408.
31 Yoder, *Personnel Management*, 615–702.
32 Yoder, *Personnel Management*, 690.
33 [Unknown]. 1955 "The University of British Columbia Calendar." P. UBC Calendars. Vancouver: University of British Columbia. August 30. doi:http://dx.doi.org/10.14288/1.0170146, 21–22.
34 [Unknown]. 1965. "UBC Calendar." P. UBC Calendars. [Vancouver: University of British Columbia]. August 30. doi:http://dx.doi.org/10.14288/1.0169935, A12.
35 [Unknown]. 1965. "UBC Calendar." P. UBC Calendars. [Vancouver: University of British Columbia]. August 30. doi:http://dx.doi.org/10.14288/1.0169935, A17.
36 [Unknown]. 1965. "UBC Calendar." P. UBC Calendars. [Vancouver: University of British Columbia]. August 30. doi:http://dx.doi.org/10.14288/1.0169935, A32.
37 [Unknown]. 1965. "UBC Calendar." P. UBC Calendars. [Vancouver: University of British Columbia]. August 30. doi:http://dx.doi.org/10.14288/1.0169935, J21.
38 [Unknown]. 1965. "UBC Calendar." P. UBC Calendars. [Vancouver: University of British Columbia]. August 30. doi:http://dx.doi.org/10.14288/1.0169935, J21.

39 [Unknown]. 1965. "UBC Calendar." P. UBC Calendars. [Vancouver: University of British Columbia]. August 30. doi:http://dx.doi.org/10.14288/1.0169935, J22–J23.

40 UBC, Sauder School of Business Fonds, Box 46, Ledger 1960, Miss Commerce 1960.

41 [Unknown]. 1975. "The University of British Columbia Vancouver/ Canada Sixty-First Session Calendar 1975–76." P. UBC Calendars. Vancouver: University of British Columbia. August 30. doi:http://dx.doi.org/10.14288/1.0169863, 15.

42 [Unknown]. 1975. "The University of British Columbia Vancouver/ Canada Sixty-First Session Calendar 1975–76." P. UBC Calendars. [Vancouver: University of British Columbia]. August 30. doi:http://dx.doi.org/10.14288/1.0169863, 29.

43 [Unknown]. 1975. "The University of British Columbia Vancouver/ Canada Sixty-First Session Calendar 1975–76." P. UBC Calendars. [Vancouver: University of British Columbia]. August 30. doi:http://dx.doi.org/10.14288/1.0169863, 29.

44 [Unknown]. 1975. "The University of British Columbia Vancouver/ Canada Sixty-First Session Calendar 1975–76." P. UBC Calendars. [Vancouver: University of British Columbia]. August 30. doi:http://dx.doi.org/10.14288/1.0169863, 28.

45 [Unknown]. 1975. "The University of British Columbia Vancouver/ Canada Sixty-First Session Calendar 1975–76." P. UBC Calendars. [Vancouver: University of British Columbia]. August 30. doi:http://dx.doi.org/10.14288/1.0169863, 28.

46 [Unknown]. 1975. "The University of British Columbia Vancouver/ Canada Sixty-First Session Calendar 1975–76." P. UBC Calendars. [Vancouver: University of British Columbia]. August 30. doi:http://dx.doi.org/10.14288/1.0169863, 33.

47 [Unknown]. 1975. "The University of British Columbia Vancouver/ Canada Sixty-First Session Calendar 1975–76." P. UBC Calendars. [Vancouver: University of British Columbia]. August 30. doi:http://dx.doi.org/10.14288/1.0169863, 34.

48 UBC, Sauder School of Business Fonds, Box 46, File 46–3, 1976 Bachelor of Commerce Graduates.

49 [Unknown]. 1975. "The University of British Columbia Vancouver/ Canada Sixty-First Session Calendar 1975–76." P. UBC Calendars. [Vancouver: University of British Columbia]. August 30. doi:http://dx.doi.org/10.14288/1.0169863, 92.

50 [Unknown]. 1975. "The University of British Columbia Vancouver/ Canada Sixty-First Session Calendar 1975–76." P. UBC Calendars. [Vancouver: University of British Columbia]. August 30. doi:http://dx.doi.org/10.14288/1.0169863, 218–219.

51 [Unknown]. 1975. "The University of British Columbia Vancouver/ Canada Sixty-First Session Calendar 1975–76." P. UBC Calendars. [Vancouver: University of British Columbia]. August 30. doi:http://dx.doi.org/10.14288/1.0169863, 217.

52 [Unknown]. 1975. "The University of British Columbia Vancouver/ Canada Sixty-First Session Calendar 1975–76." P. UBC Calendars. [Vancouver: University of British Columbia]. August 30. doi:http://dx.doi.org/10.14288/1.0169863, 92.

53 UBC, Sauder School of Business Fonds, Box 1, File: A5.2 Executive Committee Correspondence, 1973–1977, "Plan for Development, 1973–1975".

54 [Unknown]. 1975. "The University of British Columbia Vancouver/ Canada Sixty-First Session Calendar 1975–76." P. UBC Calendars. [Vancouver: University of British Columbia]. August 30. doi:http://dx.doi.org/10.14288/1.0169863, 93.

55 [Unknown]. 1985. "The University of British Columbia 71st Session 1985–86 Calendar." P. UBC Calendars. Vancouver: Office of the Registrar, The University of British Columbia. August 30. doi:http://dx.doi.org/10.14288/1.0169975, 33.

56 [Unknown]. 1985. "The University of British Columbia 71st Session 1985–86 Calendar." P. UBC Calendars. Vancouver: Office of the Registrar, The University of British Columbia. August 30. doi:http://dx.doi.org/10.14288/1.0169975, 94–95.

57 [Unknown]. 1985. "The University of British Columbia 71st Session 1985–86 Calendar." P. UBC Calendars. Vancouver: Office of the Registrar, The University of British Columbia. August 30. doi:http://dx.doi.org/10.14288/1.0169975, 95.

58 [Unknown]. 1985. "The University of British Columbia 71st Session 1985–86 Calendar." P. UBC Calendars. Vancouver: Office of the Registrar, The University of British Columbia. August 30. doi:http://dx.doi.org/10.14288/1.0169975, 95.

59 [Unknown]. 1985. "The University of British Columbia 71st Session 1985–86 Calendar." P. UBC Calendars. Vancouver: Office of the Registrar, The University of British Columbia. August 30. doi:http://dx.doi.org/10.14288/1.0169975, 95.

60 [Unknown]. 1985. "The University of British Columbia 71st Session 1985–86 Calendar." P. UBC Calendars. Vancouver: Office of the Registrar, The University of British Columbia. August 30. doi:http://dx.doi.org/10.14288/1.0169975, 96.

61 [Unknown]. 1985. "The University of British Columbia 71st Session 1985–86 Calendar." P. UBC Calendars. Vancouver: Office of the Registrar, The University of British Columbia. August 30. doi:http://dx.doi.org/10.14288/1.0169975, 257–261.

62 [Unknown]. 1985. "The University of British Columbia 71st Session 1985–86 Calendar." P. UBC Calendars. Vancouver: Office of the Registrar, The University of British Columbia. August 30. doi:http://dx.doi.org/10.14288/1.0169975, 260.

63 [Unknown]. 1995. "The University of British Columbia 1995/96 Calendar." P. UBC Calendars. Vancouver: The University of British Columbia, Registrar's Office. August 30. doi:http://dx.doi.org/10.14288/1.0169848, 80–81.

64 [Unknown]. 1995. "The University of British Columbia 1995/96 Calendar." P. UBC Calendars. Vancouver: The University of British Columbia, Registrar's Office. August 30. doi:http://dx.doi.org/10.14288/1.0169848, 80.

65 UBC, Sauder School of Business Fonds, Box 46, File 46–5, Bachelor of Commerce Graduates 1996.

66 [Unknown]. 1995. "The University of British Columbia 1995/96 Calendar." P. UBC Calendars. Vancouver: The University of British Columbia, Registrar's Office. August 30. doi:http://dx.doi.org/10.14288/1.0169848, 57.

67 UBC, Earle D. MacPhee Fonds, Box 3, File 3–10, File: Winram, Edna E. B Comm 1943, Department of Commerce, Bureau of Recommendations.

68 UBC, Earle D. MacPhee Fonds, Box 3, File 3–10, File: Winram, Edna E. B Comm 1943, Department of Commerce, Bureau of Recommendations.

69 UBC, Earle D. MacPhee Fonds, Box 3, File 3–10, File: Winram, Edna E. B Comm 1943, Edna Jaffee (Winram) to Earle D. MacPhee, 19 January 1954.

70 UBC, Earle D. MacPhee Fonds, Box 3, File 3–10, File: Winram, Edna E. B Comm 1943, Edna Winram to E.H. Morrow, 17 July 1944.
71 UBC, Earle D. MacPhee Fonds, Box 3, File 3–10, File: Winram, Edna E. B Comm 1943, Edna Jaffee (Winram) to Earle D. MacPhee, 19 January 1954.
72 UBC, Earle D. MacPhee Fonds, Box 3, File 3–10, File: Winram, Edna E. B Comm 1943, Edna Jaffee (Winram) to Earle D. MacPhee, 19 January 1954.
73 UBC, Earle D. MacPhee Fonds, Box 3, File 3–11, File: Deguefe, Taffara 1947–1976, registrar document.
74 UBC, Earle D. MacPhee Fonds, Box 3, File 3–11, File: Deguefe, Taffara 1947–1976, V. R. Purser to George A. Garbutt, 25 February 1947.
75 UBC, Earle D. MacPhee Fonds, Box 3, File 3–11, File: Deguefe, Taffara 1947–1976, N.A.M. MacKenzie to Registrar C.B. Wood, 24 June 1947.
76 UBC, Earle D. MacPhee Fonds, Box 3, File 3–11, File: Deguefe, Taffara 1947–1976, E.H. Morrow to G.A. Blowers, 1 August 1947.
77 UBC, Earle D. MacPhee Fonds, Box 3, File 3–11, File: Deguefe, Taffara 1947–1976, Assistant Registrar Edith Allan to Taffara Degeufé, 10 November 1970.
78 UBC Archive, Earle D. MacPhee Fonds, Box 3, File 3–11, File: Deguefe, Taffara 1947–1976, Taffara Deguefe to C.C. Gourlay, Faculty of Commerce and Business Administration, 20 February 1974.
79 UBC, Earle D. MacPhee Fonds, Box 3, File 3–11, File: Deguefe, Taffara 1947–1976, Colin C. Gourlay to Kurt Waldheim, 1976 (draft). It was revealed subsequent to Waldheim's two terms as United Nations Secretary General that he had been involved to some extent in wartime atrocities committed by the German Army in World War II, see Jonathan Kandell, Kurt Waldheim dies at 88; "Ex-UN chief hid Nazi Past," *New York Times*, accessed 30 January 2018, www. nytimes.com/2007/06/14/world/europe/14iht-waldheim.3.6141106.html.
80 Taffara Degeufé obituary, *Vancouver Sun*, accessed 30 January 2018, www. legacy.com/obituaries/vancouversun/obituary.aspx?pid=174350588.
81 UBC, Earle D. MacPhee Fonds, Box 3, File 3–11, File: Deguefe, Taffara 1947–1976, Taffara Deguefe to UBC Faculty of Commerce and Business Administration, 15 November 1969.
82 [Unknown]. 1995. "The University of British Columbia 1995/96 Calendar." P. UBC Calendars. Vancouver: The University of British Columbia, Registrar's Office. August 30. doi:http://dx.doi.org/10.14288/1.0169848, 157.
83 For example see Brian Bemmels.
84 [Unknown]. 1995. "The University of British Columbia 1995/96 Calendar." P. UBC Calendars. Vancouver: The University of British Columbia, Registrar's Office. August 30. doi:http://dx.doi.org/10.14288/1.0169848, 382–385.
85 Pierre Harvey, *Histoire De L'Ecole Des Hautes Études Commericales De Montréal, Tome II: 1926–1970* (Montréal: Presses HEC, 2002).
86 Harvey, *Histoire De L'Ecole Des Hautes Études Commericales De Montréal, Tome II: 1926–1970*, 11.
87 Pierre Harvey, "The Founding of the École des Hautes Études Commerciales de Montréal", Barbara Austin, ed., *Capitalizing Knowledge: Essays on the History of Business Education in Canada* (Toronto: University of Toronto Press, 2000), 98.
88 École des hautes études commerciales de Montréal (HEC) Archive (hereafter HEC), Box 20591, File A007/G-01–0095, Cours de Preparation aux Affairs, 1957–1957, 12–13.
89 HEC, Box 20591, File A007/G-01–0095, Cours de Preparation aux Affairs, 1957–1957, 16.
90 HEC, Box 20591, File A007/G-01–0095, Cours de Preparation aux Affairs, 1957–1957, 17.

91 HEC, Box 20591, File A007/G-01–0095, Cours de Preparation aux Affairs, 1957–1957, 18–19.

92 HEC, Box 20591, File A007/G-01–0095, Cours de Preparation aux Affairs, 1957–1957, 18–19.

93 HEC, Box 20591, File A007/G-01–0095, Cours de Preparation aux Affairs, 1957–1957, 18.

94 HEC, Box 20591, File A007/G-01–0095, Cours de Preparation aux Affairs, 1957–1957, 19.

95 HEC, Box 20591, File A007/G-01–0095, Cours de Preparation aux Affairs, 1957–1957, 10.

96 HEC, Box 20591, File A007/G-01–0095, Cours de Preparation aux Affairs, 1957–1957, 8.

97 HEC, Box 20591, File A007/G-04–0095, Enseignements aux adultes a L'Ecole Des Hautes Etudes Commerciales de Montréal De 1999–1967 A 1973–1976, 7–9.

98 HEC, Box 20222, File A052/W1, Classes du Jour 1975–1976, 9–13.

99 HEC, Box 20222, File A052/W1, Classes du Jour 1975–1976, 9–13.

100 HEC, Box 20222, File A052/W1, Classes du Jour 1975–1976, 27.

101 HEC, Box 20222, File A052/W1, Classes du Jour 1975–1976, 45.

102 HEC, Box 20222, File A052/W1, Classes du Jour 1975–1976, 28.

103 HEC, Box 20222, File A052/W1, Classes du Jour 1975–1976, 31–38.

104 HEC, Box 20222, File A052/W1, Classes du Jour 1975–1976, 36.

105 HEC, Box 20222, File A052/W1, Classes du Jour 1975–1976, 31–32.

106 HEC, Box 20222, File A052/W1, Classes du Jour 1975–1976, 31.

107 HEC, Box 20222, File A052/W1, Classes du Jour 1975–1976, 17.

108 HEC, Box 20222, File A052/W1, Baccalauréat en administration des affairs classes du jour, 1985–1986, 9.

109 HEC, Box 20222, File A052/W1, Baccalauréat en administration des affairs classes du jour, 1985–1986, 10.

110 HEC, Box 20222, File A052/W1, Baccalauréat en administration des affairs classes du jour, 1985–1986, 11.

111 HEC, Box 20222, File A052/W1,Baccalauréat en administration des affairs classes du jour, 1985–1986, 11.

112 HEC, Box 21452. File 3–400, Sociologie du Travail, Hiver 1987, 1.

113 HEC, Box 21452. File 3–400, Sociologie du Travail, Hiver 1987, 3.

114 HEC, Box 21452. File 3–400, Sociologie du Travail, Hiver 1987, 4.

115 Gilles Dussault, "L'analyse sociologique du professionnalisme au Québec", *Professions* vol 19, no 2 (1978), pp. 161–170.

116 HEC, Box 20222, File A052/W1,Baccalauréat en administration des affairs classes du jour, 1985–1986, 51.

117 National Institute of Standards Technology, accessed 19 October 2017, www.itl.nist.gov/div898/software/dataplot/refman1/auxillar/cochran.htm.

118 HEC, Box 20222, File A052/W1, Baccalauréat en administration des affairs classes du jour, 1985–1986, 59.

119 HEC, Box 20222, File A052/W1, Baccalauréat en administration des affairs classes du jour, 1985–1986, 74.

120 HEC, Box 20222, File A052/W1, Baccalauréat en administration des affairs classes du jour, 1995–1996, 5–6.

121 HEC, Box 20222, File A052/W1, Baccalauréat en administration des affairs classes du jour, 1995–1996, 7.

122 HEC, Box 20222, File A052/W1, Baccalauréat en administration des affairs classes du jour, 1995–1996, 10.

123 HEC, Box 20222, File A052/W1, Baccalauréat en administration des affairs classes du jour, 1995–1996, 11.

124 HEC, Box 20222, File A052/W1, Baccalauréat en administration des affairs classes du jour, 1995–1996, 49.

125 HEC, Box 21542, File 2–400, Business Law (Droit Des Affairs), Autumn 1994 to Spring 1995, 1.

126 HEC, Box 20222, File A052/W1, Baccalauréat en administration des affairs classes du jour, 1995–1996, 5.

127 HEC, Box 21542, File 2–400, Business Law (Droit Des Affairs), Autumn 1994 to Spring 1995, 2.

128 HEC, Box 21542, File 2–400, Business Law (Droit Des Affairs), Autumn 1994 to Spring 1995, 3.

129 HEC, Box 21542, File 2–400, Business Law (Droit Des Affairs), Autumn 1994 to Spring 1995, 6.

130 HEC, Box 21542, File 2–400, Business Law (Droit Des Affairs), Autumn 1994 to Spring 1995, 7.

131 HEC, Box 21542, File 2–400, Business Law (Droit Des Affairs), Autumn 1994 to Spring 1995, 9.

132 HEC, Box 20222, File A052/W1, La Touche HEC, 1997–1998, 8.

133 HEC, Box 20222, File A052/W1, La Touche HEC, 1997–1998, 12.

134 HEC, Box 20222, File A052/W1, La Touche HEC, 1997–1998, 13.

135 See Austin et al., *Capitalizing Knowledge: Essays on the History of Business Education in Canada.*

136 Doreen Sanders, *Learning to Lead: In Celebration of Seven Decades of Business Education at Western, 1923–93* (London, ON: Western Business School, 1993), 8.

137 Sanders, *Learning to Lead*, 30.

138 Sanders, *Learning to Lead*, 34.

139 Sanders, *Learning to Lead*, 12.

140 Sanders, *Learning to Lead*, 13.

141 ARCC, UWO Calendars, UWO Business School Announcement, 1950, 11.

142 ARCC, UWO Calendars, UWO Business School Announcement, 1950, 8–10.

143 ARCC, UWO Calendars, UWO Business School Announcement, 1950, 15.

144 ARCC, UWO Calendars, UWO Business School Announcement, 1950, 16.

145 ARCC, UWO Calendars, UWO Business School Announcement, 1950, 16.

146 ARCC, UWO Calendars, UWO Business School Announcement, 1950, 16–17.

147 ARCC, UWO Calendars, UWO Business School Announcement, 1950, 17.

148 ARCC, UWO Calendars, UWO Business School Announcement, 1950, 31.

149 ARCC, UWO Calendars, UWO Business School Announcement, 1950, 19.

150 ARCC, UWO Calendars, UWO Business School Announcement, 1950, 19–21.

151 ARCC, UWO Calendars, UWO Business School Announcement, 1950, 21.

152 Donald Thain interview, 16 July 2012.

153 ARCC, UWO Calendars, UWO Business School Announcement, 1960, 7–8.

154 ARCC, UWO Calendars, UWO Business School Announcement, 1960, 8.

155 McDonald, *The Golden Passport*, 226–227.

156 ARCC, UWO Calendars, UWO Business School Announcement, 1960, 18.

157 ARCC, UWO Calendars, UWO Business School Announcement, 1960, 19.

158 ARCC, UWO Calendars, UWO Business School Announcement, 1960, 19.

159 ARCC, UWO Calendars, UWO Business School Announcement, 1960, 19.

160 ARCC, UWO Calendars, UWO Business School Announcement, 1960, 28–37.

161 ARCC, UWO Calendars, UWO Business School Announcement, 1960, 19.

162 ARCC, UWO Calendars, UWO Business School Announcement, 1960, 39.

163 ARCC, UWO Calendars, School of Business Administration, 1969–70, 36.
164 ARCC, UWO Calendars, School of Business Administration, 1969–70, 11.
165 ARCC, UWO Calendars, School of Business Administration, 1969–70, 13.
166 ARCC, UWO Calendars, School of Business Administration, 1969–70, 13.
167 ARCC, UWO Calendars, School of Business Administration, 1969–70, 17.
168 ARCC, UWO Calendars, School of Business Administration, 1969–70, 17.
169 ARCC, UWO Calendars, School of Business Administration, 1969–70, 17.
170 ARCC, UWO Calendars, School of Business Administration, 1969–70, 13.
171 ARCC, UWO Calendars, School of Business Administration, 1969–70, 14.
172 ARCC, UWO Calendars, School of Business Administration, 1969–70, 19.
173 ARCC, UWO Calendars, School of Business Administration, 1969–70, 29.
174 ARCC, UWO Calendars, School of Business Administration, 1969–70, 32.
175 ARCC, UWO Calendars, 1976–1977, C-3.
176 ARCC, UWO Calendars, 1976–1977, C-4.
177 ARCC, UWO Calendars, 1976–1977, C-5.
178 ARCC, UWO Calendars, 1976–1977, C-6.
179 ARCC, UWO Calendars, 1976–1977, 83.
180 ARCC, UWO Calendars, 1976–1977, C-9.
181 ARCC, UWO Calendars, 1976–1977, C-12.
182 ARCC, UWO Calendars, 1976–1977, A-43.
183 ARCC, UWO Calendars, 1976–1977, AC-3.
184 ARCC, UWO Calendars, 1986–1987, B3.
185 ARCC, UWO Calendars, 1986–1987, B3.
186 ARCC, UWO Calendars, 1986–1987, B4.
187 ARCC, UWO Calendars, 1986–1987, B4.
188 ARCC, UWO Calendars, 1986–1987, 310–316.
189 ARCC, UWO Calendars, 1986–1987, 315.
190 ARCC, UWO Calendars, 1986–1987, B5.
191 ARCC, UWO Calendars, 1987–1988, 48.
192 ARCC, UWO Calendars, 1994–1995, 50.
193 ARCC, UWO Calendars, 1994–1995, 50.
194 ARCC, UWO Calendars, 1994–1995, 51.
195 ARCC, UWO Calendars, 1994–1995, 51.
196 ARCC, UWO Calendars, 1994–1995, 33.

5 Universities and Graduate Management Education

Graduate management education became prevalent in Canada during the post–World War II decades, and it also in key ways became the type of business education with the most prolific public profile. Management programs usually came in the form of the Master of Business Administration (MBA) degree. The MBA became a standard for management training to such an extent that it was described in the 1980s as a "union card for yuppies," which was a pejorative term used to describe young urban professional people.[1] This chapter is going to describe the evolution of graduate management education, particularly the MBA, at the University of British Columbia (UBC), the University of Western Ontario (UWO), and École des hautes études commerciales de Montréal (HEC). These institutions built on their undergraduate programs by adding MBA programs that attracted students who aspired to large incomes and success in business. The chapter will address questions similar to those considered in the preceding one on undergraduate management education: what was taught in graduate programs, was there variation or similarity between the three schools, and what did enrolling in graduate business programs qualify students to do once they entered the job market? This chapter will also examine short-duration management programs and seminars that were offered by UBC, HEC, and UWO. It will additionally describe partnerships that three schools formed at home and abroad. The role that specific people and initiatives played in shaping graduate business and management programs is clearer than with undergraduate programs, and the impact of such people will be discussed in this chapter. Canadian graduate management education, as revealed through analyses of three universities, became institutionalized and successful in many ways, but it also developed some flaws.

Graduate management education developed in Canada after undergraduate programs were initially offered. The UWO School of Business Administration introduced the MBA degree to Canadian students in 1950 and, as Donald Thain recalled, UWO graduated approximately half of people earning this degree in the country by the early 1960s.[2] UBC, surely noting UWO's success, began offering the degree in 1954.[3]

HEC introduced an MBA in 1969.[4] This meant that the MBA was offered in both of Canada's official languages. As McDonald has noted, MBA programs were proliferating in the United States and overseas by the 1960s, and Canada was part of that trend.[5] The introduction of the degree additionally reflected further maturation of business and management education in Canada, as it meant that this field would have both undergraduate and graduate study as was found in other disciplines. The MBA and short-duration management training programs would develop with similarities and differences at the three universities, just as undergraduate education had followed the same path.

The University of British Columbia

The University of British Columbia Faculty of Commerce and Business Administration was shaped by a range of variables including geography, but it was also in many ways influenced by two faculty members who led the development of the business and management programs: Ellis H. Morrow and Earle D. MacPhee. As previously noted, Morrow was influenced by his Harvard experience and joined UBC in the late 1930s.[6] He believed in general business education, and argued in a 1940 report:

> The organization of the Department must primarily be attuned to the needs of the regular B.Com. graduate who has no specialized technical equipment to assist him to find his footing in business. The problem with this type of student is to educate him and to orient him. The limits of a four-year course from matriculation does intensify the problem.[7]

Morrow went late stated in his report that "granting of a Master's degree should be a fairly early consideration" but also telling suggested that "The Department of Commerce is designed primarily for me and in some respects is unsuitable for women."[8] Morrow's views were undoubtedly crucial in shaping the direction of business and commerce studies at UBC, including the eventual introduction of an MBA. It is also quite clear that studying business was something for men, not women, and, by implication, a certain type of man that fit a stereotype defined by Morrow and others at the university. Morrow's views discriminated against women, but he was sympathetic toward people of colour. He helped Commerce graduate James Kwong to become the first Chinese Canadian to earn a Chartered Accountant designation in British Columbia.[9] UBC's leadership established a committee to examine the institution's organization in 1949.[10] That study led to the transition of the Department of Commerce into the School of Commerce in 1950.[11] Morrow was actively involved in consultations regarding the university's future structure and expressed hope that Commerce would eventually become a separate faculty.[12] It was in the context of major organizational change that the MBA program was introduced.

The 1955 MBA program was taught in a School of Commerce comprised of twenty-six faculty, and eighteen others designated as part-time lecturers. All of the faculty in full-time positions were men, and five of the part-time members were women. There was one Asian man in the full-time ranks. There were only two from the entire group who had earned degrees from Harvard. There were several with credentials from other American universities, but they came from places in the Midwest and West like Minnesota, California, and Oregon. Most interestingly, seventeen members of the school had earned at least one degree at UBC. This meant that the university had developed sufficient expertise to train people who eventually found their way into the School of Commerce as faculty. There were some faculty who had earned degrees at other major Canadian institutions like the University of Toronto, but the majority had at least one credential from UBC.[13]

The degree required applicants to have a degree in Commerce, Arts, Law, Engineering, Forestry, Agriculture or Pharmacy. Prospective students were also required to have completed five undergraduate commerce courses and one in economics, or equivalent studies. Students who were admitted were required to take three required commerce courses and one elective, three credits that were not in commerce, and complete a thesis. This last requirement is important because it illustrated that the Commerce faculty felt that MBA students should engage in graduate-level research and writing. The 1955 MBA program, while expecting students to enter with some background in commerce education, afforded the opportunity to incorporate substantial learning from disciplines in other fields.[14]

The core of the MBA program involved completing Business Finance, Policy and Administration, and a Master's Seminar. These courses seemed appropriate, but two of the courses—Business Finance and Policy and Administration—were also used at the undergraduate level. The same textbook, *Policy Formulation and Administration*, was used by undergraduate and graduate students.[15] This raises an obvious question: just how much different was the 1955 MBA from the undergraduate Bachelor of Commerce degree? The answer seems to be that there was not much difference, and that the MBA would have been redundant for students who already possessed an undergraduate business degree. In fact, a student who completed the undergraduate Commerce program would have been exposed to far more actual business study than someone in the MBA. Obtaining an MBA beyond an undergraduate bachelor's degree also involved incurring additional costs, since the former cost $240 per term.[16] The MBA was still a relatively new offering, with only three students enrolled in it in 1955.[17]

The MBA program was a key UBC business offering by the mid-1960s. Key changes had occurred at the university since the mid-1950s. The School of Commerce became the Faculty of Commerce and Business Administration in 1956.[18] Ellis Morrow's aspiration had been realized. Moreover, Earle D. MacPhee was promoted from a professor's position and appointed as the first dean of the Faculty. He was different from Morrow as he had spent most of his career in business and also earned three master's degrees from the University of Edinburgh.[19] MacPhee was somewhat of an autodidact despite having earned those degrees, as he published articles on business and economic issues beginning in the early 1930s. His 1932 article in the *Credit Men's Journal*, which was published in Winnipeg, is an early example of his work and discussed challenges to the "capitalistic" system.[20] It was principally a critique of communism and written when MacPhee was comptroller of York Knitting Mills Ltd. He had moved from business to academia and brought an applied business perspective with him.

The mid-1960s MBA program at UBC altered since 1955. There were thirty-five business faculty members in 1965. It is not evident from the faculty listing how many were women, how many more visible minority academics had been hired, or where the faculty members had earned their degrees.[21] A Bachelor of Commerce degree was the main requirement for admission, but a degree in another discipline was acceptable provided that a person first complete a series of pre-requisites:

Industrial Relations
Managerial Accounting
Merchandising and Distribution
Business Finance
Industrial Organization[22]

It was thus considered crucial for anyone entering the MBA program to have some understanding of key business functions which, in this case, involved studying industrial relations:

A study of the problems of leadership motivation, and morale in industry. Particular attention will be directed towards the role of the personnel administrator in providing for the effective utilization of manpower resources in industry.[23]

Similar issues were the subject of Industrial Organization:

A survey of the management functions involved in establishing and operating a business with particular reference to manufacturing. Special reading assignments and written reports.[24]

Working in business in 1965, as viewed by the UBC School of Business and Commerce, meant working in industry and dealing with unionized workers.

Students who were successfully admitted to the MBA program were required to complete 15 units, with each course being worth between 1.5 and 3 units, and a thesis. There were twenty-nine courses from which students could choose. Ten of them were on subjects like accounting and finance, while only three were on labour relations or organizational behaviour. The rest of the courses covered a range of topics including marketing and business policy. International business was discussed within a socio-economic context in the Seminar in International Business:

> A comparative study of the business and marketing systems employed in selected nations of the world. The seminar will deal with the relationships between business and marketing practice and the socio-economic environments of these nations.

Computers were not specifically mentioned in the 1965 course descriptions, but the use of statistical data was covered in "Seminar in Data Processing: The processing of business data; manual, tabulating, and the electronic data-processing systems." The 1965 program thus principally required students to have facility with numbers.[25]

The nature of the 1965 MBA student body is not clear from the archival documents, but the university did have 36 enrolled students in the program, and all of them were men.[26] There were eight MBA graduates in 1964, which means that there were approximately four students registered in each year of the program.[27] This was a vast increase since the mid-1950s, when about one-eighth as many students enrolled as in the mid-1960s. The thirrty-six students enrolled in 1965 paid $423 over two terms, and this was the same fee assessed for any master's degree at UBC between 18 and 21 units.[28] The fee had increased somewhat since the preceding decade, but pursuing an MBA did not represent a bigger financial challenge than other master's degrees of similar weighting. The demographics and other details of the degree would change more rapidly into the 1970s than they had since the 1950s.

The UBC Faculty of Commerce and Business offered two master's degrees by 1975: an MBA and a Master of Science in Business Administration.[29] Both degrees were two years in duration, which was a significant change since the mid-1960s, although students who had Commerce or Business Administration undergraduate degrees could be admitted into the second year of the MBA.[30] The M.Sc. was described as:

> The M.Sc. degree is designed for graduate students who wish to prepare for specialized careers in the performance of technical and analytical functions or in the administration and management of non-profit organizations. It is expected that students undertaking this degree will have one of the following objectives: (1) to prepare

in some depth for specialized functions of an analytical nature such as urban land economics or management science or (2) to prepare somewhat broadly for careers with organizational management responsibilities, such as the administration of engineering activities or health care organizations.[31]

Students were told that there was no common core in the first year of the M.Sc., and that they would instead develop the program in conjunction with an academic advisor.[32] The M.Sc. was thus a degree that was even more focused on the use of numbers and statistical methods than the MBA. For example, the Urban Land Use concentration involved completing:

Economics of Location
Seminar in Contemporary Land Investment Problems
Seminar in Government Policy in Relation to Urban Land Ownership
Seminar in Mortgage Financing[33]

Prospective MBA students faced a daunting list of pre-requisites if they did not already possess a business degree of some type:

Quantitative Methods-Analysis
Quantitative Methods-Probability and Statistics
Quantitative Methods-Statistics
Quantitative Methods-Algebra
Introduction to the Computer in Business
Introduction to Administrative Studies
Financial Accounting
Managerial Accounting
Merchandising and Distribution
Business Finance

Students were also required to complete:

Intermediate Microeconomic Theory
Intermediate Macroeconomic Theory

Students could also take Transportation Policy.[34] The degree was organized around major business functions, but those functions were obviously deemed by the Faculty of Commerce and Business to require considerable ability in mathematics.

The MBA was more structured than the M.Sc., and it was divided into concentration areas although students could choose from offerings within those areas: Urban Land Economics, Industrial Relations Management, Transportation and Utilities, Accounting and Management Information Systems, Marketing, Finance, Production, Management Science,

Management and Policy. There were sixty-six courses available to students, with Industrial Relations Management, Accounting and Management Information Systems, Finance, and Management and Policy being the three largest subject areas. Only Industrial Relations was predominantly composed of courses that resembled liberal arts content:

Organizational Behaviour and Administration
Theory Research and Methodology in the Study of Organization Behaviour
Selected Problems in Labour Relations
Seminar in Labour Relations
Organization Development
The Measurement and Evaluation of Individual Behaviour in Work Organizations
International Comparative Labour Relations
Seminar in Organizational Behaviour
Seminar in Manpower Management
Organizational Behaviour Research Seminar

It is notable that Industrial Relations was the focus of a concentration rather than Personnel Management. This emphasis, as with the undergraduate program at UBC, reflected work and employment within British Columbia in the 1970s.[35]

A liberal arts background would not have prepared someone to attempt the MBA or M.Sc. curriculums. Grounding in commerce and business studies at the undergraduate level would have been required. The master's level business programs nonetheless drew growing numbers of students in the 1970s who had the requisite academic training to at least attempt a degree. There were ninety-two students in the M.Sc. program in the 1974–1975 academic year, and 182 in the MBA.[36] This was a six-fold increase just in MBA students from the mid-1960s and reflected enormous program growth in one decade. There were eighteen women in the M.Sc. in 1974–75 and twenty-one in the MBA.[37] Men still predominated in both programs, although a significantly higher ratio of women were in the M.Sc. than in the MBA. The graduate business programs also represented the single largest group of enrollments among the various master's degrees offered by UBC in professional areas like pharmaceutical science, architecture, or engineering. Indeed, their combined enrollments of 274 students were only exceeded by the programs offered in science (283) and arts (464).[38] The UBC Faculty of Commerce and Business may not have been as significant in terms of undergraduate education as other faculties at the university, but it was a key part of graduate education. Enrollments had surged in graduate business programs, but the $510 per year tuition fee for a master's degree was the same as it was for other graduate degrees.[39]

It is also possible to glean some insights into the nature of the mid-1970s student population. There were 100 graduates between the M.Sc. and MBA in 1976, with twenty-eight in the former program and seventy-two in the latter one.[40] There was ethnic diversity within this group of graduates as thirty-four of them came from either Asian or South-Asian backgrounds.[41] There was less gender diversity as there were only ten women graduating in 1976, although four of them were Asian.[42] The largest number of students—twenty-five—had concentrated in Finance.[43] They were followed by sixteen who had focused on Accounting and Management Information Systems.[44] In contrast, there were only two students who did their concentrations in Organizational Behaviour/Industrial Relations.[45] The students were predominantly in their early to mid-twenties, and some were married. The fact that their marital status was listed along with prior employment indicates that students were expected to have some life experience prior to entering a graduate business program. The demographics and interests of students would evolve as the MBA and M.Sc. programs entered the 1980s.

The 1985 UBC graduate business programs continued to be composed of the MBA and M.Sc. offerings. The program calendar for that year provided a relatively brief description of the purpose of the MBA:

> The objective of the M.B.A. program is to offer an integrated course of study in Management and Administration and the important cognate disciplines to properly qualified persons holding a Bachelor's degree . . . The M.B.A. is intended to be a general program and narrow specialization is discouraged. Because of this general and integrated nature of the M.B.A. program mitigates against the degree of specialized study normally required for a thesis. Students interested in developing a research capability, and in writing a thesis, should consider the M.Sc. program in which it is possible to develop a more specialized course of study.[46]

This was a relatively brief summary of the purpose of the degree, but the M.Sc. description was more specific:

> The M.Sc. (Business Administration) degree is intended for graduate students who wish to prepare for specialized careers in the performance of technical and analytical functions in organizations. In contrast to the M.B.A. program whose regulations prevent excessive specialization in any one area of study, the M.Sc. program allows as much concentration in any one field of study as may be consistent with the individual student's educational goals. It is expected that students entering this program will have the objectives of developing analytical and research competence in fields of specialty such as personnel administration, management science, accounting and

management information systems, transportation, urban land economics, or market research.[47]

The terms "analytical and research competence" meant facility with numbers. The first year of the 1985 MBA program additionally reflected this quantitative orientation, even though it was presented as a general program that avoid specialization, as it stipulated:

Decision Analysis
Quantitative Methods-Analysis
Human Resources Management I
Human Resources Management II
Management Information Systems
Financial Accounting
Managerial Accounting
Marketing Management
Business Finance
Intermediate Microeconomic Analysis
Intermediate Macroeconomic Analysis[48]

Industrial Relations was now gone from the first year of the program, having been supplanted by the more general Human Resource Management. It was still a possible concentration in the M.Sc. program.[49] Human Resources Management I was presented as:

> Provides overview of the management of individuals, groups and organizations in the absence and presence of labour unions. Deals with the functions of management and with issues such as conflict, efficiency, leadership, interpersonal relations and negotiation.[50]

This was likely the only time that students specifically heard about people programs in organizations, as other required courses like Decision Analysis were more numerous:

> The use of quantitative methods to analyze decision problems. The analysis of decisions under uncertainty using the methods of probability and statistical decision theory. Techniques for analyzing data such as hypothesis testing and regression analysis. The analysis of allocation problems using the techniques of mathematical programming. Features of quantitative analysis of managerial significance are emphasized.[51]

The 1985 program could only be called general if mathematics was considered the most common aspect of commerce and business.

Both the M.Sc. and MBA had become two-year degrees, without advanced standing for work that had been completed at the undergraduate level, and the MBA could be completed on a part-time basis.[52] The length of the degrees and the content of the programs was not a deterrent as UBC had 364 students enrolled in its MBA in 1985, and forty-eight in the M.Sc.[53] The proportion of women in both programs had also increased, with fifteen in the M.Sc. and ninety-nine in the MBA.[54] More detailed demographic information is not available for 1985, but the major increase in women from 10 to 28 percent of enrollments since the mid-1970s is notable. It is also clear that a higher ratio of women saw value in pursuing an MBA over an M.Sc. The MBA had the second-highest enrollments of any master's degree at UBC by 1985 and was only surpassed by the Master of Arts in Education (M.Ed.).[55] It was a key part of graduate education at the university. The tuition charged to MBA and M.Sc. students was $3,375 for both years, which was the same fee for every other master's degree offered by the university other than Dentistry.[56]

The master's level business and management programs offered by UBC in the mid-1990s were markedly different from what had preceded them in the 1950s. The Faculty of Business and Commerce still offered an MBA and M.Sc., but the content of the programs had altered since they were introduced. This was especially true of the MBA. The 1995 MBA program was described as:

> It is anticipated that a revised M.B.A. program will be offered in the 1995/96 academic year on a full and part-time basis. The program will include an integrated core, specializations, internships, professional development weeks and modular course offerings . . . The objective of the M.B.A. program is to offer an integrated course of study in Management and Administration and the important cognate disciplines to properly qualified persons holding a Bachelor's degree . . . The M.B.A. is intended to be a general program and narrow specialization is discouraged. The general integrated nature of the M.B.A. program mitigates against the degree of specialized study normally required for a thesis. Students interested in developing a research capability, and in writing a thesis, should consider the M.Sc. program in which it is possible to develop a more specialized course of study.[57]

The M.Sc. description was the same as in 1985. The description for the MBA had altered somewhat from 1985, but the changes in program content for the first year were evident:

Decision Analysis 1
Decision Analysis II
Quantitative Methods-Analysis
Human Resources Management I
Human Resources Management II
Information Systems for Management

Financial Accounting
Managerial Accounting
Marketing Management
Business Finance
Intermediate Microeconomic Analysis
Intermediate Macroeconomic Analysis[58]

Students were advised that they should take a broad range of courses in their second year, but they would have already been influenced to believe that managing was driven by numbers. There was more quantitative content in the 1995 curriculum than ever before. Both master's programs attracted more students that they had in 1985. The tuition fee for the M.Sc. had increased to $4,558, while the MBA was $7,000.[59] This was a 35 percent increase for the M.Sc. since 1985, and a 52 percent increase for the MBA. There were 335 MBA enrollments in 1994 to 1995, and fifty-one in the M.Sc.[60] The proportion of women was essentially the same as in 1985, with 119 in the MBA and twenty in the M.Sc.[61] MBA enrollments had slipped somewhat in relation to other graduate programs—the M.Ed continued to be the largest single master's program at UBC—but the MBA and the M.Sc. continued to be significant components of graduate education.

The demographics of the graduate business students also continued to evolve into the mid-1990s. The 1996 graduating master's programs class included fifty-eight people, and twenty-three were women.[62] Most notably, women of Asian and South Asian descent were the most numerous in that group. In fact, there were more Asian and South Asian women graduating than there were men from with those backgrounds. This is important because it suggests that women from diverse cultural backgrounds saw value in pursuing an MBA. Indeed, the fact that close to half of the graduating class were women indicates that the MBA was viewed by them as a good experience that would improve their career prospects. It was clearly not viewed as a field of study that favoured men.[63] The career interests of the 1996 graduates revolved around three areas: International Business, Finance, and Consulting.[64] Urban Land Economics, Transportation and Logistics, and Policy and Strategic Management attracted the least amount of interest.[65] Students were choosing careers in various types of service industries and also wanted to perhaps work in other countries as well.

The UBC master's level commerce and business programs changed considerably from the 1950s to the 1990s. The Faculty of Commerce and Business grew out of a department, and the students coming into it could expect to participate in programs that would grow in size and complexity. Students also likely saw many of their career aspirations realized. A 1976 MBA graduate named Lindsay Gordon is a particularly prominent example of the type of career to which UBC commerce students could aspire. Gordon was born in the United Kingdom and had worked in a range of jobs including truck driving and sales before coming to Canada.[66] He then worked in administrative jobs in Canada before entering the MBA program at UBC. Gordon was 24 years old in 1976 and indicated interests in international banking and financial management in his graduate profile.[67] While there were surely people from every UBC MBA graduating class who did not realize their career aspirations, Gordon had a very distinguished career after leaving the graduate business program. He eventually rose to the position of president and CEO of HSBC Bank Canada, was a governor of the Business Council of British Columbia, and eventually became chancellor of UBC.[68]

The students who enrolled in the master's level programs further benefited from their time at the university due to their exposure to faculty who worked to achieve scholarly accomplishments. UBC was home to some notable business faculty at different periods in its post-war history. Anil Verma was one example. He completed a Ph.D. at the Massachusetts Institute of Technology and joined the UBC faculty as an assistant professor in 1984.[69] Verma would subsequently join the faculty at the University of Toronto in 1989 and become director of that university's Center for Industrial Relations and Human Resources.[70] He would eventually author a considerable body of work on industrial relations in Canada and Asia and developed a significant international profile.[71]

Students who wished to take a shorter program than an MBA, or who had an MBA and wished to acquire some additional knowledge on a specific management area, could take one of the Faculty of Commerce and Business's many executive seminars. A range of programs were offered by the mid-1970s. There were several reasons cited for offering such programs, including to keep middle and senior executives informed of new trends in administration, offer faculty opportunities to interact with practitioners, show the unique aspects of the faculty, and "provide a source of support for a variety of Faculty activities."[72] That latter point at least partially meant that seminars would hopefully be a source of revenue for the university. Early programs, such as those offered in the 1970s, benefited from British Columbia government support. A report on 1974–75 programs noted how assistance from the BC Minister of Consumer Services, in the form of a grant, had enabled the executive programs to run on a break-even basis.[73] Running seminars in conjunction with government departments was viewed as a viable programming option.[74]

There were also management education and training agreements concluded with specific organizations and others that were oriented toward different business themes. Several programs were developed in the late 1970s and into the 1980s that dealt with topics such as identifying and training a good secretary. That particular 1979 program, called "The Effective Secretary," was three days long, taught by someone who held an MBA, and cost $425 to attend.[75] A 1986 two-day seminar titled "Dealing

With Troubled and Troublesome Employees" is another example of what the UBC Faculty of Commerce and Business offered outside of regular degree programs. Attendees at that seminar were taught by a faculty member with a Ph.D. in Organizational Behaviour, paid $395 to be there, and were taught how to use methods such as "positively oriented discipline" to deal with people problems at work.[76] Those programs clearly had the potential to generate significant revenues for UBC, with relatively little cost in terms of time and resources. The 1986 programs were run in conjunction with the University of Victoria.

UBC also sought to export its business and management education acumen abroad. A partnership that UBC began in 1960 in conjunction with the University of Malaya is an early example of the type of international initiative that Canadian business programs would pursue. Subsequent discussion will show that HEC and UWO explored similar partnerships; sometimes with mixed results. The Malaysian program was a result of another deliberate government policy initiative, indeed one influenced by international governmental discussions. Governments from across the British Commonwealth met in Colombo, Ceylon (later Sri Lanka), in 1950 to discuss ways of improving economic development in South and Southeast Asia.[77] The Colombo Plan was the result of that meeting. Thwarting the possible spread of Communism was a key objective, and Canada was an early contributor to the plan.[78] Canadian universities became part of Colombo Plan efforts as they were encouraged to forge links with their counterparts in less economically developed Commonwealth nations, and Malaya (later Malaysia) was one of them.

The 1960 agreement that UBC concluded with the University of Malaya in Kuala Lumpur was initiated at the direct request of the Canadian government. Canada would sponsor UBC as it helped with the formation of a Department of Business Administration at the Malaysian university. The Canadian Department of Trade and Commerce provided funding to UBC, and the Canadian high commissioner in Malaya was also involved in direct discussions with local authorities. The contract signed with the Canadian government specified that the partnership would initially last for five years and would cost the Canadian government $242,972. The estimated budget was developed by UBC.[79]

Earle MacPhee discussed the University of Malaya project in his history of the Faculty of Commerce and Business and, while referring to the Colombo Plan and involvement of the Canadian government, did not indicate the purpose of the plan or that Canada was covering the cost of the program. He did note that faculty travelled from Canada to Kuala Lumpur in 1961 to teach Accounting and Business Management.[80] The Colombo Plan, meaning the Canadian government, also provided scholarships starting in 1962 for Malaysian students.[81] Students did so to attend UBC, earn MBAs, then return home to work as assistant lecturers at the University of Malaya.[82] UBC continued to work with its Malaysian counterpart into the early 1970s, with the Canadian International Development Agency (CIDA) providing funding in 1972 for further education program development.[83] The twelve-year duration of the UBC and University of Malaya project—funded by the Canadian government—illustrates that it was considered a success and met the objectives of the Colombo Plan. Non-governmental funding also supplemented what was contributed by countries like Canada that participated in the Colombo Plan. Correspondence involving the University of Singapore—Singapore was part of Malaysia until 1965—shows that the Ford Foundation also sponsored Malaysian students who wished to study abroad.[84]

UBC's Faculty of Business and Commerce also formed partnerships at home. A 1985 Senior Manager's Development program was developed for the native community and was intended for "persons holding senior management of administrative positions with Bands, Tribal Councils or Indian Organizations."[85] The program was offered in conjunction with the Centre for Indian Training and Research, which was an affiliate of the British Columbia Tribal Forum. There were three, four-day long sessions: Decision Analysis and Policy Development, The Management of Information Resources, and Management of Human Resources.[86] The sessions were led by full-time faculty, and cost $100 each. This particular partnership program led to others with BC's first nations community. By 1998, UBC was invited through its Centre for Management Development to begin working on a Certificate in First Nations Leadership.[87] Native groups obviously saw value in working with UBC to offer management and leadership training, and the university had the same view. The programs that were offered did not necessarily require prior business knowledge but were intended for people working in leadership roles that required management skills.

The Faculty of Commerce and Business pursued partnership ideas that were brought forward by external non-governmental organizations as well. An Aviation Professional Management Development Program proposal was developed in 1996 in partnership with the International Aviation Management Training Institute.[88] The idea of offering programs with the Land Research Institute of Korea Land Corporation was also explored in 1996.[89] The Faculty of Commerce and Business noted that the university had previously enjoyed success with educating students from Korean companies including Lucky GoldStar (later LG) and Hanjung (Korea Heavy Industries Ltd.). Some programs were not necessarily intended to generate revenue and instead provided links that added to student learning experiences. For instance, the Faculty of Commerce and Business placed student interns from the Industrial Relations Management Division in work study at the International Woodworkers of America (IWA) union in BC in the early 1990s. The union was not the only organization in which students were placed, but it is somewhat striking that business school students had the choice of interning with a union. The IWA reported back that the students did exemplary work while on placement, and obviously felt that having some links to a business school was worthwhile.[90]

The UBC Faculty of Commerce and Business grew enormously from the 1940s to the 1990s in terms of number of students and faculty and also due to the range of graduate programs that it offered. The programs were taught by a group of faculty that expanded considerably, and there were people on faculty who built stature in their fields. The student body markedly altered from the 1950s to the 1990s. Women gradually entered UBC's graduate business and management programs, with many of them showing particular interest in earning an MBA. There was evolving diversity among the women who studied in the graduate management programs as women from Asian and South Asian backgrounds eventually out-numbered their peers with European ancestry. Indeed, graduate business and management programs at UBC attracted a lot of men and women who reflected Canada's growing post–World War II ethnic diversity. The Faculty of Business and Commerce formed partnerships with a range of different groups, both within British Columbia and overseas. The state, in the form of both provincial and federal governments, played a key role in some of those partnerships.

The graduate business and management degrees became increasingly quantitative in nature as decades passed, and students coming into them would have needed substantial ability with mathematics. The M.Sc. was described as a more specialized degree than the MBA but, in practice, neither was really a general management degree. The eventual dominance of finance and accounting diminished the role of other fields like organizational behaviour and industrial relations, and those were fields that were associated with people problems at work. Students learned how to manage functions like finance and to interpret the operation of organizations through numeric methods. This approach was obviously deemed effective by the Faculty of Business and Commerce, as more of it was included as time progressed, and the number of business and management students increased. Somewhat similar trends would also emerge in Québec at HEC.

École Des Hautes Études Commerciales De Montréal

École des hautes études commerciales de Montréal (HEC) offered its first graduate program in 1968. This was later than UBC, and much later than the University of Western Ontario. This section will focus solely on HEC's MBA program, although the school also offered an M.Sc and Diplôme en sciences administratives (DSA), because of the larger amount of archival sources on the MBA. HEC's development of a Maîtrise en Administration des Affairs (MAA in French, MBA in English) program was part of the general post-war introduction of graduate business and management education in Canada, although, as with the school's undergraduate program, there were distinct aspects its graduate programs. The introduction of HEC's graduate program coincided with the implementation of the new undergraduate degree in administrative affairs (BAA). The creation of both programs was presented as a new step for the school.[91]

The new MBA program was described as:

> In an environment characterized by change, the growing interdependence of the public and private sectors, the internationalization of markets and the multiplicity of multinational enterprises, the HEC master's course aims to train administrative executives who can occupy managerial positions or act as advisers to those who will occupy these functions. The master's program in business administration, lasting two years, is an integrated and autonomous whole characterized by an interdisciplinary approach where we find the existence of a common core and optional courses.[92]

This description differed from the UBC MBA program as it placed the study of business and management within a context that included the public sector. The description was broad, but also included some other specific objectives including the need to place issues within an international context. Most notably, it suggested that it could train people who would advise managers as well as those who exercised managerial functions. This implies that the framers of the program identified considerable nuance in the practice of management and that managing need not actually mean being a manager.

Students entering the HEC program in 1971 had several study options. They could pursue a general master's degree without a thesis, one in international business without a thesis, or a specialized degree with a thesis in one of these fields:

Human Resource Management
Marketing
Finance
Control
Production
Operational Research
Applied Economics[93]

Human Resource Management was the only concentration that included more social science content such as courses in human relations. Organizational Theory was a core course in that concentration and was presented as:

> The administrator sets goals and seeks to achieve them by regularly making decisions. It is important to study how he plans, organizes his

resources, uses his authority, divides and share his tasks with his subordinates, coordinates the activities of his collaborators and controls the use of his resources to introduce corrective measures. In addition, part of the course will be devoted to the study of the cultural and social environment in which he evolves. Finally, the study of various types of economic or non-economic organizations in the private and public sectors will enable the student to question the universality and transferability of administrative concepts.[94]

This course was aligned with the overall program objective of placing management within a broad social and cultural context. Furthermore, although the emphasis was on what administrators do in their daily duties, the course would place this analysis within a wider theoretical framework.

Courses such as Organizational Theory and Human Relations were two of thirteen courses that had at least some social science orientation, with the others including Personnel and Labour Relations, Economics, Problems in Personnel Administration, Management Policy, International Management, and Comparative Leadership in International Perspective. This last course listing—Le leadership comparé dans une perspective international—was important because it clearly used the term "leadership" in its title. This was something that had not yet occurred at UBC and, as later analysis will show, at UWO. It is also interesting that "leadership" was in the title even though the rest of it was in French. That title reflected the fact that, while management was taught and practiced in many languages, English predominated in management literature.[95]

The course on International Management was important because it implied two things: that HEC graduates would perhaps work internationally and do so in French, and that Québec-based businesses could be international. The course included:

> The first part of the course in International Management develops and integrates certain disciplines in international perspective: economics, finance, and marketing. These subjects are treated from the perspective of the businessman and company. The second part of the course shows how to isolate and resolve problems of administrative policy, financial policy, and commercial policy that are specifically relevant to international business.[96]

The balance of the early 1970s MBA program was composed of courses that required students to have facility with numbers, including three mathematics courses, one in finance, and one in computer programming.[97] Other courses that dealt with broader aspects of how organizations operate, such as Administrative Policy, rounded out the curriculum.

The early 1970s faculty teaching in the HEC MBA program were overwhelmingly francophone, with a slight amount of diversity evident among them. There was one Asian man named Joseph K. Chang, and a woman named Jeannine MacNeil.[98] The composition of the MBA student body is not evident from the 1969 brochure, nor is the amount that students paid to attend HEC. The MBA degree was two years in duration, and potential students were advised that they should have already earned an undergraduate degree with distinction along with possessing a foundation in administrative sciences, mathematics, economics, and social sciences.[99] Students with a range of different undergraduate degree concentrations could have potentially applied based on those criteria, but a firm grounding in subjects like mathematics would have indeed been necessary to attempt the first year of the program. It is again noteworthy that familiarity with social sciences was encouraged, which suggests that HEC incorporated at least some social science methodology in its pedagogical methods. There would be similar trends that would continue in further iterations of the program.

The 1970s were a period of considerable deliberation within HEC about the nature of the school's programs, including the direction of graduate education. Since some of these discussions can be revealed, it is more appropriate for this part of this analysis to focus on what was being said within HEC rather than what was found in the program guides. The discussion over the place that social sciences would occupy within the school's programs was perhaps the most striking deliberation to occur in the early 1970s. A committee on the place of social sciences was formed in August 1973 and produced an interim report in June 1974 that made some comments about HEC's curriculum. The committee's report indicated that its membership had been interdisciplinary, and the report aimed to reflect the members' different views and positions.[100]

The report presented some key arguments, including:

> The social sciences have two roles to play. It is firstly important to know how to derive from the various human sciences valuable references to human activity. It is secondly important to be able to make useful transfers (of knowledge) for a better learning of what is administration.[101]

The committee essentially did not question the place of social sciences at HEC, but noted student concerns regarding this subject area, stating, "They (the students) mention that at CEGEP, they are taught theory, so they expect to come here to find practice."[102] This is an important observation because, as the chapter on community colleges showed, the CEPEG system was supposed to be more oriented to practical learning than theory. Some students coming out of CEGEP, at least in the early 1970s, obviously experienced something different.[103]

The committee on the role of the social sciences drew a distinction between the social sciences and management:

> The committee made a distinction between humanities and management. The role of administration as a function is surely to ensure the profitability of the organization and to do this, it is normal to look in the social sciences for what can be useful in management, independently of what is found in social sciences fundamentals. The social sciences, on the other hand, are more oriented towards man and society. The goal is not instrumental. There is therefore a certain tension between the two approaches that must be able to transform into drive. This distinction made by the committee, however, does not imply a gap between the two.

There is a contradiction in this statement. The committee was attempting to say in a nuanced way that social sciences mattered in management education but that they would play an applied role and not be incorporated to the fullest possible extent. It is also clear that the HEC committee members thought that they had student interests in mind when they articulated that position, and their belief was that students wanted applied learning coming out of CEGEPs. Management, regardless of the program, was to be taught as an applied vocation with only as much theory as necessary.[104]

The fact that an MBA could be earned in French at HEC drew media attention in Québec, including the English-language press. The *Montréal Star* devoted a lengthy 1971 article to the HEC MBA program and described how it complemented other new offerings at the University of Sherbrooke and Laval University. The article noted how people interested in taking a graduate business degree previously would have had to apply to an English-speaking university either in Québec or elsewhere in Canada. HEC was "at the crossroads of European and American ways of thinking" and, as the MBA program director argued, "many Québec administrators, especially French people, look upon our graduates (current BA graduates) as theorists who can be of no help to them." HEC saw itself as responding to the needs of the province, the business community, and students by providing what it considered to be a unique degree that would impart marketable skills.[105]

The MBA program attracted students, so the structure of the program held appeal for people wanting to study business. There were some criticisms of it, including from potential students. For example, one 1977 applicant to the program expressed enormous indignation over having to respond to the question: "In your opinion, what role does profit play in our society?" The prospective student considered the question "insidious and misplaced" and that it was equivalent to asking someone his or her political affiliation or religious orientation. The question posed was intriguing because it required an answer informed by at least some theoretical understanding of management and capital, yet HEC was supposed to have adopted a more practical orientation a few years earlier. This particular example also indicates that HEC could attract highly opinionated applicants who were not reluctant to challenge the school's leadership.[106]

This pattern of challenging the school's practices also occurred in more subtle ways as well. In 1970, sixteen students signed a petition asking that a course be made optional in the second semester.[107] In another instance in 1973, the students objected to one of their peers being prevented from continuing with the second year of the MBA program because of academic reasons. In a two-page letter, the MBA students' association advocated for the student who was not being permitted to proceed with the program.[108] This letter, while much more respectful in tone to the one sent by the enraged 1977 program applicant, is extraordinary as it challenged pedagogical decisions made by the faculty. It implied, in the case of the student who was obliged to leave the program, that the other graduate students knew how to better handle the case than the faculty. It is entirely possible that the student in question appealed to the MBA students' association for help, and the association responded with solidarity rather than indifference.

The 1970s were a key decade for HEC, and the programs that were offered in the late 1970s and into the 1980s expanded on what was introduced in earlier years. The school was offering a Master of Science in Management by 1978. That degree was described as for students:

> Who desire to specialize in a particular area of management and acquire distinctive competence in the application of techniques of scientific analysis to problems specific to management. It aims to train specialists in one or the other of the following fields: applied economics, finance, international management, public sector management, human resource management and marketing.[109]

There was one common required course for all of the concentration areas called Economics of the Business Organization, with the concentrations having their own specific expectations.[110] For instance, the human resource management stream required:

Forecasting and Development of Human Resources
Conflict Management
Seminar on Social System Techniques
Labour Economics
Problems of Personnel Administration
Problems of Labour Relations
Management, Leadership and Personality
Research and Consultation Methods in Management
Management of Public Services[111]

Social sciences appeared in titles like Labour Economics and was clearly evident in the description of courses such as Economics of the Business Organization:

> The purpose of this course is to study the enterprise, conceived in the broadest sense, as an organization which responds to imperatives and desires expressed in economic terms or whose behavior is evaluated in similar terms. The problems of existence, purpose and forms of enterprise are examined under various aspects related to the characteristics and conditions of the coherence between the internal structures and the objectives of the enterprise: the translation of individual and social desires in economic terms, the study of the constraints imposed by the environment of the company, the relations between the characteristics and the forms of enterprise (cooperative, socialist, capitalist, etc), the analysis of the contributions of the sciences of the behavior, the theory economic and operational research to the problem of the organization of the enterprise, etc.[112]

This was a course substantially informed by social science methodology. The idea that forms of business enterprise other than capitalist would be examined was important because it demonstrated a willingness to include a range of viewpoints.

The MBA program also developed from its origins in the early 1970s. Students entering it in 1989 were required to have much more quantitative ability than their 1970s predecessors. There were six required preparatory courses that had to be completed before entering the program:

Introduction to Computers
Preparation in Quantitative Methods
Mathematics of Interest
Probability Calculus
Statistics for Decisions
Probability and Statistics

Requiring students to have such a degree of mathematics and related subjects was a serious change from what the program required when it was founded. Students who possessed undergraduate degrees in subjects like mathematics, statistics, engineering, or a science discipline would have been able to meet the learning expectations placed on them, but students with training in social science or humanities subjects would have found the program to be difficult.[113]

The MBA underwent further expansion by 1989 and included five program concentrations: Marketing, Finance, Human Resource Management, Operations and Production Management, and Information

Systems. The Human Resource concentration most closely approximated a social science approach to management education:

Personnel Management Problems
Labour Relations Problems
Seminar in Human Resource Management in International Perspective
Compensation and Benefit Administration
Management, Leadership and Personality
Seminar in Management and Culture[114]

There was one course available in the MBA program called Business Law that dealt with the legal environment in which corporations would operate:

This course, oriented toward the launching of businesses, mainly aims to familiarize the student from concrete management situations with the main notions of company law and to teach him to identify and prevent current legal problems inherent in the structure, organization and operation of the company. The legal aspects of partnership, shareholding and business combinations will also be addressed. The discussion of practical cases (from the experience of the participants) is privileged.[115]

There was also a course called Legislative Environment that was an elective in the MBA program:

Study of the legal context in which the manager is called to work. In a business law approach, some of these themes will be seen: duties and categories of the law; the division of powers in constitutional law and the exercise of those powers; the administration of justice; economic law; property; contracts and obligations as a result; consumer protection; the civil and criminal liability of the director and the company. The discussion of cases drawn from the experience of the participants is encouraged.[116]

Those courses, if an MBA student chose to take them both, would have provided a clear understanding of the legal environment in which management operated. They would have linked the internal functions of the firm to a wider social and legal context. These courses also were obviously not quantitative in nature, but quantitative ability would still be a core requirement into the 1990s.

The HEC MBA program of the mid-1990s reflected more change from the 1980s. It required incoming students to complete preparatory courses:

Introduction to Computers
Preparation in Quantitative Methods

Mathematics of Interest
Probability and Statistics[117]

This was slightly fewer preparatory courses than had been required in 1989, so HEC had obviously decided that less direct exposure to mathematics was required by 1995. There were a series of required courses before students were able to diverge at all in the third step (semester) of the program:

Administration
Organizational Behaviour
Mathematics for Decision Making
Microeconomics
Accounting Information and Management
Marketing
Finance
Personnel Administration and Industrial Relations
Operations and Production Management
Information Systems[118]

Those courses would have covered the basic functions of a business, and it is notable that industrial relations and production management were still core requirements. This suggests that HEC felt that students needed to know something about dealing with unions and working in a manufacturing environment. The same five program concentrations existed in 1995 as in 1989: Marketing, Finance, Human Resource Management, Operations and Production Management, Information Systems.[119]

The HEC MBA program provided a generalist overview with concentration options. HEC did not include enrollment numbers in its yearly program guides, but the gradual expansion in the range of programs and the options within the MBA suggested stable enrollment growth. The nature of the students enrolling in the MBA also evolved. The first MBA program brochure did not include images, but later ones did include them, and there was diversity evident in terms of race and gender. However, the fact that the program was taught entirely in French meant that it principally attracted francophone students or anglophones with second-language fluency. One curiosity of HEC's program brochures is that they provide scant information about tuition costs. This is a major difference from UBC and, as will be seen, with the program offered by UWO. HEC attracted interest in its MBA program from overseas applicants, specifically those residing in French-speaking countries. For instance, inquiries were received from Algeria in the mid-1970s.[120]

HEC did think about what students wanted from the MBA program. For example, a survey conducted in 1977 of incoming MBA students found a range of expectations for graduate study. It also crucially found that expectations differed between anglophone and francophone Canadian students. The study involved students at McGill University, the University of Ottawa, and Laval University.[121] McGill's program was offered in English, Ottawa's in English and French, and Laval's in French. The results of the study were written in English. Thirty percent of the students who responded to the survey listed French as their first language.[122] Overall, the people leading the survey felt that they had identified a sample student group that reflected the broader MBA student population in Eastern Canada.[123]

The teaching ability of a program's faculty and the program's reputation were the two leading concerns for all students surveyed.[124] However, English-speaking students were found to be more interested in the case teaching method and less concerned with the research reputation of a program's faculty members.[125] French-speaking students were found to place more emphasis on the cost of a program.[126] The study concluded that programs serving French-speaking students needed to think carefully about using the case method.[127] HEC seems to have taken that advice because, while it was an early user in Canada of the case method, it was not the sole pedagogical method used in its MBA courses.[128]

The HEC faculty did include people who developed scholarly and public reputations for different reasons. For example, from the mid-1970s to the late 1980s, its faculty ranks included Jacques Parizeau. He would eventually become leader of the sovereigntist Parti Québécois and a Québec premier. Parizeau was an economist and earned his doctorate at the London School of Economics.[129] He was the exception, as other faculty members, such as Jean-Pierre Hogue, developed stature in their fields (industrial psychology in Hogue's case) without public profiles like Parizeau's.[130] While there were still comparatively few female faculty at HEC by the mid-1990s, Francine Harel-Giasson had achieved the rank of full professor after completing both an MBA and Ph.D. at the school.[131] Overall, the HEC faculty collectively built a body of formidable scholarly work that would have been accessible to francophone students.

HEC offered a wide range of short-duration certificates and seminars by the 1990s, which is a practice that it shared with UBC. For example, certificates were offered in topics such as Business Management, Marketing Management, and Financial Management.[132] HEC also offered programs in conjunction with professional associations such as the Institute of Canadian Bankers.[133] The short-duration seminars dealt with specific, special interest topics. As seen in Figure 5.1, one example was a mid-1990s seminar that focused on political skills for female managers. The price for seminars was clearly indicated on brochures, unlike with the MBA program, and the one on political skills cost $875 for two days.[134] That last offering may have been perceived as somewhat sexist because it implied that women needed to be taught political skills separate from men, but it in fact addressed a specific challenge facing women in the workplace.

Figure 5.1 Political Skills for Women Managers seminar

Source: Used with permission of the HEC Archive.

HEC developed a range of range of graduate and short-duration programs between the 1970s and 1990s that were intended to prepare people for leadership roles, principally in business organizations. Those programs were created with the intent of providing learning opportunities for francophone students in Québec, and that objective was successfully met. The school also built on its undergraduate programs in the process. HEC's faculty helped create a body of academic business knowledge that was written in French but was also rooted in Québec business and management. The school's stature was sufficient to attract interest from students in other French-speaking countries. The study of business and management in Canada would not just be in English due to HEC and other schools in Québec. On the other hand, HEC was not attempting to attract students from across Canada during the period under consideration nor was it attempting to describe itself as the country's leading business school. It wanted to be Québec's business school. There was a university in Ontario that did view itself as Canada's business school.

The University of Western Ontario Business School

The University of Western Ontario Business School began offering an MBA program in 1950, which made it a pioneer for the degree in English Canada. As Donald Thain noted, UWO was first to offer the degree in Canada.[135] UWO was receptive to teaching business administration, but other leading universities in the country like the University of Toronto, McGill, and Queen's "took a very dim view of it" in the 1950s.[136] Thain was one of four faculty recruited at the same time to come to UWO.[137] As discussed in the chapter on undergraduate programs, the formation of the UWO Business School was the result of very deliberate policy decisions by the university's leadership and also by leading business figures in London, Ontario. The MBA was the only graduate program offered by the business school from 1950 onward, and it was meant to be a generalist degree. It was also meant to attract people who would become leaders in Canadian business. The 1950 MBA program offered by UWO was described as:

> The graduate program in Business Administration leading to the degree, Master of Business Administration, may be built either on an undergraduate degree program in Business (or Commerce) or on a Bachelor's degree program in Arts, Science or Engineering. For the non-business graduate, however, two years' work will normally be required. In all instances, admission will be governed by individual application, and special cases will be considered on their own merits.[138]

Students were advised that they would take a series of required courses in their first year that dealt with different areas of business including "production, marketing, finance and controls (the use of figures in management)."[139] Students were assured that they would have more latitude over their course choices in their second year of the program, but that there were two required courses nonetheless: Business Policy and Public Relationships and Responsibilities.[140] The latter course was presented as:

> This course is designed to train the prospective business administrator in appraising the demands placed upon him from the public point of view. Out of this course of study should come a better appreciation of the responsibilities which businessmen carry with respect to government controls in the various areas of business enterprise.[141]

This course was important as it encouraged students to place business activity within a broader social context. The 1950 program prospectus indicated that students would pay $300 per year in tuition fees, with books and other ancillary expenses being similar to those associated with the undergraduate program.[142] The language describing the 1950 MBA program was less expressive than what was employed to present the undergraduate program, but interested students would have had an understanding that they would be taught the basic functions of business at a different level than was done at undergraduate level.

Specific details on who came into the UWO MBA program in 1950 are not available, but there is on who graduated eight years later in 1958. The class that year was comprised of fifty-eight graduates, including one woman.[143] They were all white, and only three were not anglophone. UWO had, however, succeeded in drawing students from across Canada:

Ontario—20
Québec—18
British Columbia—8
Alberta—5
Saskatchewan—3
Nova Scotia—2
New Brunswick—1
Manitoba—1[144]

Prince Edward Island and Newfoundland were the only two provinces that were not represented in the 1958 graduating class. In terms of background, the students were an average of 27 years old, and the overwhelming majority of them were married. They ranged in age from 21 to 53, although the latter student was very much the exception within his class.[145] The students came into the MBA program with a variety of backgrounds, with seventeen having earned Bachelor of Arts degrees before applying to the business school.[146] They had earned undergraduate degrees at twenty different universities.[147] Fourteen students had Bachelor of Commerce degrees, and nineteen had Science or Engineering degrees.[148] The leading career interests for the graduates were finance and accounting, sales, and marketing.[149]

Donald Thain recalled introducing content into courses that would expose students to alternate views of business. He described a new course that he introduced in 1957 called Public Relations and Responsibilities that included such features as focusing on Karl Marx's *Communist Manifesto* and also discussed the social responsibilities of corporations. Thain decided that he needed to take this approach:

> Because most of these people (the students) hated unions, they had no appreciation for labour problems—very little—the union was the enemy. So I started at square one and said "hey, there's this whole other system in the world" . . . this was seen as very far out and controversial, but it got across the idea that there's an environment out there where capitalism is ruling but it's very much in question philosophically and morally and economically.[150]

This was a bold teaching move by Thain because, as Richard Marens has noted in the American context, discussions of Marxism have generally been avoided in business schools.[151] Coming to UWO to enroll in a management program was thus supposed to involve exposure to new ideas and not simply reinforce what students already believed. The UWO program at that time eschewed theory, and Thain further stated:

> The thing that made what we were doing great was that we said that there was no theory that we can teach you. There are no X Y propositions, there are no rules. There is simply some currently useful generalization that are all derived and what we do is write three of four cases and you put the three of four cases together and you get some currently useful generalizations. Anybody at Chicago, or Wharton, or Stanford or anywhere else in the world that is trying to teach you that there is a theory under this and that there are immutable guidelines, just don't even listen to them.[152]

This was an insightful observation by Thain, considering that he was talking about an era when management theorists like Peter Drucker were becoming increasingly influential.

The 1958 graduating UWO MBA class was surely demographically representative of the students who were admitted in the 1950s and early 1960s. They were in the early stages of their careers, and they represented the business school's success in creating a program with national appeal. A significant proportion of the 1958 graduating class came into the program with backgrounds in subjects that would have equipped them to attempt courses in areas like finance and accounting, since they had science and engineering degrees, and they wanted to go into fields that involved quantitative analysis.

Changes occurred by the 1960s as the program further developed. The 1961 MBA program description had not markedly changed since 1950:

> The graduate program in Business Administration which leads to the degree of M.B.A. is designed to cover two academic years. To enter this program a student should have a recognized undergraduate degree from an accredited University plus an undergraduate record which demonstrates that he has the ability to do good graduate work. Moreover, as the case method of teaching is employed which involves daily class discussion, a good command of the English language is a necessity.[153]

No specific pre-requisite courses were specified, but students were all expected to take the same five courses in the first year of the program:

Marketing
Finance
Production
Control
Administrative Practices[154]

The last course was deemed especially important as it would "give the student a 'feel' for administrative situations . . . it is 'human relations' course in a very real sense."[155]

The program guide did not specify streams for the second year of the program. Student took an additional five courses, and one had to be Business Policy.[156] That course was presented as:

> This course approaches the production problem from a top-level policy point of view. Emphasis is on the making of production decisions in the light of marketing, financial, organizational, and general economic aspects as well as the more purely "production" factors. The course material is oriented around six industries—furniture, oil, textiles, plastics, radio and television, and steel—rather than around specific production problems. The material on each industry comprises notes and pictures on the manufacturing process; notes on the general economic structure, problems, and trends in the industry; and three to five cases on companies in the industry. This approach provides the student with the opportunity to learn to recognize a variety of production problems involved in integrated and non-integrated structured, centralized and decentralized organizations, conventional

and unique marketing ventures, old and young, stable and unstable, multi-company and few-company industries, and industries in which legal pressures may be strong or weak. The task of the students is to recognize the problems and to come to production decisions which are harmonious with the situation in the company and with the industry as a whole. The student may be required to write at least one test and at least one term report.[157]

This was a lengthy course description, and its loquacity tells much about what students would learn and do in a key required MBA course. They were being taught to look at problems from the perspective of senior leaders, even though there were probably very few of them who had much leadership experience. The reading load was light; the implication was that executives assessed problems and made decisions from reading notes and looking at photographic images. They furthermore would not have to complete a lot of work to assess their grasp of the course content. The expedited method of assessing problems that students learned could be employed regardless of the industries in which they worked. Students from across Canada obviously saw value in pursuing the UWO MBA and taking courses like Business Policy, and they only paid $490 per year to do so in 1961.[158]

Moving ahead to the 1970s reveals significant change occurred in the UWO MBA program since the 1960s. The 1975 program description was more expansive about the purpose of the degree than what was presented in 1961:

> The Master of Business Administration program is keyed toward the concurrent development of decision-making skills and the ability to make things happen. Toward these ends, extensive knowledge in specialized fields such as finance, marketing, operations management, management science, planning information and control systems, economics and organizational behaviour is provided.

Applicants needed to possess an undergraduate degree and also write the Admissions Test for Graduate Study in Business. Students were required to take seven courses in the first year of the program:

Marketing
Operations Management
Finance
Planning Information and Control Systems
Managing Human Resources
Management Science
Economics

This was an increase from the early 1960s, and it also illustrated that, while applicants only needed to hold undergraduate degrees to apply to the MBA program, they needed to have a firm grounding in quantitative methods and mathematics. Business Policy was still required in the second year, but students had discretion over their other course selections.[159]

The second-year courses were mainly designated as half-courses, and they were overwhelmingly oriented toward topics related to mathematics. Of the thirty-eight possible options listed, only one on Business and Society appeared to have a clear social science orientation.[160] Titles such as Mathematical Programming or Financial Institutions were more common. Students paid considerably more to be in the MBA program, with tuition in 1975 costing $661 per year.[161] The amount was remarkably lower than what was paid by students in UWO's other graduate programs. The graduate calendar is silent on who those students were, but they would have been exposed to quantitatively focused analytical skills to analyze business problems.

The 1980s UWO MBA program represented a continuing evolution from what was initially created in 1950, but there were three key changes shown in the 1984 to 1986 program description:

> The graduate program in Business Administration which leads to the degree of MBA is designed to cover two academic years. To enter this program, a candidate must hold a recognized undergraduate degree from an accredited university or have equivalent qualifications. Moreover, his or her record must indicate that he or she is capable of doing graduate work. Admission to the MBA program may be offered by the School of Business Administration to candidates without an undergraduate degree if they can demonstrate that their previous work experience and leadership qualities clearly indicate a high potential for management.

The description went on to indicate that the Graduate Management Admissions Test (GMAT) would also have to be written by anyone applying to the program. This was difference from UBC and HEC, neither of which explicitly required the GMAT in their program guides. This was an obvious decision by HEC, considering that the GMAT was written in English. The first change involved the idea that someone could apply without holding an undergraduate degree, the inclusion of both male and female pronouns was the second change, and the use of the term leadership was the final difference. Removing the requirement that applicants need not necessarily possess an undergraduate degree provided that they had significant work experience meant that essentially apprenticing in management was sufficient preparation. The decision not to necessarily require an undergraduate degree clearly differentiated the MBA from other graduate degrees at UWO. It also made it different from program requirements at other schools like UBC and HEC. It also implied that the necessary background for entry into the MBA program could be acquired through other credentials, or even through applied experience. The inclusion of the term leadership was noteworthy because it had not previously been used but would become ubiquitous in management literature and popular business discourse as the 1980s passed and the 1990s began.[162]

There were some new differences in the 1980s program content. The first year required that students complete:

Marketing
Operations Management
Finance
Managerial Accounting and Control
Management Behaviour
Management Science
Economic Environment of Business[163]

The second year was composed of ten half-courses, and two of them had to be Business Policy and Political Environment of Canadian Business.[164] This latter addition was a major change as it added social science content to the MBA program, but it was also another required course that reduced the number of possible electives. The degree had overall become more structured.

UWO was also offering what it described as a "special, limited enrollment" combined MBA and law degree (LLB) program by the mid-1980s.[165] Students had to meet the admissions requirements of both the law school and business school in order to be admitted, and they could complete the combined degree in four years rather than doing them separately over five years.[166] There were forty-nine elective choices in 1984–1986, and some new trends were evident among them. For instance, there was a course called Managers of Change and another one titled Career Planning and Personal Growth.[167] Most of the electives were, however, still oriented toward traditional topics like accounting, finance, and marketing. Students were still enjoying a relative bargain when they pursued the UWO MBA in the mid-1980s, as the tuition cost had only increased to $700 per term since the mid-1970s, which meant paying $2,800 over two years.[168]

The 1990s were a period in which further changes were ushered into the MBA program. UWO regarded it as one of several professional master's degrees that it offered; others included a Master of Education and a Master of Public Administration in Local Government.[169] The 1994 to 1996 MBA program description had again changed since 1985:

The graduate program in Business Administration leading to the degree of MBA is designed to cover two academic years. To enter this program, a candidate must hold a recognized undergraduate degree, GMAT/TOEFL/TSE scores and full-time work experience.

The admissions committee also places considerable weight on the applicant's professional accomplishments, leadership and interpersonal skills. A few applicants without a degree, who have a minimum of seven years of challenging full-time work experience, some university courses with an overall average of B and other strong management qualities, may gain admission.

Applicants were further advised that:

> The vision of the business school is to be recognized worldwide for developing decisive leaders, who think globally, act strategically and communicate effectively. The goal is to be at the forefront of business schools worldwide in providing a general management education with global perspective.

There were some key changes in what was required to apply for the MBA, including a clearer requirement for people who did not have undergraduate degrees. Gender neutral language was used, and leadership was further emphasized. The UWO Business School also articulated ambitious goals for itself and, by extension, its students. The program was presented more than ever before as a venue for achieving great career success.[170]

The program content had again altered since the 1980s. In their first year, students were required to take:

Marketing
Operations Management
Finance
Managerial Accounting and Control
Management Behaviour
Management Communication
Management Information Systems
Economic Environment of Business[171]

The required first-year courses would have required more mathematics ability than at any time in the history of the MBA program. If anything, UWO was late in requiring a course in information systems in comparison to UBC and HEC. Business Policy was the only required second-year course, and there were forty-three other elective courses that students could take.[172] The mid-1990s electives included some new choices that were less quantitative, including Career Management, Environmental Business Management, and Creative Business Leadership.[173] It does seem unusual that teaching students how to manage their careers could count toward degree credit, but it likely appealed to students who were told that they were destined for important leadership roles if they were admitted into the MBA program. One other interesting fact about the mid-1990s program was that UWO stopped including a schedule of fees in the graduate calendar after having done so in previous years.

UWO's MBA program altered from the 1950s to the 1990s as it became more oriented toward quantitative methods. The program was consistently presented as a general management degree, and it did not develop any concentration areas. The combined MBA/LLB degree was the only other graduate degree option at this time. The UWO Business School set very ambitious objectives from the 1950s onward as it sought to be a presence in the global graduate business community. It closely followed Harvard by using the case teaching method. UWO also attracted students from across Canada, and it was not focused on one area of country. On the other hand, the students whom it attracted were a homogenous group as they were mostly male and white. However, the fact that tuition and fees were essentially in line with UWO's other graduate programs meant that a student with the ability to be admitted to the business school could pursue an MBA as easily as any other program.

The students who attended the UWO Business School were taught by faculty who had significant reputations in their fields. For instance, Al Mikalachki conducted research in human resource management and was also the business school's first Ph.D. student.[174] Donald Thain also published extensively on management topics.[175] The faculty were also involved in developing partnerships at home and abroad. Walter Thompson was one of the faculty members heavily involved in developing partnerships and participating in non-degree training programs.[176] The nature of teaching in a business program often led to close links between faculty and business. Thain indicated that there was "tremendous resistance" from companies when it came to securing their cooperation with writing early cases used at UWO, as they were worried about issues like confidentiality, and faculty had to "sell the case method."[177] He also said that he had served on sixteen corporate boards, which helped alert him to new topics for cases and provided topics for journal articles.[178] Thain was consequently closely tied to the organizations that he studied.

Thain began his teaching at UWO in the business school's Management Training Course (MTC). Less can be said about UWO's MBA program in comparison to UBC's and HEC's due to source limitations, but much more can be said about UWO's early executive training programs and its efforts to spread Canadian management education abroad. Executive education was central to UWO's business school from the time of its founding. Describing every executive program that the school offered is beyond the scope of this analysis, but looking at the early years of the MTC reveals much about what students wanted when they came to UWO and what the university was prepared to give them. The Management Training Course—a fundamental part of the business school's mission—was where Clarence Fraser made his main contribution to

UWO, the field of university management education, and the professionalization of management. He brought the materials that he developed at Bell Canada with him. The MTC, as the program was known within the university, was the forerunner of the Executive MBA (EMBA) program that UWO eventually established. The MTC was first offered in 1948 as a kind of summer school. It was three weeks in duration. It initially drew fifty-one students, all of whom were employed in mid-level managerial positions. The program grew to eighty-five students by the summer of 1951. Those participating frequently came from the same companies that funded the business school's establishment.[179]

The university created sophisticated promotional materials for the training course by early 1950s standards. Glossy brochures that included photo images, faculty and student biographies, and an appealing overview of the program were produced. They were lodged in Huron College (an affiliated college) dormitories, but they were also provided with temporary memberships at the London Hunt and Country Club and the London Garrison Mess. Parties honouring them were held at the homes of Ray Lawson, the university president, D.B. Weldon, Hugh Labatt, J. Jeffrey, Walter Blackburn, and the Ivey family. Lawson owned a range of London businesses, Labatt was associated with the eponymous Canadian brewery, Jeffrey was associated with London Life, Blackburn owned the *London Free Press* newspaper and other media outlets, and the Ivey family owned a range of businesses. There was a lot of socializing considering that the students would only be in London from August 16 to September 10, 1951.[180]

Anyone preparing to attend the training course may have pondered how he (and they were all men) would have been able to handle the pressure of the program curriculum while also participating in the associated social calendar. Attendees would have soon found that they need not have worried. The first program brochure, while going into detail about who would be present and the social events they would attend, was silent on the curriculum. It still spoke volumes about the program's purpose. As Donald Thain recalled, UWO's business school chose to adopt Harvard's case teaching method, and case-based teaching was the method used in the MTC.[181]

The 1958 brochure finally revealed that students would cover topics such as Administration, Cost and Financial Management, Marketing, Labour Relations, Policy and Planning, Finance, and Production.[182] Those seemed like weighty topics, but no assignments or other evaluations were required. Applied knowledge was emphasized. As Thain remembered, personnel was not considered significant by executives as they viewed it as a "tag-along function" required to make sure that everyone got paid on time.[183] MTC students would thus have received a smattering of management theory, but they surely received similar levels of insight in other courses. Attendance at the training course ended with a dignified graduation ceremony at which graduates were presented with a certificate by Richard Ivey. The 1958 class president wrote that the "MTC has practiced education as it has been carried on for centuries."[184] Graduates believed that they had gone through an important learning experience. They also had a good time. However, in 1951, Richard Ivey raised concerns about the level of socializing with UWO president G. Edward Hall. Hall indicated in a letter to a third party that:

> Mr. Ivey was much disturbed about the amount of so-called drinking which had taken place at the last Management Training Course and was very disturbed about the reaction in so far as it affected not only the students but the companies which they represented. Further, I have discussed this matter on several occasions with Principal O'Neil of Huron College. Principal O'Neil again states definitely that there was less drinking amongst the members of this last Management Training Course than they had experienced during the past three courses.[185]

Students attending the training course came as much for the social networking as the chance to absorb some business knowledge.

For employers and students, the real value of the training course was not so much the academic knowledge that it conveyed but the overall experience that it provided. For the executives who sent their managers to the business school's programs, detailed academic knowledge was not a priority. As an example, the president of the Quaker Oats Company of Canada wrote to G. Edward Hall in 1956 regarding a Quaker Oats manager who wished to attend one of the business school's programs:

> I hope Richard makes it, but he has a feeling that he probably flunked his Math, so, only time will tell. Richard is very good in the shall we say "non-scientific" subjects, and has more than an ordinary flair for English, and has always done very well in History, Geography, etc, but when it comes to Math. and the Sciences, he has neither the aptitude nor the interest . . . While to bring up this subject may seem like poor taste and an unwarranted advantage of your friendly letter, I have often wondered why Universities insist on Mathematics for students who are planning a business career . . . I.B.M. and Burrough's machines can add the things up, but it takes imagination, courage, sympathy and understanding of people to produce the figures for those machines.[186]

Richard's last name was not indicated in the letter but, in all probability, he found his way into his desired program. Data collected by the university about training program attendees showed that he was likely the right sort of man for the program. Most attendees in the early 1950s were from Ontario; primarily Toronto. In 1951, fifty-six were from Ontario, seventeen from Québec, nine collectively from the western provinces, and one from Newfoundland. Over half were between the ages of 36 and 45, while all married and had an average of two children. Half of them were military veterans, and slightly over half already had some university education. Many were employed in manufacturing. Richard, whoever he was, probably fit in well with those demographic numbers.[187]

Companies clearly saw value in what was taught at the management training course, and it was not cheap. The 1955 fee was $750, which was a huge sum for a one-week training program at that time.[188] The program faculty were also well-compensated. Clarence Fraser was paid $2,000 in 1948 to teach one course.[189] The men attending the training course met other like-minded peers who had common backgrounds. They overwhelming had Anglo-Saxon last names and probably held similar political views. They were eager to give up part of their summers to travel to London, Ontario— hardly a vacation destination—to further their careers. Training-course students were promised in 1951 that they would be treated "like kings" for four weeks.[190] They would have left London with a strong network of connections, the certainty that their employers had aspirations for them, and perhaps the memory of a couple of hangovers. The latter was a small price to pay for the career payoff that would have seemed to be at hand.

The Management Training Course was in many ways the foundation on which other initiatives would be based. The UWO Business School's partnership with the University of the West Indies (UWI) was an example of how the school tried to export its expertise abroad. This initiative can be viewed as an extension of the Colombo Plan that led UBC to Malaysia. Jamaica had been a British colony from 1655 to 1962. It is one of the larger islands in the Caribbean Sea. Jamaica peacefully achieved independence from the UK but, like many former colonies in economically developing areas, it lacked the resources to build and expand a major post-secondary education system. The idea of creating a university specifically to serve the higher education needs of the Caribbean population had first been inspired by the founding of the University of Puerto Rico in 1903.[191] The Caribbean islands suffered from a shortage of trained physicians by the late 1940s, to the extent that there was growing recognition that an institution should be established in the region for medical education.[192] McGill University in Montréal offered to assist with early training programs in the region.[193] The University College of the West Indies was thus the product of long-held aspiration among local policy makers in the Caribbean region to found a university, but it also reflected pressing practical needs for trained medical professionals. The institution was chartered in 1949, and it would have three main campuses, with the first in Mona, Jamaica.[194]

CIDA formed a link to the university college in 1966 following a meeting of Commonwealth heads of state. In that year, the Canadian government committed itself to $1 million per year in funding for the university over a five-year period. This money covered a range of projects, from building construction to scholarship funding. The University College of the West Indies became a degree-granting institution and university in 1962. "Social, scientific, technological, and economic development" were cited as the reasons for CIDA's five-year commitment to the University of the West Indies, with the emphasis on economic development.[195]

The commitment that CIDA made to UWI was significant. For example, a 1967 internal agency memorandum noted that, in some cases, the aid that CIDA provided to UWI students in terms of scholarships and fellowships exceeded the value of student loans that Canadian government made available for Canadian students. The amount, $1,000 per student, was intended to cover the full amount of education costs, while funding for Canadian students was only intended to cover a portion of university expenses.[196] Indeed, the UWI funding was considered reasonable considering that it cost $2,500 per year to fund a student from the West Indies to attend a Canadian university.[197] CIDA leadership decided to reach out more fully to universities and colleges in Canada in 1968 by commissioning the Association of Universities and College of Canada (AUCC) to conduct a study into how Canada's post-secondary institutions were engaging in overseas activity. The study was led by Professor Norma Walmsley, and it yielded some notable information about the range of overseas programming developed in Canada. Walmsley noted the importance of the Colombo Plan, especially how Canada was second behind the United Kingdom in funding Commonwealth scholarships and fellowships.[198]

Some Canadian universities were actively engaged in overseas program work. For example, the University of British Columbia was described as being especially active in areas including adult education, agricultural and applied sciences, Asian studies, and commerce and business administration.[199] The University of Toronto had been actively working on medical education with UWI and also pursued other overseas initiatives.[200] UWO began assisting UWI with teaching business administration in 1966, and Walmsley further noted that UWO wished to strengthen its ties with its Jamaican partner institution.[201] Universities in Québec, especially Laval, formed links with schools in francophone Africa.[202]

The Caribbean was an important source of foreign students who chose to study in Canada. Walmsley found that, in 1968, there were 27,263 overseas students studying in Canada, with 2,056 originating from the Caribbean region.[203] This was the second-highest total from so-called developing regions, with Asia coming first with 7,358 students.[204] UWI appears several times in the AUCC study, with specific reference to CIDA's contributions to the university.[205] Canada had spent a lot of money on aid through the Colombo plan: $1 billion between 1959 and 1968.[206]

There were challenges with running overseas university partnerships. Walmsley noted that "some university personnel contend that the Canadian government should concentrate within each country on a limited number of projects only."[207] Recruiting academic staff to go overseas was also at times difficult as "Canadian universities have limited resources and the government must be realistic and efficient in its approach to the recruitment and selection of personnel."[208] CIDA forged ahead regardless of the shoals that it had to navigate when interacting with universities like UWI. Universities in Canada were encouraged to form further partnerships abroad through the auspices of CIDA. This included UWO, where there was great interest in taking the business school's expertise to other countries.

UWO began discussions with CIDA in 1971 regarding offering management training in conjunction with UWI. The Ford Foundation had previously funded UWI's management studies area from 1966 to 1971.[209] Thompson took the lead role on behalf of UWO and raised key questions about how a partnership would work. This included how scholarships would work, developing teaching cases, the creation of a library, continuing education staff recruitment, and overall acclimation of UWO staff to working in Jamaica. These were key issues, especially as anyone coming from UWO would have been accustomed to teaching in a well-developed academic environment. The UWO Business School's case method be central to the management education programs at UWI as well.[210]

Financial issues were almost absent from the AUCC study written by Norma Walmsley, but had to be considered once partnership plans were developed. The estimated budget for the UWO/UWI agreement was $1.35 million from 1971 to 1976.[211] This included:

$378,000 for staffing
$227,000 for graduate training
$135,000 for case writing
$500,000 for buildings
$89,000 for a library
$20,000 for faculty exchanges and short-term consultants

These seem like substantial amounts, but Walter Thompson still observed later in 1971 that "we miscalculated on the cost of putting Canadian staff at UWI and the overall project is being squeezed very heavily" and further noted that "we see the need to watch costs." UWI was also supposed to carry some of the costs, but those amounts were unspecified in relation to what CIDA would directly cover and what UWO would indirectly incur.[212]

Thompson was obviously enthusiastic about overseas partnerships, and so was the UWO Business School. The school had already been involved with another Commonwealth country in 1959, when Pakistan approached the Canadian government about providing technical and industrial assistance. The Department of Trade and Commence then wrote to Thompson seeking advice. From there, UWO Business School eventually hosted a specific management course for managers from Pakistan in 1961. The Colombo Plan was also referenced by the Department of Trade and Commerce. Extending the school's reach into the West Indies would have seemed like a natural progression.[213]

The agreement with UWI covered some key areas. Developing a management training program was the primary objective. Additional areas included staff development at UWI, which would include faculty visiting between the two institutions. There were also plans to create a continuing education function that would focus on business and management studies. Fostering faculty research was a priority, and this would include writing teaching cases that focused on Caribbean examples. The ultimate objective was to have a program with a "full West Indian flavor and manned by West Indians in 1976."[214]

Early 1970s Jamaica clearly seemed like a good place for Canada to devote overseas development money, mostly due to the fact that both countries were members of the Commonwealth with deep historic ties to the United Kingdom, but there were important differences between the countries that shaped the partnership between UWI and UWO. Jamaica was obviously much smaller and less developed economically. It achieved independence from Britain, and there were important political differences. Michael Manley was Jamaica's prime minister from 1972 to 1980, and later again from 1989 to 1992. He came from a prominent Jamaican family but was on the political left to a greater degree than his counterpart in Canada—Pierre Trudeau. Manley would gain a reputation for challenging the emerging global economic order in the 1970s, especially by challenging the International Monetary Fund (IMF) in 1977. Trudeau and British prime minister James Callahan supported Manley in his efforts to change the terms that the IMF imposed on Jamaica in return for receiving economic assistance.[215]

Manley led a country that was markedly divided by class. Even by 1980, when Jamaica had been independent for almost two decades along with receiving development aid from countries like Canada, three-quarters of the population was considered lower class and lived in subsistence conditions. Manley was commonly known to favour economic development that would benefit all Jamaicans, but inequality prevailed in the 1970s. This key aspect of Jamaican society also shaped development policy, including UWI's partnership with UWO. The people who would attend management training programs from across the Caribbean islands were from the local business class and not subsisting economically.[216]

CIDA and UWO were aware of Manley's political orientation and sought to gain his approval for links with UWI. The Canadian High

Commissioner in Jamaica, J. M. Harrington, told Walter Thompson that, while Manley was committed to a "third world economic strategy," he was nonetheless a pragmatist. He also suggested that it would be a good idea for UWO to confer an honourary degree on Manley as an individual and also in recognition of the Commonwealth Caribbean and of Jamaica's status as a third-world country with a viable two-party system. Harrington did not also note that Manley may well have recognized CIDA and UWO's real motivation, but the prime minister accepted the offer of an honourary degree and travelled to London, Ontario, to receive it.[217]

Jamaica's business community, although only representing a small portion of the country's population, was influential and supported UWI's efforts to introduce management education programs. A 1967 survey of members of Jamaica's managerial class—mostly people in leadership positions in business—revealed what they thought was important in terms of management training. The prevailing opinion among the people surveyed at 262 different organizations was that management education should focus on broad practical skills rather than specific technical aptitudes.[218] The curriculum that was implemented in the early 1970s was composed of courses that were common across college and university business programs in the United States and Canada. The courses included Business Policy, Production Management, Marketing, and Cost and Financial Management.[219] These courses were offered in a condensed format and mirrored how the UWO Business School ran the long-standing summer management training course. Relatively sophisticated promotional materials were printed that were essentially in the same format used at UWO. Faculty were featured prominently in program brochures. It is clear that there was interest not only in training managers in the West Indies but also in developing teaching faculty. The program was intended for more senior level managers, which was also the UWO MTC model.

The 1977 UWI program, which was the last one that was offered under the CIDA/UWO agreement, was taught by eight faculty. Only two were from Canada: J.N. Fry and J.F. Graham, both of whom were full-time professors at UWO Business School.[220] The other six taught in the Department of Management Studies at UWI. In fact, one of them, named Marshall Hall, would go on to become chair of the UWI board of governors.[221] The UWI faculty involved with the management training program had all received their Ph.D.s from either Canadian or American Universities. Another UWI faculty member, G.H. Wadinambiaratchi, had completed his MBA and Ph.D. at UWO.[222]

Recruitment of qualified faculty to teach in the management program at UWI appears to have been at times quite challenging. A program summary written in 1976 noted that most of the faculty who taught in the program during its inception in 1972 were not from the Caribbean, but that situation changed by 1976 as the staff running the program were overwhelmingly from the West Indies by that year.[223] The staff had only grown from five to eight people. Relying more on faculty from the West Indies would have been preferred for a number of reasons. CIDA, despite operating in numerous countries, appears to have been quite unaware of race and ethnicity when discussing overseas development initiatives. The idea of continually sending white faculty from a developing nation to teach management, even from a friendly Commonwealth country like Canada, would surely have been eventually viewed as somewhat colonialist in Jamaica and Trinidad and Tobago.[224]

Faculty who came from Canada came from a variety of backgrounds, and not all were regular business school appointees. For instance, Walter Thompson reviewed a teaching application from UWO MBA student Roger Spriggs. Spriggs was English and had completed a law degree at Birmingham University before coming to Canada.[225] Thompson also reached out to other business schools and management faculties in Canada and the United States in an effort to identify potential faculty to teach in the UWI program, such as the Faculty of Administrative Studies at York University in Toronto.[226] In correspondence with York, Thompson tried to find graduates from the West Indies who were trained in Canada and were possibly willing to return home to teach. His success in this endeavor is regrettably unclear, including the extent to which he pursued the contacts supplied by York.

Some of the faculty employed were full-time, but on leave from universities other than UWO. It is evident that the experience of living and working in Jamaica or Trinidad and Tobago was not what some faculty expected. A particularly difficult situation arose regarding an Australian academic named Bruce Yuill. Yuill resigned from UWI, alleging that he had both suffered from racial discrimination and saw other people suffer from it as well. This episode was reported in a local newspaper under the headline " 'Racism' So Professor Quits UWI."[227] Yuill corresponded directly with Walter Thompson about the situation saying:

> I really don't know why the UWI bothered to go all of the trouble to bring me from Australia; I found the situation quite impossible. In light of the CIDA agreement there was really no reason for filling it (teaching position) until some West Indian came along. There was really nothing I could contribute, given the attitudes of Trinidadians to outsiders, expatriates, and foreigners.[228]

Another faculty member involved with the program at that time also wrote to Thompson saying:

> I include here an article that appeared in The Express of Trinidad. It is quite funny in that it represents accurately the Trinidadian journalistic endeavors. Distorted at best, it fails to point out the negativism of Yuill.[229]

Thompson appears to have felt that the episode with Yuill did not adversely affect UWO's presence in Trinidad and indicated in his response to Cukieman that "things are going along reasonably well."[230] Indeed, Thompson discussed how people from North America could be perceived the Caribbean in correspondence with another colleague by saying "I recognize that some who go down from North America have run into difficulties . . . I know one or two who certainly invite hostility and would get in any setting because of their attitudes and way of handling themselves."[231] Members of UWI's Department of Management Studies were also willing to raise questions about who taught in the management training course. For instance, UWI professor A.A. Mark complained about the teaching ability of a Canadian named K. Hill in a 1974 memo.[232] It is difficult to ascertain if situations like those involving Yuill and Hill were especially common or if they were the exception in an otherwise collegial partnership. It is likely that there was at least some friction between faculty from UWI and UWO, and some cultural challenges faced by Canadians living in the Caribbean islands while teaching at UWI.

UWO Business School faculty who traveled to Jamaica or Trinidad to teach were expected to pursue certain objectives. For example, Walter Thompson was advised in 1972 by UWO Business School dean C.B. Johnston to:

1. Teach in classes on both campuses.
2. Push and monitor the progress towards the development of continuing education program (sic) particularly in Jamaica.
3. Collect and finish unfinished cases and develop teaching notes with a view to publishing something this summer.
4. Contact the Productivity Centre while in Trinidad to see what opportunities there might be for co-operation and mutual support.
5. Ride herd on the research that has already been approved and push for the development of research plans particularly in the area of case writing with a view to having specific proposals ready for approval by the Operations Committee in the spring.
6. Develop a plan for summer employment for the UWI students here particularly with regard to development of summer case leads.
7. Make arrangements for meetings of the Operations Committee and the Continuing Education Advisory Committee probably for the end of the week of February 19.
8. Activate liaison between UWI staff and members of our Liaison Committee here and explore plans for some kind of joint meeting either on an individual or collective basis.
9. Push for the specification of faculty plans by UWI for 1973–1974 with a view to getting at some direction as to who ought to be approached regarding employment in those programs next year.
10. Push to have Sooklal moved to the UWI payroll.

11. Push planning on the Scholarship Program with a view to identifying, as early as possible, the students who may be interested in, and suitable candidates for participation in the program here next year.

As this list shows, Thompson had a lot to accomplish in one term, especially since most of these directives dealt with administrative matters not teaching. This list also suggests that UWO was obviously the senior party in the partnership.[233]

The 1977 management training course offered by UWI was the last one that involved faculty from UWO. The UWI faculty appear to have assumed full responsibility for the program by that year. The UWO Business School would go on to other overseas projects in subsequent years. The management training program in which UWO was involved, though brief, was important for several reasons. Canada, particularly the UWO Business School, was viewed as an expert source of management education. The Canadian government, in the form of CIDA, also agreed with this view. UWO's efforts in Jamaica also garnered international attention, such as mention in the Manchester Business School newsletter.[234]

Although UWI and UWO allowed MBA students to take courses at both institutions, and it was overwhelmingly students from the former going to the latter, participation in the management training course was UWO's principal contribution to the partnership. As noted earlier, CIDA identified different subject areas which Canadian universities could pursue in other countries. CIDA did not necessarily mandate that universities provide regular degree programs, but it is noteworthy that money was devoted to enabling UWO's business school to provide a copy of its management training program. The program run in Canada was not publicly subsidized and was intended to be a source of revenue for UWO.

It is also significant that CIDA funded an education program that was targeted to such a narrow slice of the population of the West Indies countries. CIDA also funded teacher training schemes. Teacher training would seem to have had much more universal application, since it was linked to improving overall levels of literacy in a country. In contrast, management training had less common applicability. The reality was that Caribbean leaders, including Michael Manley, felt that there was a pressing need to develop expertise among the managerial class in the island nations. There is both continuity and contradiction to this approach. Countries like Jamaica sought an independent voice in a global economic system that was increasingly dominated by free market capitalism, so having a capable managerial class would have been perceived as necessary, otherwise foreign managers would be the leaders of Jamaican business. Conversely, embracing management training meant contributing to the further development of free market beliefs that were viewed as being harmful to emerging economies.

The UWO Business School did not make money from its involvement with UWI, although it had hoped to do so. CIDA provided a lot of money to UWI, but the university was often in difficult financial straits despite the aid that it received. On the other hand, CIDA and UWO both judged the partnership a success when it was concluded in 1976. Karl Johansen, Director General of CIDA's Caribbean Division, wrote to Walter Thompson saying that "the Management Studies Program is generally considered the most successful project that CIDA has had at the University of the West Indies." Being involved with UWI's business programs enabled the UWO Business School to further enhance its stature. Business groups, such as the Institute of Canadian Bankers, noted the business school's efforts in the Caribbean. In that instance, the institute noted that it had around 250 independent study students in the Caribbean engaged in training who would benefit from linking to the UWI.[235] The business school had vast links to the Canadian business community, and those links extended outside of the country. So, while revenue could not be derived from the UWI agreement, it was still possible to use it to leverage further opportunities and raise the business school's global stature.[236]

UWI also surely benefited from involvement with CIDA and UWO Business School. The objective of having a program run by faculty from the West Indies was successfully met by 1976. Other aspirations, such as writing teaching cases, were also achieved. There were fifteen teaching cases written on West Indian examples by 1973 alone. UWI's Department of Management Studies would build on the foundation that CIDA and UWO helped lay and would go on to offer programs across the Caribbean in the decades following 1976.[237] Caribbean managers who attended the UWI management training programs were being shaped into a certain form just as their counterparts in Canada were molded, even if this happened in nations like Jamaica that strove to achieve economic independence. The fact that a major Canadian government agency worked with institutions in Canada and Jamaica to make students better managers reveals insights into the importance that public entities—governments and universities—placed on management practice. Management was considered part of economic development but must have also met the definition of practical training that CIDA stipulated. It is noteworthy that studies focusing on management's opposite in the post–World War II labour-relations system, organized labour, were not a high priority when CIDA funded programs abroad.

Students in the UWI/UWO partnership may have at times felt ambivalent about their studies, but UWO students in Canada must have harboured high hopes of success when they entered the MBA program, as they were essentially promised that they could look forward to rewarding careers. The nature of the student body changed over time. The entirely male groups of students who attended the MTC program in the early 1950s eventually gave way to an increasingly diverse group of people by the early 1980s. Images of student learning and social activities from 1982 show women and more people of colour involved in the MBA program. In fact, the president of the MBA Association in that year was a woman named Susan Harper. Women in UWO's MBA program surely saw the degree as a form of career mobility just as their peers at UBC viewed the degree.[238]

Three Graduate Business Programs Compared

There are similarities and differences between the graduate business programs offered by UBC, HEC, and UWO. The programs were all intended to further build upon the undergraduate degrees that each school was already offering. They usually included core courses that closely mirrored what was already being offered at the undergraduate level. An actual undergraduate business or commerce degree was not necessarily required for admission at the three schools, but there was certainly an implication that students coming from humanities and social science backgrounds would have difficulty in an MBA program if they did not have a strong grounding in subjects relating to mathematics. The graduate business programs at Sauder and UWO were part of wider master's degree options offered by their universities. HEC, while not listing programs offered by other departments and faculties, was part of the Université de Montréal and would have had to comply with wider general university regulations regarding graduate degrees.

The three schools offered degrees that held similarities in terms of program content. Courses in subjects like finance, marketing, and operations management were found in each of them. They did not equally emphasize the same areas of study. UBC and HEC offered defined streams in the second year of study, while UWO appeared resolute in its preference to emphasize general management education. UBC and HEC offered MBA and M.Sc. programs, but UWO only branched out slightly by creating a combined degree with the UWO law school. UBC also advised prospective students that it was also offering a generalist degree. The broader objectives of each school, and by extension, their graduate programs, is what most clearly differentiated them. UBC wanted to further develop its reputation as a western Canadian commerce and management school. HEC was a leader in offering graduate business education in Québec in French. UWO Business School, from its inception, aspired to be a national business school with global stature. This does mean that the first two schools limited themselves in their initial missions. The fact that HEC, in particular, offered graduate management degrees in French is important as Canada was officially bilingual.

All three schools pursued overseas partnerships or attracted students from other countries. The project that UBC developed in Malaysia and the UWO/UWI project should be viewed within the context of broader national policy objectives, as the Canadian government played a key role in exporting management education abroad. Both universities helped educate a managerial class in Malaysia and Jamaica. However, it is clear that Jamaican students were perhaps not always receptive to what they heard in their courses. CIDA promoted Canadian education programs in other countries, like teacher education, but the government also saw definite value in the teaching of business and management. Canada's involvement in the Colombo Plan and subsequent efforts by CIDA to promote management programs overseas further reinforces the importance that the state placed on this type of education and training.

This discussion of graduate business education and non-degree programs also illustrates that business schools were also businesses. UWO Business School was operating in this manner from its founding when it established the Management Training Course. UBC and HEC also developed their own short-duration programs, and attending them was proportionately more expensive than enrollment in a graduate degree. It is also in those short-duration programs and seminars where specific aspects of management, such as dealing with workplace issues, were discussed. The seminars were additionally created with certain students in mind, as shown in the policy seminar for women in management at HEC. The partnerships formed with overseas institutions were also intended to be sources of revenue.

The students who enrolled in the programs at UBC, HEC, and UWO were not homogeneous in national terms, but they were in regional contexts. In the case of UBC, there was increasing racial and gender diversity as decades passed. Asian students, including many women, thought that an MBA would help their career prospects. HEC wanted to attract francophone students which, in Canada, meant that most of them would have come from Québec and been ethnically Western European, and a majority were likely male. UWO's students were also primarily male, but they came from across Canada. Students were interested in careers in areas like finance, and fields like production management held less appeal. There were students who went on to positions of considerable stature in the private sector and in the public sphere. People like Lindsay Gordon achieved major career success after completing MBAs at UBC. UWO Business School's carefully cultivated ties to Canadian business, especially financial services, led to many graduates working for government and business. One example was Susan Harper, who graduated from the MBA program in 1983 and went on to a career as a trade commissioner and ambassador.[239] HEC had a large proportion of faculty, like Sylvie St. Onge, who completed graduate degrees at the school and then returned as full-time faculty members.[240]

The faculty teaching in graduate programs also taught undergraduate students, and many of the professors at UBC, HEC, and UWO developed considerable research and publication records. Some, such as Jacques Parizeau, became more well-known due to their non-academic career activities. Students attending any of the three schools were assured that they were receiving instruction from people who were highly current in their fields. This fact, in turn, accentuated the value of their degrees. Many faculty in the early decades of graduate management education received their Ph.Ds. at American universities, with Harvard wielding particular influence, but increasing numbers of them earned degrees at Canadian universities by the 1980s. UBC, HEC, and UWO all adopted the practice of hiring their own graduates.

The question of whether graduate business students learned to be managers and oversee functions in an organization is difficult to conclusively answer. Students in all three programs were often taught using Harvard Business School's case methodology. Indeed, in the case of UWO, they were exclusively taught by that method. Students were taught to approach business problems from the perspective of a senior administrator, even though they may not necessarily have previously been in such a role. Students usually had at least some work experience before entering the MBA program, but the three schools were essentially trying to teach management experience through the case method. The importance of case-based teaching cannot be over-emphasized. Donald Thain described case writing as "the foundation of our careers" such was the central role it played in faculty life.[241]

Students were also taught that problems could be measured and quantified and that problems seeming to pertain directly to people were best covered in personnel or human resource management electives. UBC and HEC did have streams in those areas, but areas like finance and marketing held more interest for students. This was presumably because of the types of available career options. Students emerging from these three graduate programs would have known about the different functions of a business organization. In some cases, such as UBC, the MBA was presented as an option for people working in the public sphere as well. Graduates would have known about the concepts behind marketing, finance, accounting production, and perhaps something about personnel management. They were eventually required to learn about information systems. Their programs gradually came to include international business courses. The clear message was that MBA graduates, especially from UWO, were being prepared to quickly assume positions of major responsibility without necessarily having to gradually ascend organizational hierarchies. The fact that all three programs grew in size and scope over time suggests that students believed that this was the outcome that they could expect. In the case of the alumni who were mentioned here, positions of stature and responsibility were attained.

Notes

1 Robinson, *Snapshots from Hell*, 279.
2 Donald Thain interview, 16 July 2012.
3 [Unknown]. 1954. "The University of British Columbia Calendar." P. UBC Calendars. Vancouver: University of British Columbia. August 30. doi:http://dx.doi.org/10.14288/1.0169845, 197.

4 HEC, A050 W1 001, Box 20574, File 0001, Maitrise en Administration des Affairs, 1969–1970, 7.

5 McDonald, *The Golden Passport*, 193.

6 MacPhee, *History of the Faculty of Commerce and Business Administration*, 23.

7 MacPhee, *History of the Faculty of Commerce and Business Administration*, 23.

8 MacPhee, *History of the Faculty of Commerce and Business Administration*, 24.

9 MacPhee, *History of the Faculty of Commerce and Business Administration*, 36.

10 MacPhee, *History of the Faculty of Commerce and Business Administration*, 29.

11 MacPhee, *History of the Faculty of Commerce and Business Administration*, 30.

12 MacPhee, *History of the Faculty of Commerce and Business Administration*, 32.

13 [Unknown]. 1955. "The University of British Columbia Calendar", P. UBC Calendars. Vancouver: University of British Columbia. August 30. doi:http://dx.doi.org/10.14288/1.0170146, 21–22.

14 [Unknown]. 1955. "The University of British Columbia Calendar." P. UBC Calendars. Vancouver: University of British Columbia. August 30. doi:http://dx.doi.org/10.14288/1.0170146, 306.

15 [Unknown]. 1955. "The University of British Columbia Calendar." P. UBC Calendars. Vancouver: University of British Columbia. August 30. doi:http://dx.doi.org/10.14288/1.0170146, 147.

16 [Unknown]. 1955. "The University of British Columbia Calendar." P. UBC Calendars. Vancouver: University of British Columbia. August 30. doi:http://dx.doi.org/10.14288/1.0170146, 60.

17 [Unknown]. 1955. "The University of British Columbia Calendar." P. UBC Calendars. Vancouver: University of British Columbia. August 30. doi:http://dx.doi.org/10.14288/1.0170146, 416.

18 MacPhee, *History of the Faculty of Commerce and Business Administration*, 80.

19 MacPhee, *History of the Faculty of Commerce and Business Administration*, 38.

20 Earle D. MacPhee Fonds, Box 2, File 2–2, *The Credit Men's Journal*, April 1932, 403–412.

21 [Unknown]. 1965. "UBC Calendar." P. UBC Calendars. [Vancouver: University of British Columbia]. August 30. doi:http://dx.doi.org/10.14288/1.0169935, 15–53.

22 [Unknown]. 1965. "UBC Calendar." P. UBC Calendars. [Vancouver: University of British Columbia]. August 30. doi:http://dx.doi.org/10.14288/1.0169935, O42.

23 [Unknown]. 1965. "UBC Calendar." P. UBC Calendars. [Vancouver: University of British Columbia]. August 30. doi:http://dx.doi.org/10.14288/1.0169935, O42.

24 [Unknown]. 1965. "UBC Calendar." P. UBC Calendars. [Vancouver: University of British Columbia]. August 30. doi:http://dx.doi.org/10.14288/1.0169935, O42.

25 [Unknown]. 1965. "UBC Calendar." P. UBC Calendars. [Vancouver: University of British Columbia]. August 30. doi:http://dx.doi.org/10.14288/1.0169935, O42-O44.

26 [Unknown]. 1965. "UBC Calendar." P. UBC Calendars. [Vancouver: University of British Columbia]. August 30. doi:http://dx.doi.org/10.14288/1.0169935, A66.

27 [Unknown]. 1965. "UBC Calendar." P. UBC Calendars. [Vancouver: University of British Columbia]. August 30. doi:http://dx.doi.org/10.14288/1.0169935, A67.

28 [Unknown]. 1965. "UBC Calendar." P. UBC Calendars. [Vancouver: University of British Columbia]. August 30. doi:http://dx.doi.org/10.14288/1.0169935, A33.

29 [Unknown]. 1975. "The University of British Columbia Vancouver/Canada Sixty-First Session Calendar 1975–76." P. UBC Calendars.

[Vancouver: University of British Columbia]. August 30. doi:http://dx.doi. org/10.14288/1.0169863, 123.

30 [Unknown]. 1975. "The University of British Columbia Vancouver/ Canada Sixty-First Session Calendar 1975–76." P. UBC Calendars. [Vancouver: University of British Columbia]. August 30. doi:http://dx.doi. org/10.14288/1.0169863, 123.

31 [Unknown]. 1975. "The University of British Columbia Vancouver/ Canada Sixty-First Session Calendar 1975–76." P. UBC Calendars. [Vancouver: University of British Columbia]. August 30. doi:http://dx.doi. org/10.14288/1.0169863, 134.

32 [Unknown]. 1975. "The University of British Columbia Vancouver/ Canada Sixty-First Session Calendar 1975–76." P. UBC Calendars. [Vancouver: University of British Columbia]. August 30. doi:http://dx.doi. org/10.14288/1.0169863, 123.

33 [Unknown]. 1975. "The University of British Columbia Vancouver/ Canada Sixty-First Session Calendar 1975–76." P. UBC Calendars. [Vancouver: University of British Columbia]. August 30. doi:http://dx.doi. org/10.14288/1.0169863, 134.

34 [Unknown]. 1975. "The University of British Columbia Vancouver/ Canada Sixty-First Session Calendar 1975–76." P. UBC Calendars. [Vancouver: University of British Columbia]. August 30. doi:http://dx.doi. org/10.14288/1.0169863, 134.

35 [Unknown]. 1975. "The University of British Columbia Vancouver/ Canada Sixty-First Session Calendar 1975–76." P. UBC Calendars. [Vancouver: University of British Columbia]. August 30. doi:http://dx.doi. org/10.14288/1.0169863, 134–135.

36 [Unknown]. 1975. "The University of British Columbia Vancouver/ Canada Sixty-First Session Calendar 1975–76." P. UBC Calendars. [Vancouver: University of British Columbia]. August 30. doi:http://dx.doi. org/10.14288/1.0169863, 29.

37 [Unknown]. 1975. "The University of British Columbia Vancouver/ Canada Sixty-First Session Calendar 1975–76." P. UBC Calendars. [Vancouver: University of British Columbia]. August 30. doi:http://dx.doi. org/10.14288/1.0169863, 29.

38 [Unknown]. 1975. "The University of British Columbia Vancouver/ Canada Sixty-First Session Calendar 1975–76." P. UBC Calendars. [Vancouver: University of British Columbia]. August 30. doi:http://dx.doi. org/10.14288/1.0169863, 29.

39 [Unknown]. 1975. "The University of British Columbia Vancouver/ Canada Sixty-First Session Calendar 1975–76." P. UBC Calendars. [Vancouver: University of British Columbia]. August 30. doi:http://dx.doi. org/10.14288/1.0169863, 15.

40 UBC, Dean's Office—Historical, Box 46, File 46-2 Master of Business Administration Graduates 1976, 4–6.

41 UBC, Dean's Office—Historical, Box 46, File 46-2 Master of Business Administration Graduates 1976, 4–6.

42 UBC, Dean's Office—Historical, Box 46, File 46-2 Master of Business Administration Graduates 1976, 7–28.

43 UBC, Dean's Office—Historical, Box 46, File 46-2 Master of Business Administration Graduates 1976, 4.

44 UBC, Dean's Office—Historical, Box 46, File 46-2 Master of Business Administration Graduates 1976, 4.

45 UBC, Dean's Office—Historical, Box 46, File 46-2 Master of Business Administration Graduates 1976, 6.

46 [Unknown]. 1985. "The University of British Columbia 71st Session 1985–86 Calendar." P. UBC Calendars. Vancouver: Office of the Registrar, The University of British Columbia. August 30. doi:http://dx.doi.org/10.14288/1.0169975, 141.

47 [Unknown]. 1985. "The University of British Columbia 71st Session 1985–86 Calendar." P. UBC Calendars. Vancouver: Office of the Registrar, The University of British Columbia. August 30. doi:http://dx.doi.org/10.14288/1.0169975, 142.

48 [Unknown]. 1985. "The University of British Columbia 71st Session 1985–86 Calendar." P. UBC Calendars. Vancouver: Office of the Registrar, The University of British Columbia. August 30. doi:http://dx.doi.org/10.14288/1.0169975, 141.

49 [Unknown]. 1985. "The University of British Columbia 71st Session 1985–86 Calendar." P. UBC Calendars. Vancouver: Office of the Registrar, The University of British Columbia. August 30. doi:http://dx.doi.org/10.14288/1.0169975, 151.

50 [Unknown]. 1985. "The University of British Columbia 71st Session 1985–86 Calendar." P. UBC Calendars. Vancouver: Office of the Registrar, The University of British Columbia. August 30. doi:http://dx.doi.org/10.14288/1.0169975, 257.

51 [Unknown]. 1985. "The University of British Columbia 71st Session 1985–86 Calendar." P. UBC Calendars. Vancouver: Office of the Registrar, The University of British Columbia. August 30. doi:http://dx.doi.org/10.14288/1.0169975, 257.

52 [Unknown]. 1985. "The University of British Columbia 71st Session 1985–86 Calendar." P. UBC Calendars. Vancouver: Office of the Registrar, The University of British Columbia. August 30. doi:http://dx.doi.org/10.14288/1.0169975, 141–142.

53 [Unknown]. 1985. "The University of British Columbia 71st Session 1985–86 Calendar." P. UBC Calendars. Vancouver: Office of the Registrar, The University of British Columbia. August 30. doi:http://dx.doi.org/10.14288/1.0169975, 34.

54 [Unknown]. 1985. "The University of British Columbia 71st Session 1985–86 Calendar." P. UBC Calendars. Vancouver: Office of the Registrar, The University of British Columbia. August 30. doi:http://dx.doi.org/10.14288/1.0169975, 34.

55 [Unknown]. 1985. "The University of British Columbia 71st Session 1985–86 Calendar." P. UBC Calendars. Vancouver: Office of the Registrar, The University of British Columbia. August 30. doi:http://dx.doi.org/10.14288/1.0169975, 34.

56 [Unknown]. 1985. "The University of British Columbia 71st Session 1985–86 Calendar." P. UBC Calendars. Vancouver: Office of the Registrar, The University of British Columbia. August 30. doi:http://dx.doi.org/10.14288/1.0169975, 22.

57 [Unknown]. 1995. "The University of British Columbia 1995/96 Calendar." P. UBC Calendars. Vancouver: The University of British Columbia, Registrar's Office. August 30. doi:http://dx.doi.org/10.14288/1.0169848, 232.

58 [Unknown]. 1995. "The University of British Columbia 1995/96 Calendar." P. UBC Calendars. Vancouver: The University of British Columbia, Registrar's Office. August 30. doi:http://dx.doi.org/10.14288/1.0169848, 232.

59 [Unknown]. 1995. "The University of British Columbia 1995/96 Calendar." P. UBC Calendars. Vancouver: The University of British Columbia, Registrar's Office. August 30. doi:http://dx.doi.org/10.14288/1.0169848, 59.

60 [Unknown]. 1995. "The University of British Columbia 1995/96 Calendar."
    P. UBC Calendars. Vancouver: The University of British Columbia, Regis-
    trar's Office. August 30. doi:http://dx.doi.org/10.14288/1.0169848, 81.
61 [Unknown]. 1995. "The University of British Columbia 1995/96 Calendar."
    P. UBC Calendars. Vancouver: The University of British Columbia, Regis-
    trar's Office. August 30. doi:http://dx.doi.org/10.14288/1.0169848, 81.
62 UBC, Sauder School of Business Fonds, Box 46, File 46–6, Masters Program
    Graduates 1996, 6–34.
63 UBC, Sauder School of Business Fonds, Box 46, File 46–6, Masters Program
    Graduates 1996, 6–34.
64 UBC, Sauder School of Business Fonds, Box 46, File 46–6, Masters Program
    Graduates 1996, 4.
65 UBC, Sauder School of Business Fonds, Box 46, File 46–6, Masters Program
    Graduates 1996, 5.
66 UBC, Sauder School of Business Fonds, Box 46, File 46–2 Master of Business
    Administration Graduates 1976, 4.
67 UBC, Sauder School of Business Fonds, Box 46, File 46–2 Master of Business
    Administration Graduates 1976, 4.
68 University of British Columbia, accessed 12 December 2017, www.alumni.
    ubc.ca/about/board/lindsay-gordon-ba73-mba76/.
69 University of Toronto, accessed 11 December 2017, www.rotman.utoronto.
    ca/FacultyAndResearch/Faculty/FacultyBios/Verma.
70 University of Toronto, accessed 11 December 2017, www.rotman.utoronto.
    ca/FacultyAndResearch/Faculty/FacultyBios/Verma.
71 For representative work see Anil Verma and Richard P. Chaykowski, ed.,
    Industrial Relations in Canadian Industry (Toronto: Dryden, 1992).
72 UBC, Sauder School of Business fonds, Box 49, File 49–5, Executive pro-
    grams annual report 1974 to 1975, 1.
73 UBC, Sauder School of Business fonds, Box 49, File 49–5, Executive pro-
    grams annual report 1974 to 1975, 2.
74 UBC, Sauder School of Business fonds, Box 49, File 49–5, Executive pro-
    grams annual report 1974 to 1975, 2.
75 UBC, Sauder School of Business fonds, Box 50, File 50–1(1), Professional/
    Executive Programs—Misc Brochures, 1977–88, The Effective Secretary.
76 UBC, Sauder School of Business fonds, Box 50, File 50–1(1), Professional/
    Executive Programs—Misc Brochures, 1977–88, Management Seminars for
    Executives Spring 1986.
77 Chancellor of the Exchequer, *The Colombo Plan for Co-Operative Economic
    Development in South and South-East Asia, Report by the Commonwealth
    Consultative Committee, London: September—October 1950* (London: His
    Majesty's Stationary Office, 1950).
78 Chancellor of the Exchequer, *The Colombo Plan*, 99.
79 UBC, Earle D. MacPhee Fonds, File 3–9 Malaya Project Correspondence,
    Reports, January 1964 to August 1965, Earle D. MacPhee memorandum
    1960.
80 MacPhee, *History of the Faculty of Commerce and Business Administration*, 94.
81 MacPhee, *History of the Faculty of Commerce and Business Administration*, 94.
82 MacPhee, *History of the Faculty of Commerce and Business Administration*, 94.
83 MacPhee, *History of the Faculty of Commerce and Business Administration*,
    95.
84 UBC, Earle D. MacPhee Fonds, Box 3, File 3–9 Malaya Project Correspond-
    ence, Reports, January 1964 to August 1965, 10 June 1963 letter from the
    Ford Foundation in Malaya to Professor Leslie Wong.

85 UBC, Sauder School of Business Fonds, Box 50, File 50–1(1), Senior Managers Development Program.
86 UBC, Sauder School of Business Fonds, Box 50, File 50–1(1), Senior Managers Development Program.
87 UBC, Sauder School of Business Fonds, Box 31, File 31–6, First Nations Leadership Program, 14 September 1998.
88 UBC, Sauder School of Business Fonds, Box 2, File, 2–14, Aviation Management, Discussion Paper, 16 August 1996.
89 UBC, Sauder School of Business Fonds, Box 2, File 2–10 Korea, 1995–1996, Fax from Grace Wong, Associate Dean of International Programs to Mr. Kee Min, 4 January 1996.
90 UBC, Sauder School of Business Fonds, Box 2, File 2–2, letter from IWA President J.J. Munro to Dean Peter Lustig, 26 March 1991.
91 HEC, Fonds de la Direction du Programme M.B.A, Box 20574, file A050/W1 0001, Maitrise en Administration des Affairs 1969–1970, 7.
92 HEC, Fonds de la Direction du Programme M.B.A, Box 20574, file A050/W1 0001, Maitrise en Administration des Affairs 1969–1970, 28.
93 HEC, Fonds de la Direction du Programme M.B.A, Box 20574, file A050/W1 0001, Maitrise en Administration des Affairs 1969–1970, 28.
94 HEC, Fonds de la Direction du Programme M.B.A, Box 20574, file A050/W1 0001, Maitrise en Administration des Affairs 1969–1970, 32.
95 HEC, Fonds de la Direction du Programme M.B.A, Box 20574, file A050/W1 0001, Maitrise en Administration des Affairs 1969–1970, 30.
96 HEC, Fonds de la Direction du Programme M.B.A, Box 20574, file A050/W1 0001, Maitrise en Administration des Affairs 1969–1970, 33.
97 HEC, Fonds de la Direction du Programme M.B.A, Box 20574, file A050/W1 0001, Maitrise en Administration des Affairs 1969–1970, 32.
98 HEC, Fonds de la Direction du Programme M.B.A, Box 20574, file A050/W1 0001, Maitrise en Administration des Affairs 1969–1970, 22.
99 HEC, Fonds de la Direction du Programme M.B.A, Box 20574, file A050/W1 0001, Maitrise en Administration des Affairs 1969–1970, 28.
100 HEC, Fonds du Departement du Management, Box 20994, File E017/G-04–0003, Report Interimaire du Comite sur la Place des Sciences Humaines a l'Ecole.
101 HEC, Fonds du Departement du Management, Box 20994, File E017/G-04–0003, Report Interimaire du Comite sur la Place des Sciences Humaines a l'Ecole.
102 HEC, Fonds du Departement du Management, Box 20994, File E017/G-04–0003, Report Interimaire du Comite sur la Place des Sciences Humaines a l'Ecole.
103 HEC, Fonds du Departement du Management, Box 20994, File E017/G-04–0003, Report Interimaire du Comite sur la Place des Sciences Humaines a l'Ecole.
104 HEC, Fonds du Departement du Management, Box 20994, File E017/G-04–0003, Report Interimaire du Comite sur la Place des Sciences Humaines a l'Ecole.
105 Alain Pinard, "New Era Opens for Québecois MBAs", *The Montréal Star*, 21 December 1971.
106 HEC, Fonds de la Direction du Programme MBA, Box 20079, File A050/13, 0005, Letter to MBA Program Director Denis Lussier, 10 March 1977.
107 HEC, Fonds de la Direction du Programme MBA, Box 20078, File A050/B, 0011, 12 November 1970 petition.

108   HEC, Fonds de la Direction du Programme MBA, Box 20078, File A050/D, 0001, 22 June 1973 letter to MBA program director M.O. Diorio.

109   HEC, MSc. Guides, Box 20819, File A053 W1, 001, MSc 1978 to 1979, 43.

110   HEC, MSc. Guides, Box 20819, File A053 W1, 001, MSc 1978 to 1979, 48.

111   HEC, MSc. Guides, Box 20819, File A053 W1, 001, MSc 1978 to 1979, 51.

112   HEC, MSc. Guides, Box 20819, File A053 W1, 0001, MSc 1978 to 1979, 60.

113   HEC, MBA Guides, Box 20574, File A050 W1, 0002, MBA and DSA 1989 to 1990, 13.

114   HEC, MBA Guides, Box 20574, File A050 W1, 0002, MBA and DSA 1989 to 1990, 16.

115   HEC, MBA Guides, Box 20574, File A050 W1, 0002, MBA and DSA 1989 to 1990, 39.

116   HEC, MBA Guides, Box 20574, File A050 W1, 0002, MBA and DSA 1989 to 1990, 31.

117   HEC, MBA Guides, Box 20574, File A050 W1, 0003, MBA and DSA 1995 to 1996, 11.

118   HEC, MBA Guides, Box 20574, File A050 W1, 0003, MBA and DSA 1995 to 1996, 13.

119   HEC, MBA Guides, Box 20574, File A050 W1, 0003, MBA and DSA 1995 to 1996, 14.

120   HEC, Fondes de la Direction du Programme MBA, Box 20079, File A050/A1 0008, letter to Salah Ferrat 4 February 1976.

121   HEC, Fondes de la Direction de Programme MBA, Box 20078, File A050/B, 0005, "Relationship Between M.B.A. Program Attributes and Personal Characteristics of Students", 6.

122   HEC, Fondes de la Direction de Programme MBA, Box 20078, File A050/B, 0005, "Relationship Between M.B.A. Program Attributes and Personal Characteristics of Students", 9.

123   HEC, Fondes de la Direction de Programme MBA, Box 20078, File A050/B, 0005, "Relationship Between M.B.A. Program Attributes and Personal Characteristics of Students", 10.

124   HEC, Fondes de la Direction de Programme MBA, Box 20078, File A050/B, 0005, "Relationship Between M.B.A. Program Attributes and Personal Characteristics of Students", 10.

125   HEC, Fondes de la Direction de Programme MBA, Box 20078, File A050/B, 0005, "Relationship Between M.B.A. Program Attributes and Personal Characteristics of Students", 15.

126   HEC, Fondes de la Direction de Programme MBA, Box 20078, File A050/B, 0005, "Relationship Between M.B.A. Program Attributes and Personal Characteristics of Students", 15.

127   HEC, Fondes de la Direction de Programme MBA, Box 20078, File A050/B, 0005, "Relationship Between M.B.A. Program Attributes and Personal Characteristics of Students", 19.

128   École des hautes études commerciales de Montréal, accessed 20 December 2017, www.hec.ca/en/about/our-history/the-beginnings-of-a-proud-his tory/index.html.

129   HEC, Annuaires (BAA program), Box 20222, File A052 W1 0001, BAA 1975, 10.

130   For representative work see Jean-Pierre Hogue, *Les Relations Humanes dans L'Entreprise* (Montréal: Beauchemin, 1971).

131   For representative work see Francine Harel-Giasson, Nicole Forget, and Francine Séguin, *Justine Lacoste-Beaubien et l'Hôpital* (Sainte-Foy, PQ: Presses de l'Université du Québec, 1995).

132   HEC, Certificate Program Guides, Box 20239, 1977–1978, pp. 54–57.

133 HEC, Certificate Program Guides, Box 20239, 1977–1978, pp. 77.
134 HEC, Workshop and Seminar Guides, Box 21010, File A072/W3 0411, Political Skills for Women Executives.
135 Donald Thain interview, 16 July 2012.
136 Thain interview.
137 Thain interview.
138 ARCC, UWO Business School Announcement 1950, 22.
139 ARCC, UWO Business School Announcement 1950, 22.
140 ARCC, UWO Business School Announcement 1950, 23.
141 ARCC, UWO Business School Announcement 1950, 49.
142 ARCC, UWO Business School Announcement 1950, 24.
143 ARCC, The University of Western Ontario Business School: An Invitation to Employers, 1958.
144 ARCC, The University of Western Ontario Business School: An Invitation to Employers, 1958.
145 ARCC, The University of Western Ontario Business School: An Invitation to Employers, 1958.
146 ARCC, The University of Western Ontario Business School: An Invitation to Employers, 1958, 8.
147 ARCC, The University of Western Ontario Business School: An Invitation to Employers, 1958, 8.
148 ARCC, The University of Western Ontario Business School: An Invitation to Employers, 1958, 8.
149 ARCC, The University of Western Ontario Business School: An Invitation to Employers, 1958, 8.
150 Thain interview.
151 Richard Marens, "He Who May Not Be Mentioned: Marx, History, and American Business Schools", Patricia Genoe McLaren, Albert J. Mills, and Terrance G. Weatherbee ed., *The Routledge Companion to Management and Organizational History* (Abingdon: Routledge, 2015), pp. 84–95.
152 Thain interview.
153 ARCC, UWO Calendars, UWO Business School MBA Program 1961, 14.
154 ARCC, UWO Calendars, UWO Business School MBA Program 1961, 15.
155 ARCC, UWO Calendars, UWO Business School MBA Program 1961, 15.
156 ARCC, UWO Calendars, UWO Business School MBA Program 1961, 18.
157 ARCC, UWO Calendars, UWO Business School MBA Program 1961, 21.
158 ARCC, UWO Calendars, UWO Business School MBA Program 1961, 31.
159 ARCC, UWO Calendars, Faculty of Graduate Studies 1975, 65.
160 ARCC, UWO Calendars, Faculty of Graduate Studies 1975, 66.
161 ARCC, UWO Calendars, Faculty of Graduate Studies 1975, 14.
162 ARCC, UWO Calendars, Faculty of Graduate Studies 1984–1986, I-32.
163 ARCC, UWO Calendars, Faculty of Graduate Studies 1984–1986, I-32.
164 ARCC, UWO Calendars, Faculty of Graduate Studies 1984–1986, I-32.
165 ARCC, UWO Calendars, Faculty of Graduate Studies 1984–1986, III-7.
166 ARCC, UWO Calendars, Faculty of Graduate Studies 1984–1986, III-8.
167 ARCC, UWO Calendars, Faculty of Graduate Studies 1984–1986, III-8–9.
168 ARCC, UWO Calendars, Faculty of Graduate Studies 1984–1986, I-18.
169 ARCC, UWO Calendars, Faculty of Graduate Studies 1995–1997, I-24.
170 ARCC, UWO Calendars, Faculty of Graduate Studies Social Science Division1995–1997, III-9.
171 ARCC, UWO Calendars, Faculty of Graduate Studies Social Science Division1995–1997, III-9.
172 ARCC, UWO Calendars, Faculty of Graduate Studies Social Science Division1995–1997, III-9–10.

173 ARCC, UWO Calendars, Faculty of Graduate Studies Social Science Division1995–1997, III-9–10.
174 Alexander Mikalachki, "Group Cohesion Reconsidered: A Study of Blue Collar Work Groups" (Ph.D. Thesis, University of Western Ontario, 1964).
175 For example see Donald Thain, John J. Wettlaufer, and Samuel A. Martin, *Business Administration in Canada* (Toronto: McGraw-Hill, 1961).
176 Sanders, *Learning to Lead*, 34–35.
177 Thain interview.
178 Thain interview.
179 ARCC, UWO President's Office Collection, AFC 40–55/1, "Fourth Management Training Course, Summer 1951", 1.
180 ARCC, UWO President's Office Collection, AFC 40–55/1, "Fourth Management Training Course, Summer 1951", 12.
181 Thain interview.
182 ARCC, Clarence Fraser Papers, B5084, "11th Management Training Course, Summer 1958", 1.
183 Thain interview.
184 ARCC, Clarence Fraser Papers, B5084, "11th Management Training Course, Summer 1958", 1.
185 ARCC, UWO President's Office Collection, AFC 40–55/1, G. Edward Hall to D.B. Greig, 15 October 1951.
186 ARCC, UWO President's Office Collection, AFC 40–55/23, R. R. Faryon to G. Edward Hall 9 July 1956.
187 ARCC, UWO President's Office Collection, AFC 40–55/1, Management Training Course—1951, Statistical Summer of Class.
188 ARCC, UWO President's Office Collection, AFC 40–55/19, "Announcing the Eighth Session of the Management Training Course, August 1 to September 2, 1955", 10.
189 ARCC, Clarence Fraser Papers, B5081–1, Walter A. Thompson to Clarence Fraser, 5 March 1948.
190 ARCC, UWO President's Office Collection, AFC 40–55/1, "Fourth Management Training Course, Summer 1951", 12.
191 Phillip Sherlock and Rex Nettleford, *The University of the West Indies: A Caribbean Response to the Challenge of Change* (London: Macmillan, 1990), 12.
192 Sherlock and Nettleford, *The University of the West Indies*, 28.
193 Sherlock and Nettleford, *The University of the West Indies*.
194 Sherlock and Nettleford, *The University of the West Indies*, 35.
195 Library and Archives of Canada (hereafter LAC), RG 19, volume 5284, Canadian Development Assistance Programs, University of the West Indies, "Country Reviews: University of the West Indies, 1969".
196 LAC, RG 19, volume 5284, Canadian Development Assistance Programs, University of the West Indies, J.F. Grandy memorandum to the Minister of External Affairs, 23 January 1967.
197 LAC, RG 19, volume 5284, Canadian Development Assistance Programs, University of the West Indies, J.F. Grandy memorandum to the Minister of External Affairs, 23 January 1967.
198 AUCC, "Canadian Universities and International Development: A Report Prepared for the Canadian International Development Agency by Professor Norma Walmsley on Behalf of the Association of Universities and Colleges of Canada" (Ottawa: AUCC, 1970), 3.
199 AUCC, "Canadian Universities and International Development", 22–23.
200 AUCC, "Canadian Universities and International Development", 54.
201 AUCC, "Canadian Universities and International Development", 61.
202 AUCC, "Canadian Universities and International Development", 67.

203 AUCC, "Canadian Universities and International Development", 119–120.

204 AUCC, "Canadian Universities and International Development", 119.

205 AUCC, "Canadian Universities and International Development", 227.

206 AUCC, "Canadian Universities and International Development", 229.

207 AUCC, "Canadian Universities and International Development", 231.

208 AUCC, "Canadian Universities and International Development", 246.

209 ARCC, Walter Thompson fonds, A12–031–001, file: Project Officer UWI, "Assistance to the Faculty of Management Studies UWI/UWO".

210 ARCC, Walter Thompson fonds, A12–031–002, file: Williams, Hugh, Walter Thompson to Randolph L. Williams, 1 October 1971.

211 ARCC, Walter Thompson fonds, A12–031–001, file: Miscellaneous UWI, memo, Walter Thompson to All Faculty Members (UWO School of Business Administration), 5 February 1971.

212 ARCC, Walter Thompson fonds, A12–031–002, file: Williams, Hugh, Walter Thompson to Randolph L. Williams, 1 October 1971.

213 ARCC, Walter Thompson fonds, A12–031–001, file: Pakistan Middle Management, Ian Hodson to Walter Thompson, 3 December 1959.

214 ARCC, Walter Thompson fonds, A12–031–001, W.A. Thompson to Dean J.J. Wettlaufer, memorandum, 8 June 1972.

215 Michael Kaufman, *Jamaica Under Manley: Dilemmas of Socialism and Democracy* (London: Zed Books, 1985), 141–142.

216 Kaufman, *Jamaica Under Manley: Dilemmas of Socialism and Democracy*, 19.

217 ARCC, Walter Thompson fonds, A12–031–002, file: Manley—Jamaica—Prime Minister, J.M. Harrington to Walter Thompson, 20 February 1974.

218 ARCC, Walter Thompson fonds, A12–031–002, "Management Survey, 1967".

219 ARCC, Walter Thompson fonds, A12–031–004, file: Continuing Education, UWI, "UWI Management, 4th Annual Senior Management Course".

220 ARCC, Walter Thompson fonds, A12–031–004, file: Continuing Education, UWI, "UWI Management, 4th Annual Senior Management Course".

221 Howard Campbell, "UWI Lobbies Gov't for Project Funds Despite Budget Cut", *The Gleaner*, accessed 23 May 2015, http://old.jamaica-gleaner.com/gleaner/20110311/business/business92.html.

222 ARCC, Walter Thompson fonds, A12–031–004, file: Continuing Education, UWI, "UWI Management, 4th Annual Senior Management Course".

223 ARCC, Walter Thompson fonds, A12–031–004, file: Courses, UWI.

224 ARCC, Walter Thompson fonds, A12–031–004, file: Courses, UWI.

225 ARCC, Walter Thompson fonds, A12–031–002, file: University of the West Indies, 1971.

226 ARCC, Walter Thompson fonds, A12–031–001, file: Enrollment of West Indian Students in MBA Programs in US and Canada, Don Hathaway to Walter Thompson, 6 December 1971.

227 ARCC, Walter Thompson fonds, A12–031–004, file: *Express*, 3 October 1973.

228 ARCC, Walter Thompson fonds, A12–031–002, file: B.F. Yuill, B.F. Yuill to Walter Thompson, 13 January 1974.

229 ARCC, Walter Thompson fonds, A12–031–004, file: Cukieman, Sam, San Cukieman to Walter Thompson (no date shown).

230 ARCC, Walter Thompson fonds, A12–031–004, file: Cukieman, Sam, Walter Thompson to Sam Cukieman, 16 October 1973.

231 ARCC, Walter Thompson fonds, A12–031–001, file: Miscellaneous, UWI, Walter Thompson to Ray Jones, 3 August 1972.

232 ARCC, Walter Thompson fonds, A12–031–002, file: Kerry Hill, A.A. Mark to All Members of the Department of Management Studies, 29 October 1974.

233 ARCC, Walter Thompson fonds, A12–031–001, C.B. Johnston to W.A. Thompson, memo, 22 December 1972.
234 ARCC, Walter Thompson fonds, A12–031–001, file: UWI, Manchester Business School Newsletter 1973 (no month shown).
235 ARCC, Walter Thompson fonds, A12–031–001, file: Miscellaneous UWI, A. Rudi Kuhlmann to Walter Thompson, 30 October 1974.
236 ARCC, Walter Thompson fonds, A12–031–001, file: UWI, Karl Johansen to Walter Thompson, 30 September 1976.
237 ARCC, Walter Thompson fonds, A12–031–004, file: Case Materials UWI, 13 September 1973.
238 UWO MBA Association, *Western MBA* (September 1982), 5.
239 Richard Ivey School of Business Administration, accessed 10 January 2018, www.ivey.uwo.ca/alumni/intouch/2014/3/going-public/.
240 École des hautes études commerciales de Montréal, accessed 10 January 2018, www.hec.ca/en/profs/sylvie.st-onge.html, accessed 10 January 2018.
241 Thain interview.

6   The Meaning of
Management Education
and Training in Canada

This analysis of management education in Canada from 1945 to 1995 reveals some common themes, but also crucial differences in programs and practices. Educating and training managers in Canada occurred in important institutional environments: companies, colleges, and universities. This final chapter will summarize what was presented thus far in this narrative. It will also place management education and training into the wider social context of Canada in the five decades after World War II. Management became an important form of education, fundamental to the running of corporations, and a varied and significant type of employment. It was usually portrayed as something associated with the private sector, but the state clearly considered management to be a social institution in Canada because governments actively supported it through education and training. Being a manager was something to which many people aspired, and they were able to pursue their career ambitions through a range of programs. They could choose to participate in management education and training of different types, but doing so did not necessarily mean that they knew how to manage. They collectively formed a managerial class and, recalling Edward Thompson, managers experienced similar productive relations as they were engaged at different levels in running corporations. Thompson further argued that "class is a relationship, and not a thing," and management education and training facilitated the development of a managerial class in Canada.[1]

Examining what management education in training meant in Canada also means considering what potential and current managers were not taught. Corporations sent messages through training about what they considered their role to be in Canadian society, and how managers should view their roles in companies. Universities and colleges emphasized different aspects of management, but they also sent messages about what it meant to be in managerial roles. The end result was that, while managers were trained in ways that reflected their places in corporate hierarchies, they still formed a broad but identifiable group within Canadian society that was taught to share a common outlook on the importance of business and corporations. A managerial class existed in Canada prior to 1945, and it became much more developed as subsequent decades progressed and important institutions sought to enhance it. This narrative has so far been able to identify specific students who attended community colleges and undergraduate and graduate university programs. People who participated in corporate programs remain much more anonymous, but they appear in census data on management. As Table 6.1 shows, the number of managers in Canada increased significantly from 1951 to 1991. The most marked increase was in the number of women working in managerial jobs. By 1991, there were 14.4 million people in Canada's workforce, and 1.7 million of them were managers of some type.[2]

The institutions that offered management training and education in Canada shared some common characteristics but also major differences. Corporations were private entities that were owned by shareholders and did not have the provision of training programs as their core mission, while community colleges and universities were public institutions that were supposed to operate on a non-profit basis and had education as their reason for existence. The programs offered by all three types of organization emphasized that management was important, but they approached the idea of being a manager and the function of management from very different perspectives. Training for managers working in corporations was integrated into their overall job duties, and they did not pay for it. They were compensated if they attended programs that required them to be away from the usual job site. In contrast, anyone attending a college or university management course of some type had to pay for it and attend on his or her own time. Management training and education programs offered by companies, colleges, and universities reflected stratification within management as an occupation even as managers existed in the same social class.

Table 6.1 Managerial Employment in Canada by Gender, 1951–1991

Year	Total Number of Managers	Male	Female
1951	407,191	369,934	37,257
1961	539,040	481,379	57,661
1971	679,843	593,488	86,355
1981	1,060,0015	797,830	262,190
1991	1,739,165	1,086,150	653,020

Source: Dominion Bureau of Statistics, Ninth Census of Canada 1951, Volume IV, Table 4, Labour Force; Dominion Bureau of Statistics, 1961 Census of Canada, Series 3.1, Table 17, Labour Force; Statistics Canada, 1971 Census of Canada, Occupations, Table 1; Statistics Census of Canada 1981 Census Divisions and Subdivisions, Selected Social and Economic Characteristics; Statistics Canada, Census of Canada 1991, Table 1, Industry and Class of Worker, Table 1.

Corporations

The three corporations discussed here adopted different methods of providing training that evolved over time, largely in response to changes in technology. Bell Canada operated a sophisticated management training program in the 1950s and 1960s that enabled selected participants to actually participate in training programs outside of their daily work. The Bell program included some theory and described how Bell operated internally and in the areas of Canada where it provided phone service. Managers going away for several days of training were given thick binders full of flow charts, case studies, and other documents that they could use on the job. Bell's leadership wanted to convey a message that the company was central to Canada's economic prosperity. As a company that was built on communication technology, managers were taught enough about how the Bell system's infrastructure functioned so that they could credibly respond to technology issues that they faced in their jobs. The Bell training materials were usually based on what had already been implemented at AT&T, and the content was thus based on American management thought. Bell managers were taught that being in management and operating the company's infrastructure was important. The company was unionized, but it was clear to anyone reading a management training manual that its leaders felt that unions had a limited role to play in the organization. Employer paternalism appeared in Bell's training materials as managers were encouraged to help employees solve their problems. While Bell did not develop extensive systems of welfare capitalism like companies such as Kodak, paying for managers to attend training at a resort was certainly a basic form of it.

Eaton also used print materials that were usually produced internally and reflected values and attitudes that were important to the company's leadership. The company encouraged supervisory staff in the 1950s to view Eaton as a social institution. The pursuit of profit was secondary to the firm's status in Canadian society. Eaton practiced employer paternalism, and long-service supervisory staff in the late 1940 and early 1950s could perhaps look forward to meeting members of the owning family at their country estate. The teaching methods that Eaton used in its training programs altered by the 1970s as the use of film and video became more common, and those resources were often internally developed. The company continued to represent itself as an important national institution, and its sponsorship of events like the Santa Claus parade in Toronto made it appear that way to Canadian consumers. Eaton did not show much diversity in its 1970s training resources, and it instead presented to current and prospective managers images of what the firm's leadership thought Canada was like at that time. Eaton changed in the 1980s and was clearly trying to portray itself as more diverse, technologically advanced, and still the leader of Canada's retail industry.

Douglas Eichar examined the history of corporate social responsibility, and the Eaton family would have liked the term had they heard it while their firm was still operating. However, anyone in middle and lower management who watched Fredrik Eaton talk about the state of the company may have felt some consternation over what his views were on what they experienced on a daily basis. Theory was not explicitly mentioned in Eaton training materials, but it was still evident throughout. There was little evidence of Frederick Winslow Taylor, but Elton Mayo and the Human Relations School hovered over Eaton's approach to management. The company was paternalistic, and the emphasis placed on making a long-term career and fitting into the company's ethos were ways of making employees feel special. Eaton's approach to management did not appear punitive, but the firm's absolute resistance to unionization showed that policies regarding the employment would be determined by management and nobody else. Eaton managers were not told that they could not expect long tenure with the firm, but they eventually received messages that the pace of their work should increase. Seeing a winning football coach say on a video that he thrived on stress sent a clear signal that managers should also develop a taste for it. Eaton managers were reminded, right into the 1990s, that they needed to be in control of communication with and between employees. For instance, such was the need for maintaining control that managers were told that they should take minutes at staff meetings and not delegate this task. There were changes over time as women were portrayed in managerial roles, even if it involved taking meeting minutes.[3]

Labatt did not always portray itself as a major cornerstone of Canada's economy. It instead emphasized its long history in Canada and its role as a leader in the country's beer industry. Labatt, like Eaton, was started as a family business, although that family's role was not central to the firm's management like the Eaton family's position at the retail company. Labatt made extensive use of non-print training methods from the late 1960s onward. Those materials were generally created in the United States, with the company occasionally making its own films and videos. The messages conveyed in the Labatt materials was markedly different from what was said in those used by Bell and Eaton. Whereas Bell and Eaton managers were encouraged to think about the importance of their firms and ensuring that internal policies and procedures were followed, Labatt managers received conflicting messages. They were told to cooperate with each other, but that they were foolish to believe that they would have jobs for life. Managers had to compete for jobs and be willing to embrace constant change. The way in which these messages was conveyed illustrated the role of training by the early 1970s. Audio cassette tapes could be listened to at home or in a car stereo, and managers could very well have been expected to have a tape running while on personal time or while performing other work tasks.

Bell and Eaton did not talk at length in their training programs about competition in their industries. Bell was a regulated monopoly, and Eaton considered itself to the most important retailer in Canada while acknowledging that it had competitors. Labatt's senior management was concerned in the 1990s about the future of the beer industry to such an extent that they paid to convene a management conference that featured several guest speakers. That company was also unionized, like Bell, and had a similar outlook on unions. Labatt management sought to encourage cooperation between labour and management, and labour at the time appeared to agree with that approach. Workplace health and safety was discussed in Labatt training resources, whereas it was not evident in the materials used by Bell or Eaton.

Methods for dealing with employee issues in the workplace frequently appeared in Labatt's training resources. The examples used were often situational, much as they had been at Bell in the 1950s and 1960s. An employee encounters a problem, shows a pattern of behaviour that management considered undesirable, is applying for a new role, or some other issue. Managers were told what they should do in response based on what was conveyed on the tape or in the film or video. The purpose was not for managers to think critically about a personnel problem, but to draw on the knowledge acquired from watching a film or listening to a tape and applying it on the job. The Labatt training resources at times showed evidence of gender bias. The early 1970s film starring Van Johnson was commentary on the type of behaviour that was evident in workplaces at that time, and it says something about the organizational values at Labatt because the company chose to acquire the film and use it. The film produced locally in London, Ontario, that featured two beer sales representatives may have been the product of minds with juvenile senses of humour, but it managed to find its way into the collection of training materials retained by the company. It showed that there were at least some members of Labatt management who thought that bias toward women was still acceptable, even though almost twenty years had elapsed since Van Johnson was on screen agonizing over whether he was a professional. Julie Berebitsky has noted that the term "sexual harassment" was not coined until 1975 and that women had long been viewed as sex objects in the workplace. Training on gender issues like harassment was apparently not included in Labatt's training materials, nor did it appear at Eaton or Bell. The film about the Eaton strike, which was not made by the company but rather by the union, was the only resource used by Eaton that explicitly talked about gender issues in the workplace.[4]

The wide array of print and audio-visual training aids alone indicates that corporate management training was a big business from the 1950s to the 1990s. This fact was borne out by the memories of corporate training film veteran John. Companies routinely spent money on training aids for a range of purposes. They learned in the 1970s to rely on professional film-makers to craft the messages that they wanted to convey. Training resources were not the same as marketing tools to present to new and potential customers. The industry changed in the late 1980s as video technology became more accessible to anyone who wanted to enter the corporate film industry. A domestic corporate training video industry emerged in Canada, even though American training films were ubiquitous in management training at Eaton and Labatt.

There was no liberal arts content in the training resources used by Bell, Eaton, or Labatt, nor was there quantitative analysis. The work of some management writers was used on a limited basis by Bell. The issue of management as a profession was not always clearly referenced in training materials at Bell, Eaton, and Labatt. Training was conducted by staff from human resources in the case of in-class training sessions at Bell but using videos or audio tapes required no facilitator to lead a training session. A senior manager could have simply handed a video tape to a subordinate supervisor and advised him or her to watch it. Training occurred in environments that were specific to each company, and much of what was taught could not be easily transferred to another work environment. For instance, knowing about the vicissitudes of the brewing industry in the early 1990s would not have helped an Eaton's manager run a department in a store. This meant that stature as a manager would not have been easily recognized by another company beyond having held the actual job title. People became managers within the confines of a specific organization.

Managers were not taught much about core business functions like finance, accounting, finance, or operations management. The emphasis was on personnel problems and what it meant to be in management. In one sense, it meant indoctrinating them into the practices and beliefs of their firms. In another sense, being more familiar with a problem like the rise of craft brewing than other managers would have given someone an advantage in Labatt. The same thing was true of managers who went away for training at Bell in the 1960s or who were held in high enough esteem at Eaton to attend a reception at the Eaton family estate. Managers who received company training were professionals within the confines of their companies. The most important aspect about the management training methods taught at Bell, Eaton, and Labatt was that they were used by people who were managers and actually managed different aspects of their organizations. Management training was important in those three companies, but it is not possible to determine if it affected their profitability or future progress. Senior leadership in all three organizations consistently spent money on training managers, so it was obviously considered an investment that bore results. The managers who participated in training, in the case of the study of Bell managers, did not find that it always helped them deal with issues that they faced on the job. The views of Eaton and Labatt managers are not recorded. Nonetheless, all three companies forged ahead with training programs.

Community Colleges

The management education programs offered by Vancouver Community College (VCC), Collége Ahuntsic, and Niagara College were varied but included some important similarities. The most important difference between what community colleges offered in comparison to companies is that at least some academic credit was associated with their programs. Programs were offered on full-time and part-time bases at all three schools. Another crucial point about community college management programs pertains to when the schools themselves were founded. The mid to late 1960s witnessed the founding and rapid expansion of community colleges across Canada. The community college was considered a necessary type of institution because it provided educational opportunities to the country's large baby boom demographic cohort and also because public policy makers felt that a more educated workforce was required to ensure economic growth and prosperity.

Governments in British Columbia, Québec, and Ontario all studied their respective higher education needs. Applied education was considered a necessity, and community colleges would meet that particular need. Governments also crucially thought that training managers and supervisors was also something that community colleges should be doing. The three schools discussed here operated in provinces with differing education systems. British Columbia organized VCC in such a way that it would provide a pathway to university for students who wanted to go further in higher education, but it also offered a path that led directly to the job market. Ontario introduced a community college system that did not offer an expeditious route to university. That province's colleges were intended to offer more strictly applied programs, although educating managers was again a priority, as it was in BC. The CEGEP system in Québec was intended to be a transition from secondary school to university for those students who wished to eventually complete a degree, but it also offered applied programs that would prepare graduates for the labour market.

The impetus for offering management programs at community colleges was also related to local conditions as much as concerns about national competitiveness. In BC, VCC was founded to provide educational opportunities to young people in Vancouver and lower provincial mainland. Citizens were actively encouraged to support its founding and were advised of the benefits that the new college would bring to the community. The CEGEPs were a unique system in relation to what was developed in English Canada, but there was extensive consideration of systems that existed in other jurisdictions including the United States. Some CEGEPs were established to offer programs taught in English, but they were outnumbered by others that operated entirely in French. The fact that young francophone students could study either for a vocational occupation or prepare for university was a major advance in Québec. A school like Niagara College was also intended to make it possible for students from the Niagara Region of Ontario to pursue post-secondary education without having to move away, and to then contribute to the local economy.

The fact that management education programs of differing types were offered by community colleges in three Canadian provinces indicates that management was viewed as a vocational pursuit. The colleges offered programs during the day and, as seen in the case of Niagara College, it was not unusual for them to offer an extensive range of programs in the evening. The colleges formed links to external organizations that administered different professional designations, such as the Ontario Management Development Program (OMDP). The OMDP program was important because, while it did not enroll enormous numbers of students, it was a state-sponsored effort to create a province-wide management training program. The need for more advanced training for managers and supervisors had been identified in the 1970s by a federal government agency, and the provinces were involved in discussions regarding what should be done to address the problem. The Ontario government responded with OMDP along with further expansion of community college management programs. The OMDP program also revealed another important aspect of some community college management programs: they were intended to be sources of revenue beyond what was earned from full-time day programs. This was particularly true of OMDP since community colleges were compensated for developing courses that were used across Ontario. Programs like that one were offered in the evenings, and students could complete them at their own paces. Community college management programs, regardless of the province in which they were offered, were inexpensive, and their value clearly attracted students as more of them were developed almost every year.

The full-time community college programs did include some liberal arts content, especially in the early years that they were offered. The programs required some quantitative ability but were not overwhelmingly oriented in that direction. There was considerable emphasis on daily workplace issues in the college programs, such as personnel or human resources practices. The part-time programs addressed new workplace concerns such as diversity and issues that were felt to pertain more specifically to women. In the case of Niagara College, the Labour Studies program courses placed workplace issues within a broader analytic framework than those offered in the management programs. Programs altered, some disappeared, and new ones were introduced as time passed. The colleges endeavoured to be closely aligned with what employers hoped to see students learn. In the case of Niagara College, advisory boards were usually comprised of people from the local business community.

Students who attended management programs in the evening or on weekends were generally already working during the day. They were in management roles of some type, or aspired to be in such a role, and integrated what they learned at community college with their job tasks. This model of management learning almost resembled an apprenticeship as it tied in-class learning with on-the-job knowledge application. Community college management students came from a wide range of age groups. Students coming to full-time programs were secondary school graduates in their late teens and early twenties, while students in evening and weekend programs were older and more established in their careers.

Some people educated at community colleges were better prepared to become managers, while others were not necessarily ready to assume managerial roles. Students who came right out of secondary school and entered a management program learned about core business functions like finance, accounting, marketing, and operations management. Courses on those functional areas were found at VCC, Collége Ahuntsic, and Niagara College. Students could specialize in certain aspects of business management, such as human resources. They may not have necessarily been ready to step into managerial roles but would have been familiar with the basic aspects of business functions and thus capable of eventually assuming managerial responsibility. The colleges did not imply in their program descriptions that students could expect to quickly assume positions of great stature and authority in business organizations. They instead emphasized that students would learn about management functions. Profiles of previous students who had participated in a given management program were sometimes used in program guides, and those former students were often working in front-line and middle-level managerial roles. There was no question that they were capable of managing at least small-scale business functions, as they were already doing so and came to college outside of working hours to become better at their jobs and perhaps further their careers. In this regard, they were like managers who participated in training programs at companies like Bell, Eaton, and Labatt. Indeed, some of them may have worked for those companies. They were different from students who enrolled in undergraduate university business and management programs, as they balanced other life commitments including jobs in order to attend classes.

Undergraduate

The undergraduate business and management programs offered by the three universities discussed here—UBC, UWO, and HEC—shared some similarities with those run by corporations or offered by colleges, but there were some differences between them. The undergraduate programs all led to a bachelor's degree, which in the hierarchy of academic credentials was at a higher status than non-credit corporate training or community college certificates and diplomas. Undergraduate university programs were generally offered on a full-time basis to students who had recently graduated from high school. HEC did offer evening study options, but UBC and UWO were firmly focused on teaching young people who had not yet been in the workforce on a full-time basis.

University management education preceded other forms of credentialed management education in Canada by several decades. The founding of business and management programs was closely linked to concerns about regional and national competitiveness and the needs of Canada's growing twentieth-century business sector. UBC was founded in order to make it possible to pursue a university education in British Columbia and alleviate the need to attend a university in eastern Canada or perhaps the United States. The establishment of UBC was an accomplishment for the province. British Columbia students were able to stay close to home to study if they wished. The founding of the UBC Commerce program was propelled by concerns about the province's economic development. HEC was created to provide commerce education in French and to help develop the development of capital in Québec at a time when English language universities were the only places where business could be studied. The founding of HEC consequently was an important development for the province and for its business community.

There were key similarities shared by UBC and HEC when it came to formation of their business and management programs, and those traits reflected wider patterns in Canada's socio-economic development. Ontario was an economic rival to Québec and also home to the largest number of Canada's leading English-language universities in the early twentieth century. Countering Ontario's economic influence, and the influence of the English-speaking business class in Québec, required the development of institutions that would foster economic development in other parts of the country and help the francophone business class. UBC and HEC helped meet those objectives. UWO began offering undergraduate commerce programs in response to student interests and a perceived need to foster the growth of Canadian business. The difference with UWO was that it was located in southern Ontario and closer to the main centres of economic power in Canada than UBC and, unlike HEC, its programs were taught in English. UWO wanted London, Ontario, to be a preferred destination for young people who wanted to study business regardless of where they lived. All three schools ultimately sought to cast wider nets to attract students than community colleges would attempt to do in their early decades.

Undergraduate management education was presented as providing a general overview of how business functioned. It was initially rooted in liberal arts education, and students were obliged to have either completed a year of study that included courses in subjects such as history or economics or to include such subjects in their first year as actual business or commerce students. Core business functions were to be studied once students were actually admitted as business or commerce students. This was the practice from the late 1940s to the early 1960s, when program content began to markedly shift toward more numerically focused courses. Business and commerce programs continued to be ostensibly presented as having a general liberal arts basis, but anyone coming into them needed to have well-developed skills in mathematics so that they could succeed in subjects like quantitative analysis, finance, and accounting. UBC and HEC offered programs that provided students with the ability to choose defined program concentrations, but UWO did not provide that option and instead listed a series of elective courses that could be used to create an essentially individualized concentration. The list of non-quantitative options decreased at all schools, regardless of whether defined concentrations were part of a program. Of the three business schools, UWO was the most consistently emphatic in saying that its program was general in nature. The message that developed over time was clear: understanding managing business was a process driven by numbers, and knowing how to interpret and use numbers would lead to success.

The teaching methods used in undergraduate business and commerce programs had some common traits with what was offered at community colleges but were unique in other ways. The role of the case teaching method and by extension the influence of Harvard Business School (HBS) appeared at both community colleges and in undergraduate programs. Cases were also used in corporate training. Bell used actual written cases, while videos at Labatt were often based on instances of fictional business problems. The OMDP program integrated basic case study analysis as well. The cases used by UBC, HEC, and UWO were developed by academics. Indeed, UWO used case-based instruction as its core pedagogical method. Cases were not without controversy, as noted by Duff McDonald and also by Stephen Cummings, Todd Bridgman, John Hassard, and Michael Rowlinson. Often complex business problems were distilled into a few hundred words, and students were expected to grasp a case's content and then argue how the problem should be solved. The fact that cases were written with the help of the companies that were the focus of them meant that students would benefit from learning about actual business problems. The obvious negative aspect to cases was that, in the HBS model, companies had final say over what was found in cases. This means that cases could present benign narratives of management decision making.

UBC, HEC, and UWO all articulated reasons why students would value enrolling in their business programs. UWO Business School was the most effusive in its statements to potential students and basically communicated that career success was assured for anyone who graduated from its programs. UBC and UWO were not quite as bold in the claims that they made about their programs. All three had some reason to feel confident about what they were offering. Business and commerce students in the 1950s and 1960s were not a diverse group. Images found in program guides from that period portray groups of students who were white and male. There was some emerging diversity at UBC as students like Taffara Deguefé chose to come to Vancouver to study. In fact, UBC was the first program to show substantial changes in enrollment patterns in the 1970s as more women and people of colour chose to enroll in its Faculty of Commerce.

The cost of business and commerce programs from the 1950s to the 1980s was equal to what was assessed for other undergraduate programs, and increases only began by the 1990s. UBC, HEC, and UWO all cost more to attend than community colleges, but the economic issue for students was paying to attend university overall and not specifically the cost of studying business or commerce in hopes of securing a management job upon graduation. The programs at all three schools were equally developed in terms of the number of faculty who were involved with them. Whereas the facilitators for corporate training were usually anonymous, and community college faculty were also largely unknown unless their names happened to be listed in program guides, business faculty were prominently listed in undergraduate program information. UBC, HEC, and UWO all had faculty with terminal degrees and research and publication track records. All three schools employed faculty who were alumni of one or more of their programs. This was especially true of HEC, as its faculty taught and published in French.

The manner in which an institution presents information about itself says much about what its leaders prioritized. HEC's program guides tended to feature its history and the credentials and accomplishments of its faculty, then present information about its program. HEC was not concerned with quickly detailing the cost of its programs. It was instead more concerned with emphasizing its overall academic quality. In fact, HEC first talked about the school's history in its program information. UBC's undergraduate program information was listed along with others offered by different programs across the university. UBC listed its fee structure, then listed faculty with their credentials, and finally went into program descriptions. UBC and HEC both included descriptions for each course, and course texts were actually listed in the UBC program syllabi in the early years of the commerce program. UWO was as concerned with presenting lists of contacts in the Canadian business community as it was with listing the names and credentials of faculty members. Degree costs were delineated in the first few pages of a program guide and were followed by degree outlines and course descriptions. UWO Business School emphasized the marketability of its undergraduate degree and links to Canada's business community as much as any other aspects of it.

Graduates of the UBC, HEC, and UWO undergraduate business and commerce programs learned about core business functions and would have graduated equipped with well-developed skills in quantitative analysis, marketing, finance, and accounting. They were basically taught that managing was about creating, interpreting, and manipulating numbers, as every aspect of business came across as a number. There was a shift in focus from the 1950s to the 1990s that emphasized financial education and corporate profitability. Students at all three schools learned about employee issues in the workplace by taking courses on personnel, industrial relations, or human resource management, but that requirement was however gradually phased out as decades passed. HEC continued to provide an emphasis on human resources in business. Students at UBC and UWO could take electives in that subject, but it was not required. This leads to the question of whether graduates from these schools were actually capable of managing business functions or managing people. They would have known about many variables that went into running a business organization, but they were not required to learn much about dealing with the people who performed tasks in functions like marketing or finance departments. The credentials that students earned at UBC, HEC, and UWO said that they had learned something about business and what it meant to operate companies, but they largely missed learning about the crucial human aspect of organizations.

Graduate

A graduate degree in any field of study is intended to be more difficult and comprehensive in nature than an undergraduate degree. The graduate business programs offered at UBC, HEC, and UWO were obviously different from those found at community colleges, but they were not markedly different from what was offered at the undergraduate level. Graduate business programs were continuations of what was taught in undergraduate programs. UBC, HEC, and UWO created graduate degrees years after first devising undergraduate programs. The MBA was the preferred credential, with UBC and HEC both also offering M.Sc. programs. In the case of UBC, the MBA attracted far more students than the M.Sc. degree. UWO only offered an MBA, with the inclusion of a joint LLB/MBA option in later years.

The content of MBA programs altered over time and closely mirrored trends found at the undergraduate level. Students coming into all three programs needed to possess good mathematical skills in order to succeed in curriculums that were driven by quantitative subjects. They could have possessed undergraduate fields in any subject, but having earned an undergraduate business degree would have been the best possible preparation, although it meant repeating much of what a student would have already learned. In terms of curricular content, there was often little difference in what was taught, as core functions like finance, marketing, and accounting were considered foundational to understanding business and management. Courses and concentrations in problems that pertained to people were eventually as largely absent from MBA curricula as they were from those of undergraduate programs.

MBA programs performed functions different from undergraduate degrees, even if they seemed very similar in content. The MBA, despite its emphasis on numbers, enabled students who did not have undergraduate business degrees to study business at a graduate level. The MBA was also the first step in graduate education and, as seen in the preceding pages, graduates went on to complete Ph.Ds. and became business school professors. Universities with graduate programs employed faculty members who actively published and researched in their fields. In contrast, schools that focused more closely on undergraduate programs could be perceived as more oriented toward teaching and less on the creation and dissemination of knowledge. Community college faculty did not engage in research as their institutions were entirely focused on teaching.

The stature of the MBA within management education and training programs leads to the question of why people wanted to earn one. The MBA became a unique degree between its introduction in Canada in 1950 and the mid-1990s. Graduates with community college diplomas in management and holders of undergraduate commerce degrees have not written personal accounts of their time at school subsequent to collecting their diplomas. In contrast, there have been memoirs written by people who attended graduate business programs. For example, Peter Robinson wrote about this time in the MBA program at Stanford Business School.[5] An earlier example of a graduate business school memoir was written by Peter Cohen about his experience at HBS.[6] Books have been written about the careers of MBA graduates after they experienced business success, such as Laurence Shames' study of the 1949 graduating HBS MBA class.[7] The MBA conferred prestige on a manager, especially if it had been earned at a well-known school. Robinson discussed how he was able to obtain job interviews with Robert Maxwell, Steve Jobs, and Rupert Murdoch and that he would not have been able to get them without an MBA from Stanford.[8] He noted how he applied to Murdoch's organization with an undergraduate degree before attending Stanford, but never received a reply.[9] The result would have been also have been the same if he applied with a community college credential or corporate training on his résumé. For a person to have to cover the same subjects in an MBA program that he or she had already taken at the undergraduate level was a small price to pay under such circumstances.

The MBA received a lot of attention in popular media. For instance, *Canadian Business* magazine regularly published articles on graduate management education. That magazine was Canada's leading popular business periodical. Its coverage of the MBA degree was generally positive, with some occasional negative critiques. An example of the latter type of commentary was a 1993 article titled "Robots With Swollen Egos," which argued that MBA graduates lacked humility.[10] *Canadian Business* had conducted a survey of vice presidents of human resource departments and found that many felt that MBA programs needed to put more emphasis on "people skills" and that MBA graduates often held unrealistic expectations about how their careers would progress.[11] Several survey respondents felt that MBA students "would benefit from work sessions interwoven with academic studies, or by working for two or three years before taking their degrees."[12] *Canadian Business* asked "Can An MBA Run Your Company?" in a 1993 cover story.[13] That article included excerpts from a survey of corporate chief executives (CEOs) conducted by Monitor, and it noted that 75 percent of CEOs would have encouraged their sons and daughters to pursue an MBA.[14] They were also willing to help their employees cover the cost of an MBA, with 85 percent saying they would cover some costs and 40 percent indicating that they would cover all costs.[15] On the other hand, the MBA was the third choice for management training, with specialized external training and on-the-job experience being the preferred methods.[16] Of the group of CEOs surveyed, 55 percent held MBA degrees, and the UWO Business School was overwhelmingly considered to have the best program in Canada.[17]

Canadian Business also published annual commentaries on each MBA program in Canada and on the near future of graduate business education. Those reviews were often laudatory while perhaps suggesting new directions in which MBA programs should be developed. For instance, the April 1993 articles described above came from an issue devoted to graduate business programs. A detailed guide to MBA programs was published by Catherine Purcell in 1991.[18] The key point about the articles published in periodicals like *Canadian Business* and books such as Purcell's was that they were devoted to one type of graduate degree. There were no articles and guides to describe undergraduate management education programs, never mind those that were offered by community colleges.

The MBA had become a topic of some popular interest in Canada, and this helped spur student interest in the degree. It is evident from the information published in Canada's leading business magazine that many senior executives held conflicting views about MBA graduates and the impact that they had on business organizations. MBA graduates lacked skills for dealing with people and could often display a sense of entitlement. There was even preference among some executives for having managers learn on the job or participate in specialized training. However, the serious shortcomings identified with the nature of MBA training did not dissuade a large majority of executives from encouraging their offspring to pursue the degree. This was surely because they realized that it was, to paraphrase McDonald's expression, a golden passport to career success.

The fact that a survey of Canadian executives revealed UWO Business School as the best place to earn an MBA confirms that it offered the best passport up to the early 1990s. This was because of UWO Business School's stature and the status that its graduates could attain in Canada's business community and beyond. The MBA represented a route for career advancement and, over time, it attracted increasing numbers of women. The many images of women, including many who were Asian, in the pages of the UBC listing of MBA graduates in the late 1970s confirm that the degree was viewed as a path to success. UWO, in particular, communicated that its program was preparing people to quickly rise to positions of great stature, and that is the result that students coming into its MBA program would have expected.

Having a graduate business program was a platform upon which universities could build short-duration management and executive programs. Executive MBA programs had yet to proliferate during the period under consideration in this analysis, but all manner of workshops and seminars were offered by UBC, HEC, and UWO. The latter school was a pioneer in this type of management education, with the creation of its Management Training Course (MTC). The fact that it was introduced at the same time as UWO first offered its MBA program was intentional, as the two programs complemented each other. Programs like the MTC, the partnerships that UBC operated, and the seminars run by HEC represented a chance to sample advanced management education while providing universities with new sources of revenue. Business schools and faculties prized access to business leaders, and short-duration programs were additionally a method of cultivating those links.

Graduate business education became something that could be exported to other countries. It is doubtful that the UWO Business School would have been involved in the Canadian government's efforts to work with the University of the West Indies had it not operated an MBA program or had experience with its MTC. The same thing was true of UBC's partnership in Malaysia. The Canadian government's involvement in spreading management education to other countries was initiated by the Colombo Plan, which was itself an initiative to contain communism. UWO and UBC appear to have received mixed receptions to what they taught. UBC enjoyed success in Malaysia, but some Jamaican students were less enthusiastic about what UWO Business School faculty taught to them.

Canadian graduate business education from the 1940s to the 1990s shared some similarities with what was being offered in other countries, even as it was exported abroad. The impact of the United States on business management has been found in many countries. For instance, McDonald described the shift to more quantitative analysis in American graduate business programs that originated in the 1950s, and that trend has been shown to have emerged in Canada by the mid-1970s.[19] Francesca Fauri described the early influence of American business education on programs in the United Kingdom.[20] Jacqueline McGlade described the post–World War II expansion of American management education into Western Europe.[21] In contrast, as Tamotsu Nishizawa has described, Japan developed post-war managers who were highly educated, but that country's business community did not emphasize training managers in graduate schools.[22] John Wilson has argued that the United Kingdom had a management ethos prior to the 1950s that focused on the virtues of the amateur and the idea that "managers are born, not made."[23] Canada always historically felt the impact of American management thought and education, and that trend accelerated after World War II. In contrast to Japanese business, companies in Canada saw great merit in developing graduate management education. The idea that people were born to be managers may have existed in Canada, as there was often interest in ensuring that the right kind of person was chosen for leadership roles. However, the growth of management education after 1945 confirms that the idea that managers could be made became the dominant view in Canada.

The Changing Canadian Context

The development of management in Canada was described in the first chapter of this book, and returning to the late 1940s to describe how Canada progressed over the next fifty years situates management education in a wider socio-economic context. The period from 1945 to 1995 was dominated by the Cold War, and Canada formed alliances that aligned itself with the interests of the United States. American economic influence in Canada gradually increased, with US ownership of Canadian industrial assets increasing from 15 percent in 1929 to 24 percent in 1954.[24] This level remained fairly consistent into the late 1970s. Close economic links with the United States led to the integration across borders of some industries, particularly the automotive sector. As Dimitry Anastakis has described, the Canada–US Automotive Products Agreement (Auto Pact) concluded between the United States and Canada in 1965 not only integrated the auto industry, it also closely tied Canada's overall economy to that of its southern neighbour.[25] This agreement would remain in effect until its impact was initially diminished by the introduction of the 1989 Canada–US Free Trade Agreement (FTA).[26] Canada was widely recognized to have further embraced free trade with the introduction of the 1993 North American Free Trade Agreement (NAFTA) and by its membership in the World Trade Organization (WTO).

Canada's internal economic structure also changed from the late 1940s to the mid-1990s. Whereas the country's economic power was centred in Toronto and Montréal at the start of this period, new economic power centres rose in the western provinces. As Taylor and Baskerville have shown, the discovery of oil at Leduc, Alberta, in 1947 heralded enormous economic change in a region of Canada that would soon wield more national influence.[27] The socio-economic role of Québec also changed from the late 1940s to the mid-1990s. Canada adopted a policy of official bilingualism as a result of recommendations made by the Royal Commission on Bilingualism and Biculturalism in 1967.[28] Not all Canadian businesses were expected to operate in both English and French, but the effect of what was commonly called the Bi and Bi Commission was to strengthen the role of the French language in the country beyond Québec. That province's first sovereigntist government was elected in 1976, and it was more interested in nationalizing key industries than any other administration in Canada.[29] The ambitions of Québec sovereigntists would eventually be the catalyst for referenda on independence in 1980 and 1993.

Canada's demographics altered profoundly during the five decades after World War II. The baby boom generation described by Doug Owram transitioned from elementary school through to post-secondary education, then into the workforce. They were the people for whom the many management programs in companies, colleges, and universities were created. Immigration continued to be a source of population growth, with over half of immigrants settling in Toronto, Montréal, and Vancouver.[30] The impact of immigration can be seen in the reality that, in one five-year period between 1971 and 1976, the country's population increased by slightly over 1.4 million people, and immigration accounted for almost 35 percent of that number.[31] The Canadian government adopted multiculturalism as official policy.[32] The percentage of women participating in the paid labour force also vastly increased in Canada, from 24 percent in 1953 to 76 percent in 1990.[33] The women who applied to undergraduate and graduate management programs were among that group. The country overall became more diverse, with the role of immigrants and women becoming far more socio-economically important.

Government continued to occupy a central role in Canada's economy. Crown corporations were found at the provincial and federal levels into the mid-1990s. The state was also the main influence on the regulation of capital. Canadian governments generally created conditions that were amenable to business, such as the implementation of free trade agreements. The impact of government in the early nineteenth century described by Bliss continued into the late twentieth century. The interest that governments at the federal and provincial levels showed in promoting management education was another manifestation of state interest in Canada having a strong business sector. The two political parties— Liberal and Progressive Conservative—who formed national governments were pro-business. The third party, the New Democrats, formed governments in some provinces but not at the federal level. Business groups assiduously courted government assistance through groups like the Canadian Manufacturers' Association.[34]

Managers, Managing, and Management

This part of the analysis leads to the same fundamental question that pertained to internal company training programs, community colleges, and undergraduate and graduate management programs: were people who participated in them capable of being managers? The answer is that it depended on where people were educated and trained. There is also the issue of what participants in management training and education were taught as opposed to what was not included in their programs. Many issues that were found in companies were not discussed in management programs. For instance, Jeremy Milloy revealed the problem of violence in North American automotive assembly plants from 1960 to 1980, but the problem of workplace violence was not mentioned in the education and training programs discussed in this book. Many of the social and economic themes that Canada experienced in the post–World War II decades such as issues like race, gender, unionization, and technological change were not adequately discussed. This is remarkable considering that, as was shown in the second chapter, those themes along with others pertaining to human issues in companies have consistently appeared in Canadian management and labour history. For example, the use of computers in management education increased, but there was no programmatic emphasis on managing technological change. There was thus an overall lack of historical context in management education and training programs regardless of where they were taught.[35]

The way that managers progressed through their organizations profoundly changed from the mid-1940s to the mid-1990s. For instance, Donald Thain remembered that the students with whom he interacted in the UWO MTC program in the 1950s "were trained by apprenticeship and doing the job," and "functional apprenticeship" led to the top of a company's hierarchy. The emphasis changed from "running the factory to producing goods that consumers needed and wanted so distribution channels changed, product design and engineering changed, and there was a whole switch where marketing became a critical function." In the 1950s and 1960s "the most exciting place in the world for an MBA graduate to go and work was in P&G (Procter and Gamble) in marketing," as marketing was a growing function at that time. The way in which senior managers and executives were compensated also had a profound impact on how companies were run. Thain indicated that executives in the early 1960s were encouraged to borrow money to buy shares in the firms that employed them, thus giving them an ownership position. He noted that, in 1960, the General Motors board owned 5 percent of the company's stock. The idea of simply awarding stock options did not exist, and "compensation existed based on seniority." The situation changed in the 1980s:

> A whole lot of forces looked upon a salary as not being the way of compensating these people (executives). We first started giving out

bonuses and then, because they all had to be related to the market, we gave them (stock) options . . . the name of the game became one of buying and selling companies, mergers and acquisitions, financial manipulation. The price/earnings ratio became very important . . . the value of the stock ricocheted off that. Now, let's face it, creativity and financial manipulation are what matters.

Thain identified significant problems with how businesses were run by the 1980s, but in his view these issues originated within corporations and did not come from business schools. He further recalled a colleague who taught at Harvard Business School who was convinced that every problem that he saw in businesses related to people, so he trained as a psychoanalyst to try and better understand those problems. Business school faculty members like Thain and the other people described here taught students who aspired to be senior executives, but graduate management students were not interested in learning about people.[36]

There was thus an enormous contradiction in corporate priorities regarding the emphasis that should be placed on learning how to deal with people. The president of Quaker Oats Canada who wanted one of his managers accepted into the UWO Business School knew that the ability to deal with people was a major requirement for management, but he appears to have been anomalous by later standards as business schools placed more emphasis on areas like marketing because that is what corporations wanted although it was not what they needed. This leads to the broader issue of managerialism that Locke and Spender have discussed. In their view, managerialism occurs when management becomes a predatory caste, and they blame graduate business schools for creating that phenomena. The fact that graduate business schools focused on teaching knowledge that did not focus on people suggests that students could form a particular set of insular beliefs that were in contrast to the main problems facing corporations. Management became less insular as it focused more on human issues. Managerialism, as defined by Locke and Spender, would have been fostered in Canadian graduate management programs and to a lesser extent in those at the undergraduate level. It would have been less prevalent in corporate training and discouraged at community colleges because they were more prone to offer training and education programs that focused on people, even if those programs relied on scientific management or Human Relations School practices.[37]

The contradiction between what was taught in graduate business programs and corporate training materials is striking because corporations were telling business schools to place less emphasis on areas like human resource management in favour of other subjects while at the same time focusing heavily on human resource matters in their internal training. The implied view being demonstrated by senior corporate leaders was that students trained in graduate business programs did not need to worry about personnel matters. Senior people would handle wider strategic matters such as the problems facing company presidents. Dealing with workers was instead a duty for front-line and middle-level managers. A senior executive who had been promoted through the managerial apprenticeship described by Donald Thain would have known that this was an erroneous approach to running a company, but it would have been a belief reinforced by people emerging from graduate business programs. It is possible that senior executives came to the conclusion that anything that was not covered in a graduate management program could be handled through a company training program after a person was hired. That approach would not have addressed the problem of human issues not being at the core of graduate management education.

Another key issue about management education and training is what people thought would be involved when they participated in it. Students who attended part-time community college programs or enrolled in MBAs often had some prior work experience that included front-line supervisory jobs. Students who went directly from secondary school to an undergraduate management program or a full-time management program at a community college would have only known what it meant to be a manager in abstract terms since they had no direct experience of performing such roles. They may have had friends and family who worked in managerial roles, or part-time jobs in which they reported to managers, otherwise their ideas about what it meant to be in management would have been based on popular media representations. For example, students from the 1950s to the 1990s may have heard of a book like Sloan Wilson's *The Man in the Grey Flannel Suit* or Tom Wolfe's novel *The Bonfire of the Vanities* or have seen films and television shows that depicted managers. Their actual experience of working in management was more accurately reflected in academic research.[38]

The work of C. Wright Mills was referenced at the start of this book as a framework for understanding where Canadian managers fit into broader Canadian society. Mills described corporate executives as the organizers of a system of private property that had corporations located at its centre.[39] Senior corporate leaders were generalists, while middle-level managers below them had to be specialists, although it was the person who was the generalist who appeared to rise to the top of hierarchies.[40] In Mills' view, the foreman or front-line supervisor was the person in management structures who had "been so grievously affected by the rationalization of equipment and organization."[41] He also argued that middle managers were increasingly concerned with the management of people, and even want so far to say that "middle managers do not count for very much beyond their individual bureaucracies."[42]

Mills described a process of class formation within a wider managerial group. The executives whom he described were the type of people who graduated from MBA programs. They were supposed to be trained as generalists, even though their analytical skills were biased toward one skill area, and university business schools and faculties communicated messages that executive suites could await graduates of their MBA programs. Completing an MBA meant aspirations to join the power elite that Mills described in 1956 or the establishment revealed by Newman in the 1970s and early 1980s. Undergraduate business and management programs were also intended to be more general and to also prepare students to assume roles of responsibility, even if successful progress required completing an MBA after earning a bachelor's degree. Community college programs and company training were intended for different strata in the management hierarchy. College diplomas and certificates drew people who were already in middle-level roles or aspired to enter them. People who participated in corporate programs learned much more about dealing with people than the people at the top of a firm's organization chart. The problem of executives being disconnected from people in the organizations became acute in the 1980s as fewer of them rose through the ranks and instead became focused on short-term financial gains.

The state played a major role in legitimizing management in Canadian society, and it is because of the state's interest in seeing management develop that it can be regarded as a social institution. Governments at the federal, provincial, and local levels helped legitimize management in Canada, whereas in the United States funding sources like private foundations played a more important role. Master and servant laws were no longer in effect in the twentieth century, but managers still had enormous legal authority in organizations. Management was not narrowly confined to one area of society, and governments promoted its expansion throughout the country. State advocacy for developing management in Canadian society did not make it into a profession despite efforts made to develop it. Andrew Abbott argued that, by World War II, business relied on different professions such as accounting and others that contributed to functions like marketing.[43] Abbott also listed a series of events that were usually associated with the creation of a profession:

> First (national) professional association
> First governmentally sponsored licensing legislation
> First professional examinations
> First professional school separate from other professions
> First university-based professional education
> First ethics code
> First national-level journal[44]

Management in Canada involved professional schools, many different academic journals, and university-based professional education. There were no provincial agencies or organizations that regulated managers, as there were for attorneys and physicians.[45] Ethics was not taught by the companies, colleges, and universities discussed in this book during the time period that has been covered. There were courses on business law, but HEC was the only school to offer a course on the legal environment in which managers functioned. There were no professional licensing examinations or governmentally sanctioned management designations. There was instead a cornucopia of management designations that connoted some expertise in a given area. The availability of so many programs in turn helped drive management credentialism in Canada.

There is no census information on how many people participated in corporate management training programs, but there is revealing data on how many people enrolled in college and university programs. As Table 6.2 shows, enrollments in university commerce programs increased dramatically from 1965 to 1985. The increase was particularly marked for women, whose enrollments rose by over 5,000 percent. The mode of learning also changed because, by 1985, 4,856 of the students enrolled in graduate commerce programs pursued their degrees on a part-time basis. Part-time students slightly outnumbered those studying on a full-time basis, and the ratios were approximately equal for both men and women. Taking a degree such as an MBA was consequently done while also working and handling other life commitments.[46]

The most remarkable numbers to emerge about enrollments in management programs emerged in 1991 census data. Table 6.3 shows two types of credentials: those earned at universities and those earned elsewhere. Statistics Canada did not explicitly say in this data that trade and non-university occurred in community colleges, but the foregoing discussion shows that those were the places where it occurred. The number of trade and non-university qualifications held by Canadians age 15 and over constituted slightly over 40 percent of the overall national total in 1991. There were over twice as many women with educational qualifications in management as men, which means that they were better equipped academically for managerial roles than men. It is also clear that, on a proportional basis, more women earned qualifications from non-university programs than men. Community colleges, while not explicitly

Table 6.2 University Commerce Degree Enrollments in Canada by Gender, 1965–1985

Year	Undergraduate Degrees	Graduate Degrees
1965	9,949 Male	998 Male
	517 Female	8 Female
1975	24,518 Male	2,407 Male
	6,598 Female	413 Female
1985	35,312 Male	6,316 Male
	27,586 Female	2,619 Female

Source: Dominion Bureau of Statistics, *Survey of Higher Education, 1965–1966*, Part 1— Fall Enrollment in Universities and Colleges, Table 5; Statistics Canada, *Fall Enrollment in Universities, 1975–1976*, Tables 2 and 5; Statistics Canada, Universities: *Enrollment and Degrees, 1985*, Tables 7 and 9.

Table 6.3 Business Degrees, Diplomas, and Certificates in Canada, 1991 (over age 15)

Credential Type	Male	Female	Total
University Degrees, Diplomas, and Certificates	626,860	1,093,420	1,720,280
Trade and Non-University Qualifications	319,340	925,635	1,244,975
Totals	946,200	2,019,055	2,965,255

Source: Statistics Canada, *1991 Census of Canada, Major Fields of Study of Post-Secondary Graduates*, Table 1.

named, were key providers of management education of different types. It is unclear how many people participated in corporate management and supervisory programs between 1945 and 1995, but it is evident that many leading companies in Canada operated programs of different types. Company programs and those offered by community colleges were surely where most Canadian managers learned how to perform their jobs or at least make sense of them.

Universities, especially graduate management programs, were likely less influential then companies and colleges when it came to education and training. People in company training programs were also either already in managerial roles or being groomed for them. Full-time community college students would not necessarily have had management experience, but people who enrolled in part-time programs often did possess it. In terms of post-secondary education, community college graduates were likely better prepared to assume management roles than their university counterparts. Community college students learned something about being managers, which implied executing duties by directing other people. University management students learned about the functional areas of a company that required managing, but they did not learn enough about how to actually become managers and deal with people.

This book has frequently noted the cost of management education programs in different institutions over time. Table 6.4 shows the median income in Canada over a forty-year period.Community college programs have been shown to be less expensive than those offered by universities and more economically accessible to most Canadians. University programs, while more expensive than their community college counterparts, would have also been accessible to most people whether they were attending themselves or assisting a dependent who wished to pursue post-secondary education. It was not until the 1990s, and increases such as the one that occurred with the UBC MBA program, that cost began to become a barrier for students. For women, in particular, community college programs would have been attractive due to cost versus income.

Table 6.4 Average Income in Canada by Gender, 1971–1990

Year	1971	1985	1990
Male Income	$6,538	$35,606	$36,079
Female Income	$2,883	$24,041	$24,801

Source: Dominion Bureau of Statistics, *1961 Census of Canada*, Series 3–3, Table 9; Statistics Canada, *1971 Census of Canada, Labour Force and Individual Income*, Volume 18, Table 29; Statistics Canada, *1991 Census of Canada, Employment Income by Occupation*, Table 1. The 1971 amounts are for all employed workers, while the 1985 and 1990 amounts are for workers employed full-time. 1990 amounts show the value of the Canadian dollar in that year.

The manner in which management was taught to deal with personnel issues was frequently referenced in this book. The reality that MBA programs gradually placed less emphasis on educating students about personnel issues meant that executives who held MBAs would treat people the same as any other resources to be used to pursue an organization's aims. This substantiated a key critique of capitalism that was first made by Karl Marx, who argued that labour was the key to transforming other commodities so that an organization could make a profit. The converse view would be that the presence of people was implied in studies of subjects like finance, accounting, and quantitative analysis. People ultimately become numbers.[47]

There were also biases in what was taught at community colleges and in companies. The need for management was never seriously questioned in any of the management programs that have been described in this book. Management was portrayed as a good occupation and institution that helped workers and organizations succeed, and anyone who was not doing what management wanted was portrayed as a problem to be rectified. It is also abundantly clear that governments at the federal and provincial levels thought that community colleges were the institutions that would train managers and do so on a vocational basis. There is little evidence that community college graduates saw a business as less of an integrated entity than anyone graduating from an undergraduate or graduate management program.

Management education and training also became a major business between 1945 and 1995. Corporations clearly devoted considerable resources to it and, as seen in the interview with John, a supporting media industry grew around training needs. Management and supervisory training became a key area for colleges and universities and, in the case of the colleges, continuing education courses and programs were sources of profit. Graduate business programs even sought to export it. There is also the question of what would have happened if management education and training had not expanded in Canada in the post–World War II decades. It is possible that Canada could have been like Japan and not developed formal graduate business education while still experiencing economic growth and prosperity. It is more likely that Canadian business benefited from the expansion of management education and training as organizations became highly complex along the lines suggested by Chandler. The content of management education and training focused on subjects that were found in programs in the United States or other countries. Canadian management education was unique for reasons that related to the environment in which it developed, and not necessarily because of curriculum content. Canada developed management education programs that spanned companies, community colleges, and universities. That expertise included applied learning but also the development of management as an academic discipline and field of research. Canada did not rely on expertise from other countries and instead trained its own experts. Most importantly, management developed in Canada in two official languages while also reflecting concerns found in the country's different regions and with active support from the state.

The problems found within different forms of management education do not diminish the role it played in Canada in the post–World War II decades. Peter Drucker derisively said in 2004 that business schools educated mediocre graduates. The problem with observations like Drucker's is that he focused on graduate business education which, as has been shown, did not constitute the majority of the management education sphere in Canada. Management education and training was obviously considered valuable, otherwise universities and colleges would not have expanded programs focused on it. To agree with Drucker's view would mean diminishing the enormous agency showed by university students like Taffare Degeufé, Edna Winram, and Susan Harper as well as community college students like Don and Sharon Svob. It would also more broadly cast aspersions on the aspirations of hundreds of thousands of Canadian women who enrolled in management education programs to further their careers, especially women of colour, despite facing huge barriers. Deguefé can be imagined arriving in Vancouver into a decidedly white, anglo environment in which he managed to thrive. Winram in many ways broke a path for women like Harper who came after her. The Svobs, blue-collar workers who wanted to advance themselves, had to find the stamina to attend classes outside of their daily jobs and other commitments. People thought that management education had merit, otherwise students like those describe here would not have enrolled in numbers that grew significantly from 1945 to 1995.[48]

The main issue with management education and training was its content. As Chandler showed, business organizations became highly complex beginning in the late nineteenth century and running them required specialized training. Governments thought that knowing how to run such organizations was important and, more crucially, so did countless numbers of students. They did not become professionals like attorneys or physicians and instead apprenticed as managers and were often educated in vocational environments like companies and community colleges. There were programs in which they participated that lacked sufficient emphasis on the role of people in business organizations. University programs placed a particular emphasis on quantitative skills as decades passed, to the detriment of liberal arts content. People who participated in management education and training learned practices and internalized behaviours that were associated with the title of manager or responsibility for managing a function in an organization and became part of a Canadian managerial class that had common experiences and shared interests. They were men and women who assumed managerial roles, studied management, and made themselves into Canada's managers from 1945 to 1995.

Notes

1 Thompson, *The Making of the English Working Class*, 10.
2 Statistics Canada, Census of Canada 1991, Table 1, Industry and Class of Worker, Table 1.
3 Eichar, *The Rise and Fall of Corporate Social Responsibility*.
4 Julie Berebitsky, *Sex and the Office: A History of Gender, Power, and Desire* (New Haven: Yale University Press, 2012), 3.
5 Robinson, *Snapshots from Hell*.
6 Peter Cohen, *The Gospel According to Harvard Business School* (New York: Doubleday, 1973).
7 Laurence Shames, *The Big Time: The Harvard Business School's Most Successful Class and How It Shaped America* (New York: Harper and Row, 1986).
8 Robinson, *Snapshots from Hell*, 278–279.
9 Robinson, *Snapshots from Hell*, 279.
10 Susan Grimbly, "Robots With Swollen Egos", *Canadian Business* 66, 4 (April 1993).
11 Grimbly, "Robots With Swollen Egos".
12 Grimbly, "Robots With Swollen Egos".
13 Randall Litchfield, "Can an MBA Run Your Company?" *Canadian Business*, 66, 4 (April 1993).
14 Litchfield, "Can An MBA Run Your Company?"
15 Litchfield, "Can An MBA Run Your Company?"
16 Litchfield, "Can An MBA Run Your Company?"
17 Litchfield, "Can An MBA Run Your Company?"
18 Catherine Purcell, *Guide to MBA Programs in Canada: The Strengths and Weaknesses of 26 Canadian MBA Programs* (Toronto: ECW Press, 1991).
19 McDonald, *The Golden Passport*, 219–227.
20 Francesca Fauri, "British and Italian Management Education Before the Second World War: A Comparative Analysis", Lars Engwall and Vera Zamagni, ed., *Management Education in Historical Perspective* (Manchester: Manchester University Press, 1998), pp. 34–49.
21 Jacqueline McGlade, "The Big Push: The Export of American Business Education to Western Europe After the Second World War", Lars Engwall and Vera Zamagami, ed., *Management Education in Historical Perspective* (Manchester: Manchester University Press, 1998), pp. 50–65.
22 Tamotsu Nishizawa, "Business Studies and Management Education in Japan's Economic Development—An Institutional Perspective", Rolv Peter

Amdam, ed., *Management Education and Competitiveness: Europe, Japan and the United States* (Abingdon: Routledge, 1996), pp. 96–110.

23 John F. Wilson, "Management Education in Britain: A Compromise Between Culture and Necessity", Rolv Peter Amdam, ed., *Management Education and Competitiveness: Europe, Japan and the United States* (Abingdon: Routledge, 1996), 134.

24 Taylor and Baskerville, *A Concise History of Business in Canada*, 452.

25 Dimitry Anastakis, *Auto Pact: Creating a Borderless North American Auto Industry, 1960–1971* (Toronto: University of Toronto Press, 2005), 6.

26 Anastakis, *Auto Pact*, 6.

27 Taylor and Baskerville, *A Concise History of Business in Canada*, 413.

28 For a media report at the time of the release of the commission's report see Canadian Broadcasting Corporation (CBC), accessed 29 January 2018, www.cbc.ca/archives/entry/bilingualism-finally-a-report.

29 Taylor and Baskerville, *A Concise History of Business in Canada*, 426.

30 Margaret Conrad and Alvin Finkel, *History of the Canadian Peoples, volume 2, fourth edition* (Toronto: Pearson, 2006), 400.

31 Conrad and Finkel, *History of the Canadian Peoples*, 394.

32 Conrad and Finkel, *History of the Canadian Peoples*, 401.

33 Statistics Canada, "The Surge of Women in the Workforce", accessed 30 January 2018, www.statcan.gc.ca/pub/11-630-x/11-630-x2015009-eng.htm.

34 Canadian Manufacturers and Exporters, accessed 30 January 2018, www.cme-mec.ca/english/who-we-are/who-we-are.html.

35 Jeremy Milloy, *Blood, Sweat, and Fear: Violence at Work in the North American Auto Industry, 1960–80* (Vancouver: University of British Columbia Press, 2017).

36 Thain interview.

37 Locke and Spender, *Confronting Managerialism*, 2.

38 Sloan Wilson, *The Man in the Grey Flannel Suit* (New York: Simon and Schuster, 1955); Tom Wolfe, *The Bonfire of the Vanities* (New York: Farrar, Straus, Giroux, 1987).

39 Mills, *The Power Elite*, 119.

40 Mills, *The Power Elite*, 135–136.

41 Mills, *White Collar*, 87.

42 Mills, *White Collar*, 86.

43 Andrew Abbott, *The System of Professions: An Essay on the Division of Expert Labor* (Chicago: University of Chicago Press, 1988), 235.

44 Abbott, *The System of Professions*, 16.

45 In the case of Ontario, the Law Society of Upper Canada has been the regulatory body for lawyers since the late eighteenth century, accessed 29 January 2018, www.lsuc.on.ca/,. Physicians in the province have been regulated by the College of Physicians and Surgeons of Ontario since 1866, accessed 29 January 2018, www.cpso.on.ca/About-Us/A-Look-Back.

46 Statistics Canada, Universities: Enrollment and Degrees, 1985, Tables 7 and 9.

47 Karl Marx, *Das Kapital, volume 1* (London: Penguin, 1990), 129.

48 James Nelson interview with Peter Drucker, *Emerald Insight First*, accessed 1 February 2018, http://first.emeraldinsight.com/interviews/pdf/drucker.pdf.

Bibliography

Archival Sources:

Archives and Research Collection Center, Western University Canada

- Clarence Fraser Papers
- Labatt Brewing Company Collection
- University of Western Ontario President's Office Collection
- University of Western Ontario Business School Announcement, 1950–1969
- University of Western Ontario Calendars, 1950–1995
- Walter Thompson Fonds

Archives of Ontario

- T. Eaton Company Fonds

Bell Canada Archive

- Supervisor's Course on Employee Relations—Conference, May 1940, catalogue number 25449
- University Graduates' Induction Course 1955, catalogue number 21119–1
- *Bell News*, 30 May 1956
- Management Conference, Alpine Inn, 1958, catalogue number 26159
- Industrial Effectiveness Through Team Action", letter from W.M. Rankin, vice-president, to program participants, 8 March 1965

Bibliothèque et Archives nationales du Québec

- Communications-Ahuntsic. Vol, No 1 (Feb 1986—vol 29), no 1 (Autumn 2014)
- Collége Ahuntsic Guides, 1968-

École des hautes études commerciales de Montréal service de la gestion des documents et des archives

- Fonds de la direction du programme M.B.A.,1967-
- Fonds du department du management dirigeants

George Brown College Archive

- Business and Industry Training Administration and Program Records 1967–1991

Langara College Library

- Vancouver Community College, Langara Campus historical documents Boxes 1 and 2

Niagara College Library

- Archive storage room: full-time and part-time calendars, 1968–1995; College Board of Governors Minutes; Yearbooks and Reports
- Course Information Sheets, 1980s to 1990s.

Thomas Fisher Rare Book Library, University of Toronto

- *Business Compendium: Guelph Business College, 1889*
- The Ronalds Company Ltd., "The Story of Business: An informal study of the basic principles of our Canadian was of doing business, showing why Capital and Labour need each other, what responsibilities each has to the other, and why we must work together" (Montréal: 1940)

University of British Columbia Archive

- Sauder School of Business Fonds
- Earle D. MacPhee Fonds
- University of British Columbia Calendars, 1945–1995

Oral Interviews

Anonymous (John)—7 September 2016
Donald Thain—16 July 2012
Sherri Rosen—11 October 2016

Census Data

Dominion Bureau of Statistics, *Census of Canada 1961*
Dominion Bureau of Statistics, *Survey of Higher Education, 1965–1966*
Statistics Canada, *Census of Canada 1971*

Statistics Canada, *Fall Enrollment in Universities, 1975–1976*
Statistics Canada, *Census of Canada 1981*
Statistics Canada, *Census of Canada 1985*
Statistics Canada, *Universities: Enrollment and Degrees, 1985*
Statistics Canada, *Census of Canada 1991*

Secondary Sources:

Abbott, Andrew. *The System of Professions: An Essay on the Division of Expert Labor.* Chicago: University of Chicago Press, 1988.

Amdam, Roly. *Management Education and Competitiveness: Europe, Japan and the United States.* Abingdon: Routledge, 1996.

Anastakis, Dimitry. *Auto Pact: Creating a Borderless North American Auto Industry, 1960–1971.* Toronto: University of Toronto Press, 2005.

Archer, Maurice. *An Introduction to Canadian Business, fifth edition.* Toronto: McGraw-Hill Ryerson, 1986.

Armstrong, Christopher and H. Vivian Nelles. *Monopoly's Moment: The Organization and Regulation of Canadian Utilities, 1830–1930.* Philadelphia: Temple University Press, 1986.

Association of Universities and Colleges of Canada. "Canadian Universities and International Development: A Report Prepared for the Canadian International Development Agency by Professor Norma Walmsley on Behalf of the Association of Universities and Colleges of Canada." Ottawa: AUCC, 1970.

Austin, Barbara, ed. *Capitalizing Knowledge: Essays On the History of Business Education in Canada.* Toronto: University of Toronto Press, 2000.

Avery, Donald. *Reluctant Host: Canada's Response to Immigrant Workers, 1896–1994.* Toronto: McClelland and Stewart, 1995.

Barnard, Chester. *The Functions of the Executive.* Cambridge, MA: Harvard University Press, 1938.

Belisle, Donica. *Retail Nation: Department Stores and the Making of Modern Canada.* Vancouver: University of British Columbia Press, 2011.

Bellamy, Matthew. *Profiting the Crown: Canada's Polymer Corporation, 1942–1990.* Montréal: McGill-Queen's University Press, 2005.

———. "I Was Canadian: The Globalization of the Canadian Brewing Industry." Dimitry Anastakis and Andrew Smith, ed. *Smart Globalization: The Canadian Business and Economic History Experience.* Toronto: University of Toronto Press, 2014:pp. 206–230.

Berle, Adolph and Gardiner Means. *The Modern Corporation and Private Property.* New York: Macmillan, 1932.

Blanchard, Kenneth and Spencer Johnson. *The One Minute Manager.* New York: Berkley, 1983.

Bliss, Michael. *Northern Enterprise: Five Centuries of Canadian Business.* Toronto: McClelland Stewart, 1987.

Braverman, Harry. *Labor and Monopoly Capital: The Degradation of Work in the Twentieth Century.* New York: Monthly Review Press, 1974.

Brech, Edward, Andrew Thomson and John F. Wilson. *Lyndall Urwick, Management Pioneer: A Biography.* Oxford: Oxford University Press, 2011.

Bray, Douglas W., Richard Campbell, and Donald L. Grant. *Formative Years: A Long-Term AT&T Study of Managerial Lives.* New York: Wiley-Interscience, 1974.

Burley, Edith. *Servants of the Right Honourable Company: Work, Discipline and Conflict in the Hudson's Bay Company, 1779–1870*. Toronto: Oxford University Press, 1997.

Cameron, David M. *More Than an Academic Question: Universities, Government, and Public Policy in Canada*. Halifax: The Institute for Research on Public Policy, 1991.

Campbell, Howard. "UWI lobbies Gov't for Project Funds Despite Budget Cut." *The Gleaner*. Accessed 23 May 2015. http://old.jamaica-gleaner.com/gleaner/20110311/business/business92.html.

Canadian Broadcasting Corporation (CBC). Accessed 29 January 2018. www.cbc.ca/archives/entry/bilingualism-finally-a-report.

Canadian Institute of Management (CIM). Accessed 30 December 2017. www.cim.ca/organization/about-cim-chartered-managers-canada.

Canadian Manufacturers and Exporters. Accessed 30 January 2018. www.cme-mec.ca/english/who-we-are/who-we-are.html.

Chancellor of the Exchequer. *The Colombo Plan for Co-Operative Economic Development in South and South-East Asia, Report by the Commonwealth Consultative Committee, London: September—October 1950*. London: His Majesty's Stationary Office, 1950.

Chandler, Alfred. *The Visible Hand: The Managerial Revolution in American Business*. Cambridge, MA: Belknap, 1977.

Chinoy, Ely. *Automobile Workers and the American Dream*. Garden City, NY: Doubleday, 1955.

Cohen, Lizabeth. *Making a New Deal: Industrial Workers in Chicago, 1919–1939*. Cambridge: Cambridge University Press, 1990.

College of Physicians and Surgeons of Ontario. Accessed 29 January 2018. www.cpso.on.ca/About-Us/A-Look-Back.

Cookson Peter W. Jr. and Caroline Hodges Persell. *Preparing for Power: America's Elite Boarding Schools*. New York: Basic Books, 1985.

Corbo, Claude. *L'education pour nous: une anthologie du Rapport Parent*. Montréal: Presses de l'Université de Montréal, 2002.

Crainer, Stuart and Des Dearlove. *Gravy Training: Inside the Business of Business Schools*. San Francisco: Jossey-Bass Publishers, 1999.

Craven, Paul. "The Law of Master and Servant in Mid-Nineteenth Century Ontario," D.H. Flaherty, ed. *Essays in the History of Canadian Law I*. Toronto: University of Toronto Press, 1981, pp. 175–211.

Craven, Paul. "Labour and Management on the Great Western Railway," Paul Craven, ed. *Labouring Lives: Work and Workers in Nineteenth-Century Ontario*. Toronto: OHSS, 1995, pp. 335–336.

Creighton, Donald. *Empire of the St. Lawrence*. Toronto: Macmillan, 1956.

Cronon, William. *Nature's Metropolis: Chicago and the Great West*. New York: W.W. Norton, 1991.

Cummings, Stephen, Todd Bridgman, John Hassard and Michael Rowlinson. *A New History of Management*. Cambridge: Cambridge University Press, 2017.

Dalton, Melville. *Men Who Manage: Fusions of Feeling and Theory in Administration*. New York: John Wiley and Sons, 1959.

Daniel, Carter. *MBA: The First Century*. Lewisburg: Bucknell University Press, 1998.

Drucker, Peter. *The Practice of Management*. New York: Harper and Brothers, 1954.

Dussault, Gilles. "L'analyse sociologique du professionnalisme au Québec." *Professions* vol. 19, no. 2 (1978), 161–170.

Eatonia. Accessed 17 August 2016. www.eatonia.ca.

École des hautes études commerciales de Montréal. Accessed 20 December 2017. www.hec.ca/en/about/our-history/the-beginnings-of-a-proud-history/index.html.

———. Accessed 10 January 2018. www.hec.ca/en/profs/sylvie.st-onge.html.

Eichar, Douglas M. *The Rise and Fall of Corporate Social Responsibility*. Abingdon: Routledge, 2015.

Engwall, Lars and Vera Zamagni, ed. *Management Education in Historical Perspective*. Manchester: Manchester University Press, 1998.

Fauri, Francesca. "British and Italian Management Education Before the Second World War: A Comparative Analysis." Lars Engwall and Vera Zamagni, ed. *Management Education in Historical Perspective*. Manchester: Manchester University Press, 1998, 34–49.

Fayol, Henri. *Industrial and General Administration*. Paris: SRL Durand, 1916.

Folts, Franklin E. *Introduction to Industrial Management: Texts, Cases, and Problems*. New York: McGraw-Hill, 1949.

Gillespie, Richard. *Manufacturing Knowledge: A History of the Hawthorne Experiments*. Cambridge: Cambridge University Press, 1991.

Goutor, David. *Guarding the Gates: The Canadian Labour Movement and Immigration, 1872–1934*. Vancouver: University of British Columbia Press, 2007.

Green, Venus. *Race on the Line: Gender, Labor and Technology in the Bell System, 1880–1980*. Durham: Duke University Press, 2001.

Grimbly, Susan. "Robots with Swollen Egos." *Canadian Business* vol. 66, no. 4 (April 1993).

Harding, Nancy. *The Social Construction of Management: Texts and Identities*. London: Routledge, 2003.

Harel-Giasson, Francine, Nicole Forget and Francine Séguin. *Justine Lacoste-Beaubien et l'Hôpital*. Sainte-Foy, PQ: Presses de l'Université du Québec, 1995.

Harris, Howell John. *The Right to Manage: Industrial Relations Policies of American Business in the 1940s*. Madison: University of Wisconsin Press, 1982.

Harvey, Pierre. "The Founding of the École des Hautes Études Commerciales de Montréal." Barbara Austin, ed. *Capitalizing Knowledge: Essays on the History of Business Education in Canada*. Toronto: University of Toronto Press, 2000.

———. *Histoire De L'Ecole Des Hautes Études Commerciales De Montréal, Tome II: 1926–1970*. Montréal: Presses HEC, 2002.

Hay, Douglas and Paul Craven, ed. *Masters, Servants, and Magistrates in Britain and the Empire, 1562–1955*. Chapel Hill: University of North Carolina Press, 2004.

Heron, Craig. *Working in Steel: The Early Years in Canada, 1883–1935*. Toronto: McClelland and Stewart, 1988.

———. *The Canadian Labour Movement: A Short History, second edition*. Toronto: Lorimer, 1996.

———. *Lunch-Bucket Lives: Remaking the Workers' City*. Toronto: Between the Lines, 2015.

Hochschild, Arlie Russell. *The Managed Heart: Commercialization of Human Feeling*. Berkeley: University of California Press, 1983.

Hogue, Jean Pierre. *Les Relations Humanes dans L'Entreprise*. Montréal: Beauchemin, 1971.

Innis, Harold Adams. *The Fur-Trade of Canada*. Toronto: Oxford University Press, 1927.

Jackall, Robert. *Moral Mazes: The World of Corporate Managers*. Oxford: Oxford University Press, 1988.

Jacoby, Sanford. *Modern Manors: Welfare Capitalism Since the New Deal*. Princeton: Princeton University Press, 1997.

Kandell, Jonathan. "Kurt Waldheim Dies at 88; 'Ex-UN Chief Hid Nazi Past'." *New York Times*, 14 June 2007. Accessed 30 January 2018. www.nytimes.com/2007/06/14/world/europe/14iht-waldheim.3.6141106.html.

Kaufman, Michael. *Jamaica Under Manley: Dilemmas of Socialism and Democracy*. London: Zed Books, 1985.

Kealey, Greg and Bryan Palmer. *Dreaming of What Might Be: The Knights of Labor in Ontario, 1880–1900*. Cambridge: Cambridge University Press, 1982.

Khurana, Rakesh. *From Higher Aims to Hired Hands: The Social Transformation of American Business Schools and the Unfulfilled Promise of Management as a Profession*. Princeton: Princeton University Press, 2007.

Klimm, Lester F., Otis P. Starkey and Norman F. Hall. *Introductory Economic Geography*. New York: Harcourt, Brace and Company, 1937.

Kuyek, Joan Newman. *The Phone Book: Working at the Bell*. Toronto: Between the Lines, 1983.

Laird, Pamela Walker. *Pull: Networking and Success Since Benjamin Franklin*. Cambridge, MA: Harvard University Press, 2006.

Larrowe, Charles P. "A Meteor on the Industrial Relations Horizon: The Foremen's Association of America." *Labor History* vol. 2, no. 3 (1961), 259–294.

Law Society of Upper Canada. Accessed 29 January 2018. www.lsuc.on.ca/.

Lewis, Roy and Rosemary Stewart. *The Boss: The Life and Times of the British Business Man*. London: Phoenix House, 1961.

Litchfield, Randall. "Can an MBA Run Your Company?" *Canadian Business* vol. 66, no. 4 (April 1993).

Locke, Robert. *Management and Higher Education Since 1940: The Influence of America and Japan on West Germany, Great Britain, and France*. Cambridge: Cambridge University Press, 1989.

Locke, Robert and J.C. Spender. *Confronting Managerialism: How the Business Elite and Their Schools Threw Our Lives Out of Balance*. London: Zed Books, 2011.

Lowe, Graham. "Mechanization, Feminization, and Managerial Control in the Early Twentieth Century Canadian Office." Craig Heron and Robert Storey, ed. *On the Job: Confronting the Labour Process in Canada*. Montréal: McGill-Queen's, 1986. pp. 177–209.

Mackenzie King, William Lyon. *Industry and Humanity: A Study in the Principles Underlying Industrial Reconstruction*. New York: Houghton-Mifflin, 1918.

MacPhee, Earle D. *History of the Faculty of Business Administration at the University of British Columbia*. Vancouver: University of British Columbia Press, 1976.

Marens, Richard. "He Who May Not Be Mentioned: Marx, History, and American Business Schools." Patricia Genoe McLaren, Albert J. Mills and Terrance G. Weatherbee, ed. *The Routledge Companion to Management and Organizational History*. Abingdon: Routledge, 2015, 84–95.

Marx, Karl. *Das Kapital, volume 1*. London: Penguin, 1990.

Mayo, Elton. *The Human Problems of an Industrial Civilization*. New York: Macmillan, 1933.

McCallum, Margaret. "Corporate Welfarism in Canada: 1919–1939." *Canadian Historical Review* vol. 71, no. 1 (March 1990), 46–79.

McDonald, Duff. *The Golden Passport: Harvard Business School, the Limits of Capitalism, and the Moral Failure of the MBA Elite*. New York: Harper Collins, 2017.

MacDonald, John B. *Higher Education in British Columbia and a Plan for the Future*. Vancouver: University of British Columbia Press, 1962.

McGlade, Jacqueline. "The Big Push: The Export of American Business Education to Western Europe After the Second World War." Lars Engwall and Vera Zamagni, ed. *Management Education in Historical Perspective*. Manchester: Manchester University Press, 1998, 50–65.

McLaren, Patricia Genoe and Albert J. Mills. "History and the Absence of Canadian Management Theory." Patricia Genoe McLaren, Albert J. Mills, and Terrance G. Weatherbee, ed. *The Routledge Companion to Management and Organizational History*. Abingdon: Routledge, 2015, 304–331.

Mikalachki, Alexander. "Group Cohesion Reconsidered: A Study of Blue Collar Work Groups." Ph.D. Thesis, University of Western Ontario, 1964.

Milloy, Jeremy. *Blood, Sweat, and Fear: Violence at Work in the North American Auto Industry, 1960–80*. Vancouver: University of British Columbia Press, 2017.

Mills, Albert J. and Jean Helms Mills. "When Plausibility Fails: Towards a Critical Sensemaking Approach to Resistance." Robyn Thomas, Albert J. Mills, and Jean Helms-Mills, ed. *Identity Politics at Work: Resisting Gender, Gendering Resistance*. Abingdon: Routledge, 2004, 141–157.

Mills, C. Wright. *White Collar: The American Middle Classes*. New York: Oxford University Press, 1953.

———. *The Power Elite*. Oxford: Oxford University Press, 1956.

Mintzberg, Henry. *Managers Not MBAs: A Hard Look at the Soft Practice of Managing and Management Development*. San Francisco: Berrett-Koehler Publishers, 2004.

Moss Kanter, Rosabeth. *Men and Women of the Corporation*. New York: Basic Books, 1977.

National Institute of Standards Technology. Accessed 19 October 2017. www.itl. nist.gov/div898/software/dataplot/refman1/auxillar/cochran.htm.

Nelson, James. Interview with Peter Drucker, *Emerald Insight First*. Accessed 1 February 2018. http://first.emeraldinsight.com/interviews/pdf/drucker.pdf.

Nerbas, Don. *Dominion of Capital: The Politics of Big Business and the Crisis of the Canadian Bourgeoisie, 1914–1947*. Toronto: University of Toronto Press, 2013.

Newman, Peter C. *The Canadian Establishment, volume one*. Toronto: McClelland and Stewart, 1975.

———. *The Canadian Establishment, volume two: The Acquisitors*. Toronto: McClelland and Stewart, 1981.

Nishizawa, Tamotsu. "Business Studies and Management Education in Japan's Economic Development—An Institutional Perspective." Rolv Peter Amdam, ed. *Management Education and Competitiveness: Europe, Japan and the United States*. Abingdon: Routledge, 1996, 96–110.

Noble, David. *America By Design: Science, Technology, and the Rise of Corporate Capitalism.* Oxford: Oxford University Press, 1977.

Norman, Andrew. *The Story of George Loveless and the Tolpuddle Martyrs.* Tiverton: Halsgrove, 2008.

Owram, Douglas. *Born at the Right Time: A History of the Baby Boom Generation.* Toronto: University of Toronto Press, 1996.

Packard, Vance. *The Pyramid Climbers.* New York: McGraw-Hill, 1962.

Parent Commission. Accessed 30 December 2017. http://classiques.uqac.ca/con temporains/Québec_commission_parent/commission_parent.html.

Patrias, Carmela and Larry Savage. *Union Power: Solidarity and Struggle in Niagara.* Edmonton: Athabasca University Press, 2012.

Penfold, Steven. *A Mile of Make-Believe: A History of the Eaton's Santa Claus Parade.* Toronto: University of Toronto Press, 2016.

Pentland, H. Clare. *Labour and Capital in Canada, 1650–1860.* Toronto: James Lorimer and Company, 1981.

Pettigrew, Andrew. "Context and Action in the Transformation of the Firm." *Journal of Management Studies* vol. 24, no. 6 (November 1987), pp. 649–670.

Phenix, Patricia. *Eatonians: The Story of the Family Behind the Family.* Toronto: McClelland and Stewart, 2002.

Pinard, Alain. "New Era Opens for Québecois MBAs." *The Montréal Star.* 21 December 1971.

Pollard, Sidney. *The Genesis of Modern Management: A Study of the Industrial Revolution in Great Britain.* Cambridge, MA: Harvard University Press, 1965.

Portis, Bernard. "Management Training Through Organization Development." *Business Quarterly* (Summer 1965), pp. 44–55.

Purcell, Catherine. *Guide to MBA Programs in Canada: The Strengths and Weaknesses of 26 Canadian MBA Programs.* Toronto: ECW Press, 1991.

Radforth, Ian. *Bushworkers and Bosses: Logging in Northern Ontario, 1900–1980.* Toronto: University of Toronto Press, 1987.

Rinehart, James. *The Tyranny of Work: Alienation and the Labour Process, fourth edition.* Toronto: Harcourt Canada, 2001.

Russell, Jason. *Our Union: UAW/CAW Local 27 from 1950 to 1990.* Edmonton: Athabasca University Press, 2011.

———. "Organization Men and Women: Making Managers at Bell Canada from the 1940s to the 1960s." *Management and Organizational History* vol. 10, no. 3–4 (2015), 213–229.

Sanders, Doreen. *Learning to Lead: In Celebration of Seven Decades of Business Education at Western, 1923–93.* London, ON: Western Business School, 1993.

Sefton-McDowell, Laurel. "Company Unionism in Canada." Bruce E. Kaufman and Daphne Gottlieb Taras, ed. *Nonunion Employee Representation: History, Contemporary Practice, and Policy,* Armonk: M.E. Sharpe, 2000. pp. 96–120.

Sherlock, Phillip and Rex Nettleford. *The University of the West Indies: A Caribbean Response to the Challenge of Change.* London: Macmillan, 1990.

Skolnik, Michael. "A Look Back at the Decision on the Transfer Function at the Founding of Ontario's Colleges of Applied Arts and Technology." *Canadian Journal of Higher Education* vol. 40, no. 2 (2010), 1–17.

Statistics Canada. "The Surge of Women in the Workforce." Accessed 30 January 2018. www.statcan.gc.ca/pub/11-630-x/11-630-x2015009-eng.htm.

Stern, Phillip J. *The Company-State: Corporate Sovereignty and the Early Modern Foundations of the British Empire in India.* Oxford: Oxford University Press, 2011.

Storey, Robert. "Unionization Versus Corporate Welfare: The 'Dofasco Way'." *Labour/Le Travail* vol. 12 (Autumn, 1983), 7–42.

Sufrin, Eileen. *The Eaton Drive: The Campaign to Organize Canada's Largest Department Store, 1948 to 1952.* Toronto: Fitzhenry and Whiteside, 1982.

Sugiman, Pamela. *Labour's Dilemma: The Gender Politics of Auto Workers in Canada, 1937–1979.* Toronto: University of Toronto Press, 1994.

Surtees, Lawrence. *Pa Bell: A Jean de Grandpré and the Meteoric Rise of Bell Canada.* Toronto: Random House, 1992.

Taylor, Frederick Winslow. *The Principles of Scientific Management.* New York: Harper and Brothers Publishers, 1911.

Taylor, Graham T. and Peter Baskerville. *A Concise History of Business in Canada.* Oxford: Oxford University Press, 1994.

Taylor, Jeffrey. *Union Learning: Canadian Labour Education in the Twentieth Century.* Toronto: Thompson Educational Publishing, 2001.

Thain, Donald, John J. Wettlaufer, and Samuel A. Martin. *Business Administration in Canada.* Toronto: McGraw-Hill, 1961.

Thompson, E.P. *The Making of the English Working Class.* London: Penguin, 1991.

Timothy Eaton United Church. Accessed 1 August 2016. www.temc.ca/.

Tonn, Joan C. *Mary Parker-Follett: Creating Democracy, Transforming Management.* New Haven: Yale University Press, 2003.

Tucker, Eric. *Administering Danger in the Workplace: The Law and Politics of Occupational Health and Safety Regulation in Ontario, 1850–1914.* Toronto: University of Toronto Press, 1990.

Tucker, Eric and Judy Fudge. *Labour Before the Law: The Regulation of Workers' Collective Action in Canada, 1900–1948.* Oxford: Oxford University Press, 2001.

University of British Columbia. Accessed 12 December 2017. www.alumni.ubc.ca/about/board/lindsay-gordon-ba73-mba76/.

University of Exeter. Accessed 3 February 2018. http://elac.ex.ac.uk/fecolleges/index.php.

University of Toronto. Accessed 11 December 2017. www.rotman.utoronto.ca/FacultyAndResearch/Faculty/FacultyBios/Verma.

Urwick, Lyndall. "Management *Can* Be an Intelligent Occupation." *Advanced Management* (February 1956).

———. *Leadership in the Twentieth Century.* London: Sir Issac Pitman and Sons, 1957.

UWO MBA Association. *Western MBA.* September 1982.

Verma, Anil and Richard P. Chaykowski, ed. *Industrial Relations in Canadian Industry.* Toronto: Dryden, 1992.

Vosko, Leah. *Temporary Work: The Gendered Rise of a Precarious Employment Relationship.* Toronto: University of Toronto Press, 2000.

Way, Peter. *Common Labour: Workers and the Digging of North American Canals, 1780–1860.* Cambridge: Cambridge University Press, 1993.

Whitley, Richard Alan Thomas and Jane Marceau. *Masters of Business?: Business Schools and Business Graduates in Britain and France.* London: Tavistock Publications, 1991.

Whyte, William H. *The Organization Man.* New York: Simon and Schuster, 1959.

Willis, Paul. *Learning to Labour: How Working Class Kids Get Working Class Jobs.* Westmead, Farnborough, Hampshire, England: Gower, 1980.

Wilson, John F. "Management Education in Britain: A Compromise Between Culture and Necessity." Rolv Peter Amdam, ed. *Management Education and Competitiveness: Europe, Japan and the United States*. Abingdon: Routledge, 1996, 133–149.

Wilson, John F. and Andrew Thompson. *The Making of Modern Management: British Management in Historical Perspective*. Oxford: Oxford University Press, 2006.

Wilson, Sloan. *The Man in the Grey Flannel Suit*. New York: Simon and Schuster, 1955.

Wolfe, Tom. *The Bonfire of the Vanities*. New York: Farrar, Straus, Giroux, 1987.

Yoder, Dale. *Personnel Management and Industrial Relations*. New York: Prentice-Hall, 1945.

Index

Page numbers in *italic* indicate a figure and page numbers in **bold** indicate a table

Abbott, Andrew 224
Accounting 73–74, 77, 84, 111, 113, 114, 115, 119, 150; Fundamentals of 127, 128, 130
Accounting and Business Management 157
Accounting and Management Information Systems 108, 151, 152
Accounting, Finance and Investment program 71–72
Administrative Science 76
Administrative Studies 76, 77, 150, 186
Agriculture 99, 147
Air Canada 47
AMA *see* American Management Association
Amdam, Rolv 5
American Bell 36, 40
American Federation of Labor (AFL) 16, 21
American Management Association (AMA) 25, 52, 53
American Telephone and Telegraph (AT&T) 3, 25, 36, 205; "Net Change Study" 39
Anastakis, Dimitry, 219
Applied Arts and Technology 89
Archer, Maurice: *An Introduction to Canadian Business* 83
Armstrong, Christopher 6, 19
Arts and Applied Arts 72
AT&T *see* American Telephone and Telegraph
Austin, Barbara 5

average income in Canada by gender **227**
Aviation Professional Management Development Program 158

Barnard, Chester 3–4, 26, 30, 40, 41
Baskerville, Peter 6, 19, 20, 219–220
Bassett-Spiers, Ronald 39
Belisle, Donica 18
Bell Canada 7, 35, 36–42, 59, 61, 179, 205; compensation package 37; corporate training comparison 59–63; employment relations and handling personnel problems 36–37; "Net Change Study" 39; Human Relations School 41–42; women absent from training films 60
Bell Telephone 24, 28, 47
Bemmels, Brian 112
Berebitsky, Julie 207
Berle, Adolph 21, 22, 30
Bibliothèque et Archives nationales du Québec (BAnQ) 7, 67
Blackburn, Walter 179
Blanchard, Kenneth: *The One Minute Manager* 50
Bliss, Michael 14, 19, 20–21, 220
Blowers, G. A. 110
Boffa, Peter 56
Braverman, Harry 17, 119
Brewery, General, and Professional Workers' Union 52
Bridgman, Todd 4, 213
Brown, Ellis 38–39, 67

Burley, Edith 13
Business Council of British Columbia 156
business degrees, diplomas, and certificates **226**
Business Law, 122, 123, 166
Business Logistics 105
Business Management 73, 74, 83, 86, 128, 157, 168, 177

CAAT *see* Colleges of Applied Arts and Technology
Canada-US Free Trade Agreement 219
Canadian Bankers 168, 189
Canadian Business 216, 217
Canadian Department of Trade and Commerce (CIDA) 157, 158, 181–182, 183, 184–185, 186, 188, 189, 191
Canadian General Electric 125
Canadian Institute of Management (CIM) 88, 91
Canadian International Development Agency 158
Canadian Manufacturers' Association 220
Canadian Studies 74, 75
Canada Trust 58
Canadian Pacific Railway 16
capitalism 2, 3, 20, 52, 100, 172, 227; free market 188; industrial 14; welfare 18, 19, 26, 30, 101, 205
Career Management program 177
Catelli Pasta 55
Catholic Church 68, 75
CEGEP *see* Collège d'enseignement général et professionnel
Center for Industrial Relations and Human Resources 156
Centre for Indian Training and Research 158
Chandler, Alfred 3, 4, 17, 19, 22, 29, 228
Chateaugay Wines 55
Chinoy, Ely 22
CIDA *see* Canadian Department of Trade and Commerce
CIM *see* Canadian Institute of Management
CIS *see* course information sheet
Cohen, Lizabeth 19
Cohen, Peter 216
Cold War 219

Collective Bargaining 77, 83, 105
Collège Ahuntsic 7, 67, 71–78, 84, 89, 90, 93, 209, 211
Collège d'enseignement général et professionnel (CEGEP) 67, 68, 75, 76, 78, 89, 115, 136, 137, 162, 163, 209–210
College of Physicians and Surgeons of Ontario 230n45
Colleges of Applied Arts and Technology (CAAT) 78, 89, 91
Colombo Plan 157, 158, 181, 182, 184, 191, 218
Commerce 98, 99, 100, 102, 104–106, 113, 124, 147, 148, 172, 212, 214, **225**
Commerce and Business Administration 106, 107–109, 111, 146, 148, 149, 150, 151, 154, 155, 156, 157, 158, 159
community colleges 67–93; management as an applied vocation 89–93; perspectives 68–70; *see also* Collège Ahuntsic; Niagara College; Vancouver Community College
companies 35–63; *see also individual company names*
Computer Applications 83
Computer Applications in Business 106
Computer Operations 83
Congress of Industrial Organizations (CIO) 21, 37
Conservative Party 12
Cookson, Peter W. 6
Corbo, Claude 76
corporate social responsibility 26, 47, 52, 206
corporate training comparison 59–63
corporate welfarism 18
course information sheet (CIS) 68, 84, 86
Crainer, Stuart 5
Craven, Paul 12–13, 15
Creative Business Leadership program 177
Creighton, Donald 12
Cronon, William 12
Cummings, Stephen 4, 213
Currie, Archibald W. 102

Dalton, Melville 4
Daniel, Carter 5

Dartnell Sales Training Films 54
Data Processing Management 79, 84
Davis, Bill 68, 78, 89
Dawson College 68
"Dealing with Troubled and Troublesome Employees" 156
Dearlove, Des 5
Decision Analysis 153, 158
Decision Analysis I 112
Decision Analysis II 112
Deguefé, Taffara 109–110, 111, 214, 228
Department of Commerce 146
Department of Trade and Commerce 184
Dofasco 18
Dominion Securities 125
Dominion Stores 47, 125
Drucker, Peter 3–4, 23, 26, 27, 50, 52, 62, 172, 228
Dussault, Gilles: "L'analyse sociologique du professionnalisme au Québec" 119

Eaton, Fredrik 51
Eaton, George 51
Eaton, John Craig 42
Eaton, Timothy 35, 42; *see also* Eaton (T.) Company
Eaton Credit Corporation "Eaton Credit Corporation Recruitment Video" 51; University 51; women absent from training films 60
Eaton family 52, 60
Eaton (T.) Company 7, 19, 35, 42–52; bankruptcy 51; "Christmas Sales Presentation" 48; community profile 47; corporate social responsibility 47, 52, 206; corporate training 59; corporate training comparison 59–63; employee military service 43; female sales staff directed by male managers 60; "First Class Male" 49; Hamilton plan 46; lack of French language training films 60; Management Guide to Personnel Policies 46–47; "Managing to Win" 49; *No Small Change* 50; "One Minute Manager Excerpts" 50; Santa Claus parade 42, 48, 64n32, 205; "Staff Training Spring 1974" 49; "Twice Across Canada

Annually" 48; unionization 50, 60; veterans 43–44; "Welcome to Eaton's" 47; "Your Career at Eaton's" 44, *45*
École des Hautes Études Commerciales de Montréal (HEC): graduate management education 159–170, *169*; Master of Business Administration 159–168, 190–192, 215–219; undergraduate management education 112–124
"The Effective Secretary" 156
employer paternalism 15, 18, 26, 42, 205
engineering profession 3, 14, 36
Engwall, Lars 5
Environmental Business Management 177
Evoy, Peggy 39
Executive Secretary program 71

Fayol, Henri 26–27, 28, 30, 40, 41
FBDB *see* Federal Business Development Bank
Federal Business Development Bank (FBDB) 85, 87
Field, Frederick 102
Financial Management 79, 168, 179
Folts, Franklin E.: *Introduction to Industrial Management* 101
Ford Foundation 158, 183
Ford Glass 79
Ford Motor Company 21, 29, 47, 125
Ford Rouge Plant 22
foreman 1, 22, 223
Foreman's Association of America 22
Fortran 83
Fox, W. Sherwood 124
Fraser, Clarence 23–26, 27, 28–29, 34n101, 36, 38, 40–41, 178, 181; "A Career Plan for Every Man" 25; "god-father relationship" 25, 39
French 7, 28, 40, 60, 68, 76, 90, 112, 113, 116, 119, 123, 124, 136, 159, 161, 163, 167, 168, 170, 190, 210, 212, 214, 220
front-line supervisor 1, 36, 44, 223
Fry, J. N. 185
Fundamentals of Accounting 127, 128, 130

Gantt, Henry 28
General Arts 76

General Motors 21, 25, 26, 29, 79, 88, 221
General Motors Diesel 124
George Brown College 67
GMAT *see* Graduate Management Admissions Test
Gordon, Lindsay 155–156, 191
Goutor, David 16
Governmental and Institutional Accounting 117
Graduate Management Admissions Test (GMAT) 175
graduate management education 145–192; three business programs compared 190–192; *see also* École des Hautes Études Commerciales de Montréal; University of British Columbia; University of Western Ontario (UWO) Business School
Graham, J. F. 185
Great Western Railway 15
Guelph Business College 15

Hall, Marshall 185
Hall, Norman F.: *Introductory Economic Geography* 99, 100
Hanjung 158
Harding, Nancy 5, 102
Harel-Giasson, Francine 168
Harper, Susan 190, 191, 228
Harrington, J. M. 185
Harris, Howell 21
Hart, Rose 39
Harvard Annex 27
Harvard Business School (HBS) 4, 5, 101, 102, 108, 116, 120, 124, 127, 129, 135, 146, 147, 170, 178, 179, 192, 213, 216, 222
Harvey, Pierre 112
Hassard, John 4, 213
Hay, Douglas 12–13
Hayes-Dana 79
HBC *see* Hudson's Bay Company
HBS *see* Harvard Business School
Health Sciences 76
Heron, Craig 17
Hill, K. 187
Holtz, Lou 49
Hospitality Management Accounting 82
Hotel and Restaurant Administration 82, 92
Howe, C. D. 20

Hudson's Bay Company (HBC) 13, 15, 21, 47
Human Relations in Industry 80
Human Relations School 4, 18, 25, 32n59, 41–42, 206, 222
Human Resource Management 81, 105, 117, 133
Human Resources 92, 105, 118
Hyde Park declaration 20
hydroelectric power 19

Imperial Munitions Board 19
Industrial Economics 81
Industrial Management 76–77, 80, 84, 100, 101, 102
Industrial Management Clubs of Canada 80
Industrial Psychology 80
Industrial Relations 79, 80, 81, 84, 103, 105, 106, 152, 153
Industrial Relations Management 107, 108, 150, 151, 158
Industrial Revolution 3
Innis, Harold Adams 12; *Introductory Economic Geography* 99
International Aviation Management Training Institute 158
Ivey, Richard 180
Ivey family 179

Jeal, Margaret 39
Jeffrey, J. 179
Jobs, Steve 216
John Labatt Brewing Company *see* Labatt's
Johnson, Van 54, 57, 207
Jute Bag Company 101

Kealey, Greg 16
Khurana, Rakesh 5, 90–91
King, William Lyon Mackenzie 18, 23
King Edward Centre 71
King Edward Senior Matriculation and Continuing Education Centre 71
Klimm, Lester E.: *Introductory Economic Geography* 99, 100
Knights of Labor (KoL) 15–16
Kodak 19, 205
Kwong, James 146

Labatt, Hugh 179
Labatt, John 52, 55, 57–59

Labatt's (aka John Labatt Ltd.; John Labatt Brewing Company) 7, 35, 52–57, 58, 124, 125, 206–207; corporate training comparison 59–63; "Do It Right" 56; lack of French language training films 60; Management by Objectives 52–53, 54, 62; "The Professional" 54; quality of work life 56; sources of management training 57–59; training resources 208–209, 211, 213; unionization 60; women absent from training films 60; *see also* Catelli Pasta; Chateaugay Wines; The Sports Network; Toronto Blue Jays
Labour Studies 74, 75, 81, 91, 210
Laird, Pamela Walker 38
Land Research Institute of Korea Land Corporation 158
Langara College 7, 67, 70, 71, 72, 73, 74, 75, 84
Larose, Michèle 122
Laurentian Thesis 12
Laval University 119, 163, 168
Law Society of Upper Canada 230n45
Le Collège Saint-Ignace 76
Levins, Edward 114
Lewis, Roy 4
L'Institut des Arts Graphiques 76
L'Institute de Technologie Laval 76
Locke, Robert 5, 7, 222
Lockwood Films 58, 59
London Life 58, 124, 125, 179
Lorrain, Jean 122
Lowe, Graham 18
Lucky GoldStar 158

MacDonald, John A. 12, 16
MacDonald, John B. 70, 71
MacDonald Commission 70, 75–76
MacNeil, Jeannine 162
MacPhee, Earle D. 146, 148, 157
making managers 6–8
management education and training, meaning of *see* meaning of management education and training
management education history 4–6
Management of Human Resources 81, 105, 158
Management Policy and Practice 71, 72, 74
Management Policy and Procedure 73

management to 1945 11–30; late 1940s 29–30; thinking about management theory 23–29
Management Skills for Women Supervisors 83
Management Training 81
Management Training Course (MTC) 178, 179–180, 181, 189, 191, 218, 221
management training sources 57–59
managerial employment by gender 204
Managers and Management Practice 122, 123
Managers of Change 176
Manley, Michael 184–185, 188
Marceau, Jane 5
Mark, A. A. 187
Marketing Analysis 105
Marketing Management 79, 168
Marx, Karl 227; *Communist Manifesto* 172
Marxism 3, 172
Maslow, Abraham 25
Master of Business Administration (MBA) 5, 102, 104, 109, 116, 125, 127, 129, 223–224, 225, 227; École des Hautes Études Commerciales de Montréal 159–168, 190–192, 215–219; Procter and Gamble 221; University of British Columbia 145–152, 153–156, 157, 159, 190–192, 215–219; University of Western Ontario Business School 170–192, 215–219, 226
Maxwell, Robert 216
Mayo, George Elton 18, 23, 24, 30, 32n59, 80, 103, 206
McCallum, Margaret 18
McDonald, Duff 5, 101, 127, 146, 213, 217, 218
McGill University 98, 168, 181
MacPhee, Earle 109
meaning of management education and training 203–229; average income in Canada by gender 227; business degrees, diplomas, and certificates 226; changing context 219–220; community colleges 209–211; corporations 205–209; graduate 215–219; managerial employment by gender 204; managers, managing,

and management 221–225; undergraduate 211–215; university commerce degree enrollment by gender **225**
Means, Gardiner 21, 22, 30
Mess, London Garrison 179
middle managers 1–2, 223
Midvale Steel Company 27
Mills, Albert J., 23, 42
Mills, C. Wright 1, 2, 223–224
Mills, Jean Helms, 42
Mintzberg, Henry 5
modern management 3–4, 17, 18, 26, 29
Morrow, Ellis H. 102, 109, 110, 124, 146, 148
Moss Kanter, Rosabeth 4, 42
M.Sc. 149–150, 151, 152, 153, 154, 155, 159, 190, 215
MTC *see* Management Training Course
Murdoch, Rupert 216
Murray, Ray 56

National Institute of Standards and Technology 120
National Labor Relations Act 21, 22, 103
National Policy 12, 16, 20, 190
Nelles, H. Vivian 6, 19
Nerbas, Don 20
New Deal 19, 24
Newman, Peter C. 20, 224
Niagara College 7, 67, 68, 70, 78–89, 90, 91, 92, 93, 209, 210, 211
Noble, David 3
North American Free Trade Agreement 219

OMDP *see* Ontario Management Development Program
Ontario Hydroelectric Commission 19, 29
Ontario Management Development Program (OMDP) 84, 85, 86–87, 88, 89, 91, 92, 96n75, 210, 213
Ontario Public Service Employees Union 91
Operations, Recreation, Hotel and Restaurant 92
Opinion Research Corporation 22
Orr, John Leslie 28
Owram, Doug 68, 69, 220

Pacific Rim Language 74
Pacific Rim Management 74
Packard, Vance 4, 42
Packard Motor Company 22
Palmer, Bryan 16
P&G (Procter and Gamble) 221
Parent Commission 75–76
Parizeau, Jacques 168, 191
Parker-Follett, Mary 26, 27, 28, 41
Parti Québécois 168
paternalism, employer 15, 18, 26, 42, 205
Patrias, Carmela 91
Pentland, H. Clare 13, 14
Persell, Caroline Hodges 6
Personnel/Human Resources 92
Personnel Management 74, 113
Personnel Management and Industrial Relations 79, 81, 84
Personnel Management by Objectives 81
Pettigrew, Andrew 41
Phenix, Patricia 42
Philosophy 76
Policy Formulation and Administration 147
Pollard, Sydney 3, 13
Polymer Corporation 19, 33n68
Port Cares 88
Probability Statistics for business Decisions 128
Production Management 79, 150, 165, 167, 185
Progressive Conservative government 68, 78, 89, 220
Psychology 81
Psychology of Industrial Relations 80
Public Accounting 117
Public Relations at the Local Level 81
Public Relationships and Responsibilities 171, 172
Pure and Applied Science 76

Quaker Oats Company of Canada 180, 222
Quantitative Techniques in Accounting and Verification 119
Quantitative Techniques in Finance 119
Quantitative Techniques in Marketing 119, 120
Quiet Revolution 75

Radforth, Ian 21
Recreation Facilities Management 74
Research Methods 105
Retain Management 82
Retail, Wholesale, and Department Store Union 50
Robarts, John 68
Role of Women in Canadian Trade Unions 81
Ronalds Company 20
Roosevelt, President 24
Rosen, Sherri 7, 81, 91, 92, 93
Rowlinson, Michael 4, 213
Royal Commission of Inquiry on Education 75
Royal Commission on Bilingualism and Biculturalism 220

Salesmanship 71
Sauder School of Business Fonds 190
Savage, Larry 91
School of Business and Commerce 148
School of Commerce 103, 104, 146–148
Sefton-McDowell, Laurel 18
Skolnik, Michael 89
Social Psychology for Trade Unionists 81
Social Science 76, 126, 132, 134, 135
Sociology of Work 119
sources of management training 57–59
Spencer, J. C. 5
The Sports Network 55
Spriggs, Roger 186
Staples Theory 12
Starkey, Otis P.: *Introductory Economic Geography* 99, 100
State University of New York (SUNY) 70
Statistics 77, 134
Statistics Canada 225
Statute of Labourers 13
Steel Company of Canada (Stelco) 17, 18, 19, 29
Stelco *see* Steel Company of Canada
Stewart, Bryce 34n101
Stewart, Rosemary 4
Stochastic Models 106
Sugiman, Pamela 23

Supervisory Management 80, 81
Svob, Don 88, 228
Svob, Sharon 88, 228

Taft-Hartley Act 22
Taylor, Frederick Winslow 17–18, 23, 26–27, 28, 30, 103, 119, 206, 219; *The Principles of Scientific Management* 17
Taylor, Graham 6, 19, 20
Taylor, Jeff 91
Taylorism 17, 25, 41
T. Eaton Company *see* Eaton (T.) Company
Thain, Donald 7, 127, 145, 170, 172, 178, 179, 192, 221–222, 223
Thomas, Alan 5
Thompson, Edward 2, 203
Thompson, Walter 124, 178, 183–184, 185, 186–188, 189
Thompson Products 79
Thomson, Andrew 3
Toronto Blue Jays 55
Trades and Labour Congress (TLC) 37
Trade Unions Act 15
Trudeau, Pierre 184

UAW/CAW Local 27
undergraduate management education 97–137; three programs 136–137; *see also* École des Hautes Études Commerciales de Montréal (HEC); University of British Columbia; University of Western Ontario
United Auto Workers (UAW) 21
United Steel Workers of America (USWA) 21
University of British Columbia (UBC) 7; graduate management education 145–159, 160, 161, 167, 168, 175, 177, 178, 181, 190–191, 192, 215, 218, 226; Master of Business Administration 145–152, 153–156, 157, 159, 190–192, 215–219; undergraduate management education 97, 98–112, 124, 136, 137, 211, 212, 213, 214, 215
University of California at Berkeley 109
University of Malaya 157–158
University of Ottawa 168
University of Puerto Rico 181

University of Toronto 97, 98, 121, 147, 156, 170, 182
University of Western Ontario (UWO) Business School 7, 39, 56, 97, 121, 124; graduate management education 170–190; Master of Business Administration 170–192, 215–219, 226; modelled on university in United Kingdom 98; undergraduate management education 124–135; *see also* Western University Canada
University of Windsor 58
Urwick, Lyndall 25, 26, 27–28, 30, 39, 40, 41
US National Labor Relations Board 22

Vancouver Community College (Langara; VCC) 7, 67, 70–75, 76, 79, 84, 89, 90, 93, 209
Vancouver School Board 71
Vancouver School of Art 71
Vancouver Vocational Institute 71
VCC *see* Vancouver Community College
Verma, Anil 156
Victoria College 70
Vosko, Leah 23

Waldheim, Kurt 111, 141n79
Walmsley, Norma 182, 183
Way, Peter 14
Weber, Max 119
Weldon, D. B. 179
welfare capitalism 18, 19, 26, 30, 101, 205
Western Electric Hawthorne Works 18, 32n59
Western University Canada 7; *see also* University of Western Ontario (UWO) Business School
White-Collar Unionist 81
Whitley, Richard 5
Whyte, William H. 2
Willis, Paul 6

Wilson, John F. 3, 19, 219
Wilson, Sloan: *The Man in the Grey Flannel Suit* 223
Winram, Edna 109, 228
Wolfe, Tom: *The Bonfire of the Vanities* 223
women absent from training films 60
Work in Canadian Society 75
World Trade Organization 219
World War I ; Eaton employees 42–43; economic expansion 29; role of government to business production 19
World War II 20; Bell Canada 36, 37, 40; business 224; community colleges 67, 68, 70, 91; demographics 220; Eaton Company 51, 60; Eaton employees 42–43; Eaton managers 46; École des Hautes Études Commerciales de Montréal 112; economic expansion 29, 36; ethnic diversity 159; German Army 141n79; graduate management education 145, 189; Labatt's 52; management education and training 203, 219, 221, 227, 228; post– 1, 4, 5, 6, 8, 20, 21, 22, 26, 29, 30, 36, 37, 42, 43, 46, 51, 52, 60, 67, 68, 70, 91, 98, 100, 112, 136, 145, 159, 189, 203, 219, 220, 221, 227, 228; pre– 19, 23, 28, 30, 40; role of government to business production 19; undergraduate management education 100, 136; universities 98; University of British Columbia 98; women in industrial employment 23

Xerox 55, 57

Yoder, Dale: *Personnel Management and Industrial Relations* 103
York Knitting Mills Ltd. 148
Yuill, Bruce 186–187

Zamagni, Vera 5

For Product Safety Concerns and Information please contact our EU
representative GPSR@taylorandfrancis.com Taylor & Francis Verlag GmbH,
Kaufingerstraße 24, 80331 München, Germany

Printed and bound by CPI Group (UK) Ltd, Croydon, CR0 4YY

01/05/2025

01858355-0001